Shakespeare Stories

Here, in a breathtaking display of virtuoso storytelling, splendidly illustrated by Michael Foreman, Leon Garfield gives us twelve of Shakespeare's memorable plays. Presented afresh in narrative form and using the playwright's own dialogue, they will delight both all who know our greatest dramatist's work and those (especially young people) who are new to them.

Leon Garfield is the distinguished author of more than thirty books for children and adults. Widely acclaimed for his historical novels, he has also written picture book texts, short stories and novellas, as well as retellings of traditional and classical material. He has won the Carnegie Medal, the Whitbread Prize and the Children's Book Award, and several literary honours in America and Europe, including the Prix de la Fondation de France.

Michael Foreman is one of the foremost children's illustrators in this country today. He has won the Kate Greenaway Medal for outstanding children's book illustration and has been runner up for this award three times. Twice the winner of the Francis Williams Memorial Prize (awarded by the Victoria and Albert Museum), he has also won the Kurt Maschler 'Emil' Award, the Federation of Children's Book Groups' Children's Book Award, and the Bologna Book Fair Graphic Prize for Youth.

SHAKESPEARE STORIES

Leon Garfield

illustrated by

MICHAEL FOREMAN

GOLLANCZ CHILDREN'S PAPERBACKS
LONDON

To the Royal Shakespeare Company

Text © Leon Garfield 1985
Illustration © Michael Foreman 1985

First published in Great Britain in 1985
by Victor Gollancz Ltd
14 Henrietta Street, London WC2E 8QJ
Published in Gollancz Children's Paperbacks September 1988
Second impression February 1990
Third impression July 1991
Fourth impression July 1992

British Library Cataloguing in Publication Data
Garfield, Leon, *1921-*
    Shakespeare stories.
    I. Title   II. Foreman, Michael, *1938*
    III. Shakespeare, William, *1564-1616*
    823'.914[J]

ISBN 0 575 04340 7

Printed and bound in Singapore
by Imago Publishing Ltd

Contents

Colour Plates

Twelfth Night

Before you hear of the shipwreck, you must know that, inland from its wild sea coast, Illyria was a green and golden land, of thatched cottages, neat as well-combed children, of gracious mansions, and the noble palace of the Duke. Orsino was his name, and, before the shipwreck, he was fathoms deep in love with Olivia, a fair countess who dwelt nearby.

"If music be the food of love," he sighed, gazing through his windows towards the lady's house, "play on, give me excess of it . . ." and his lute-player bent low over his beribboned instrument and filled the air with song. But alas! What pleasure was there in a feast for only one? The lady would have nothing to do with him, nor, indeed, with any of his sex. That is, until the shipwreck. She was in mourning for a brother deceased, and had shut herself away in her mansion, and vowed to see no suitors for seven long years.

"What a plague means my niece to take the death of her brother thus?" complained her uncle, Sir Toby Belch, a fat bag of wind and merriment who lived in her house and floated between kitchen and cellar like a portly bubble in stained brocade. He himself had fetched his niece a suitor, a long, thin knight by name of Sir Andrew Aguecheek; but it had been to no avail. Nonetheless, Sir Andrew kept paying for Sir Toby's entertainment in the foolish hope of becoming his nephew. Though he always dressed young, it was a case of stale wine in a new bottle. To be honest, the knight was old enough to know better, and too old to do it. But Sir Toby kept him in hopes, and he kept Sir Toby in drink; which seemed a fair exchange.

Then, one day, came a shipwreck. Far out at sea, a sudden and fearful tempest sprang up. Huge winds came boiling out of black clouds and tore sea and sky to shreds. A vessel, frail as paper, lifted, plunged, turned and tossed, until at last caught between two roaring walls of water, it cracked and split! Its cargo of shrieking souls was tumbled helplessly among the waves. Some clutched at spars and broken fragments of the mast, while others clung, with streaming desperation, to the shattered vessel itself. Then the storm began to abate and the wreck, driven hither and thither by winds, was heaved up on to a beach. Some half dozen sailors, the ship's captain and a solitary passenger gave thanks to God, and limped wearily ashore.

"What country, friends, is this?" asked the passenger, as the sun came out, and made the morning gold.

"This is Illyria, lady," answered the captain.

"And what should I do in Illyria?" she wept, gazing towards the dazzled sea. "My brother he is in Elysium." Her name was Viola and her brother had been called Sebastian; but now, surely, he was drowned. They had been twins, alike as two mornings in April, full of young beauty and promise. The kindly captain tried to reassure her that her brother might still live, for he had been seen, clinging to a spar; and Viola was glad enough to clutch at this frail straw even as her brother had clutched at his.

"Knowest thou this country?" she asked. The Captain knew it well, and told her of the Duke and his love for Olivia, and of how matters stood between them. Viola sighed; dearly she would have liked to serve the lady, who mourned a brother even as she did herself. But it was not to be, as the lady would admit none to her house, so Viola begged the captain to bring her to the court of Duke Orsino where, in man's clothing, she might get employment as a page.

She called herself Cesario, and, in doublet and hose, with sword at her hip, and plumed hat in her hand, she made as handsome a youth as she had been beautiful as a girl. Gladly the Duke took her into his service; and, so much trust did he place in her that, after only three days, he sent her to the lady Olivia to plead his love. "Be not denied access," he urged her. "Stand at her doors."

"I'll do my best," promised Viola, and set off to bear her master's heart to the lady's house. It was a bitter errand; for that which she carried she would sooner have kept for herself. In the space of the three days, she had fallen in love with the Duke.

Olivia was not well pleased when she was told that there was a young man waiting at her gate who would not be sent away. Nor was she better pleased when she learned that her uncle was with him. Shrewdly she judged that the sight, smell and sound of Sir Toby would give no very favourable impression of a house in mourning. So she sent her steward, Malvolio, to tell the young man to go away, and to contradict, in his solemn person, any wild notion the young man might have got from Sir Toby. Malvolio was as sober a personage as Sir Toby was not, with a face as long as Sunday, which he wore on every day of the week. Before his important tread, the very larder mice grew serious and thought of church; but not even he could dislodge Duke Orsino's messenger from Olivia's gate.

"Let him approach," said the lady, with weary resignation; and, when Malvolio had stalked away to admit the young person, she bade Maria, her waiting-woman, to fetch her veil.

"The honourable lady of the house, which is she?" demanded Viola, coming into the chamber with a stride that was too long for her, a look that was too bold, and a voice that was too deep. Then, when she had been coldly informed which was the mistress and which was the maid, she begged the veiled one to grant an audience alone. Olivia considered the request. Although there was an impertinence in the messenger's manner, and he had, from all accounts, been impudent at her gate, there was such a manly boldness about him (bolder by far than his too-gentle master), that the lady was curious to know him better. She dismissed her maid and leaned forward so that her eyes sparkled like stars within the night of her veil.

"Good madam, let me see your face," begged Viola, stepping a little outside her office and yielding to womanly curiosity. Olivia hesitated and then, not wanting it to be thought that she wore a veil merely to hide a plain countenance, drew it back and smiled a most radiant smile.

"Is't not well done?" she asked, with quiet pride.

"Excellently done," granted Viola, none too pleased to see a beauty that almost rivalled her own, "if God did all."

"'Tis in grain, sir," returned the lady, a little taken aback that the honesty of her complexion should be called into question. "'Twill endure wind and weather."

Viola, anxious to make amends for her offence, and fearful, perhaps, that its very shrewdness might have betrayed her for a woman, began pleading the Duke's cause with such passion and ardour, with such tender fire and aching love, as any woman might have dreamed of hearing from a lover's lips, but never did. She spoke for the Duke as she longed for the Duke to have spoken to her.

"What is your parentage?" murmured Olivia faintly, when the messenger had done.

"Above my fortunes," answered Viola, somewhat surprised. "I am a gentleman."

Olivia sighed and nodded, and bade the messenger return to the Duke. "I cannot love him," she said. "Let him send no more . . ." She paused, and then added softly, "unless, perchance, you come to me again, to tell me how he takes it."

When the handsome youth had gone, Olivia gazed after him with brightly shining eyes. She summoned her steward. "Run after that same peevish messenger," she told him with a calmness that she herself marvelled at. "He left this ring behind him . . . tell him I'll none of it."

When her steward had gone with the ring, she blushed for her lie. The youth had left nothing; the ring had been her own. The messenger had pleaded the master's cause with too much success. The lady had fallen in love with the messenger, and longed for him to come again.

Malvolio, his black cloak flapping and his black stockings twinkling, like a crow to a feast, panted after the Duke's messenger. "Were not you even now, with the Countess Olivia?" he demanded when he had caught up with the youth; and, when the messenger had confessed as much, he said: "She returns this ring to you," and held out the trinket disdainfully, between finger and thumb.

Much surprised, Viola disclaimed all knowledge of the ring, so Malvolio dropped it contemptuously in the mire and hastened back to his mistress's house. Viola picked up the ring, stared at it, wondered, then guessed the reason for the sending of it. "Poor lady!" she sighed. Though the sun shone, the blossoms smiled and the air was soft, it was a sad world. She loved Orsino, who loved Olivia, who now, it seemed, loved her. In each instance, love was given, and not returned.

That night, in Olivia's house, there was another giver who got no return. Sir Andrew Aguecheek, still laying out his money for a cause that all but a fool would have known to be hopeless, was with his good friend, Sir

Toby Belch. They were both drunk and inclined to be musical: Sir Toby low, and Sir Andrew high and eager as a wren. They sat at a table in a golden cave of candlelight, that, as they breathed, swayed and tottered as if the very air was tipsy from recollected wine. Presently they were joined by Feste, Olivia's jester, an ageing Fool who earned his keep by roaming the mansion and dispensing faded laughter and sad sweet songs. All three now leaned together in their withered finery, like a bowl of old mottled fruit.

"Would you have a love-song, or a song of good life?" proposed Feste.

"A love-song, a love-song!" belched Sir Toby, with an amorous glint in his wine-rich eye.

"Ay, ay," agreed Sir Andrew eagerly. "I care not for good life."

So Feste sang them a love-song of such sweet melancholy that they fell silent; and when he finished with: "Then come kiss me, sweet and twenty, Youth's a stuff will not endure," they sighed and their eyes grew moist; it was December remembering May. But melancholy was soon blown to the winds, for they began upon a mad song that went round and round, like a blindfold child at a birthday, which required much banging of tankards and stamping of feet to keep it in motion.

"What a caterwauling do you keep here!" Maria, a cross plump morsel in her shift, had to shout to make herself heard, for the revellers had awakened the house. But she was too pretty a complainant to be taken seriously. Sir Toby staggered to his feet, caught her in his arms, and danced her about the room, singing at the top of his voice.

"For the love o' God, peace!" she shrieked, but more in laughter than reproach.

Then, when the uproar was at its height, with Feste capering, Sir Andrew whirling like a blown leaf, and the very plates upon the table jigging up and down, there appeared in the doorway a most fearful, dismal, chilling sight. Malvolio in his nightgown, with every inch of him, from tasselled cap to the shocked toes of his bare feet expressing outrage and indignation, stood and surveyed the lunatic scene. "My masters, are you mad?" he demanded; and then went on, in dreadful tones, to threaten Sir Toby, in his mistress's name, with eviction from the house unless he mended his ways.

"Dost thou think," returned Sir Toby indignantly, "because thou art virtuous, there shall be no more cakes and ale?"

Malvolio ignored him and, after having expressed strong disapproval of Maria, for being party to the drunken disorder, he stalked away like a ghost to the tomb.

"Go shake your ears!" said Maria angrily; and then, exasperated by the pompous steward, confided in Sir Toby a certain plan she had devised for humbling that odious man.

She would write a letter, in her mistress's hand, containing a passionate declaration of love for a person not named, but warmly described. She would drop this letter directly in Malvolio's way. Such was his vanity and high opinion of himself that, when he picked it up and read it, he would unfailingly see himself as being the object of the Countess Olivia's love. The conspiritors beamed happily at one another at the prospect of Malvolio's antics when he believed his mistress was his slave.

While Sir Toby and his companions were plotting to make free with Olivia's love, Viola took back the refusal of it to Duke Orsino. Her feelings were mingled. She was a little saddened for the sadness Olivia's message caused her master, and thankful that it gave her hope of, one day, gaining Orsino for herself.

The Duke would hear none but the most doleful ditties, which chimed in with his mood. He bade his page go to the Countess Olivia once more to plead his love.

"But if she cannot love you, sir?" said Viola gently. But the Duke would take no such answer; so Viola, as nearly as she dared, tried to turn Orsino's thoughts towards herself. "My father had a daughter loved a man," she said, "as it might be, perhaps, were I a woman, I should your lordship."

The Duke gazed curiously at his page. "And what's her history?" he asked.

"A blank, my lord: she never told her love."

"But died thy sister of her love, my boy?" asked the Duke, when he had heard a sad tale of unspoken affection.

"I am all the daughters of my father's house," answered Viola, mysteriously; then grief swept over her as she thought of lost Sebastian. "And all the brothers too . . ." She turned away to hide the sorrow and the love she dared not show; and was thankful to escape Orsino's eye, even though her errand, to Olivia's house, was even less to her liking than before.

Now the Countess Olivia had a garden, where close-clipped trees made green secrets of the avenues and walks. Here Sir Toby and his companions had hid themselves and were peering eagerly through a lattice-work of branches, for Malvolio was coming, and the fateful letter lay directly in his way.

He came, a blot of ink upon the bright morning, with his shadow in close attendance, like an admiring pupil. He was in a gravely sauntering mood, with his buckled shoes making stately little patterns on the path. Sometimes he paused and bowed courteously to some imaginary ac-quaintance, sometimes he made gestures as if to indicate an audience with him was at an end. He was communing with himself aloud, as men

16

He came, a blot of ink upon the bright morning

will do when they suppose their only listeners are the trees. First, Maria was in love with him; and then, advancing further into dreams, he was Count Malvolio, had beeen married to Olivia for three months, was richly dressed and had just summoned his wife's uncle to stand before him as a penitent. "Cousin Toby," he murmured reproachfully, "you must amend your drunkenness."

"Out, scab!" breathed Sir Toby, trembling with rage at the steward's presumption. Then he and his fellow watchers held their breath. Malvolio had seen the letter. He touched it with his foot; looked cautiously about him; then picked the letter up and immediately recognized his mistress's hand! With shaking fingers he broke the seal and read:

"Jove knows I love: But who?" There followed some riddling lines that ended with: "M.O.A.I. doth sway my life."

He cogitated, long and deep; and then, with a burst of excitement, he realised that M.O.A.I. were all letters that were in his own name. He read on; and every word he read convinced him more and more that the letter was from his lady and was meant for him. "If this fall into thy hand," she wrote, "revolve. In my stars I am above thee, but be not afraid of greatness. Some are born great, some achieve greatness, and some have greatness thrust upon 'em." Then she urged him to be haughty in his manner, for was not his future golden? He should smile in her presence to show that he returned her love; and she earnestly requested him to appear in yellow stockings with cross garters.

The solemn steward was transfigured with joy. He hopped, he danced, he kissed the letter and pressed it to his breast. His dearest dreams had been fulfilled. He would be his mistress's master, and lord of the mansion. He kissed the letter again and, black and flapping, capered away!

"Mark his first approach before my lady," promised Maria, as the conspirators came out of their hiding-place, weeping with laughter. "He will come to her in yellow stockings, and 'tis a colour she abhors, and cross-gartered, a fashion she detests!"

Viola, on her way to perform her master's errand, came striding through the garden; but before she could enter the mansion, Olivia herself, in mourning more gorgeous than ever, came out, together with Maria.

"Most excellent, accomplished lady," exclaimed Viola, doffing her great plumed hat and bowing low, "the heavens rain odours on you!"

Sir Toby and Sir Andrew, who were eagerly awaiting the appearance of Malvolio, looked askance at the Duke's extravagant page.

"That youth's a rare courtier," muttered Sir Andrew, enviously, "'rain odours'—well!" And even when the Countess made it plain that she wished to hear the Duke's message alone, he lingered, unnecessary as a maypole in June. At length, he was persuaded to follow his companions; and Olivia, sinking down upon a rustic bench, gazed warmly at the page.

"Give me your hand," she commanded gently.

With the utmost reluctance Viola surrendered her hand, and took it back as soon as she could, for Olivia showed every sign of pressing it to her bosom. She tried to plead her master's cause, and to avert her eyes from Olivia's ardent eyes and heaving breast. She tried to back away, but Olivia, with a silken rustle that was, in Viola's ears, more terrible than the pursuing of a tiger, followed after. "Dear lady—" pleaded Viola; but Olivia, overcome with passion, abandoned all restraint, and poured out her love for the Duke's handsome, retreating page. The more she was refused, the greater grew her desire, for it was like any other hunger that increases with denial.

"And so adieu, good madam," cried Viola, when, by a mixture of ingenious avoiding and desperate cunning, she had got herself to the gate.

"Yet come again," begged Olivia, as the youth escaped.

Sir Andrew, whose amorous hopes had been kept alight by Sir Toby, was in despair. "I saw your niece," he said to his fat comforter, "do more favours to the Count's serving-man than ever she bestowed upon me." He was all for giving up his courtship of Olivia, but Sir Toby, anxious not to lose so easy a supply of money, persuaded him otherwise. He put it to Sir Andrew that Olivia, by showing favour to the page, had meant only to stir up Sir Andrew to valour. He advised Sir Andrew to challenge the youth to a duel. Sir Andrew nodded, and, when he had gone to write out the challenge, Sir Toby reflected that no great harm would come out of the encounter; for Sir Andrew and the youth were about as fierce and warlike as each other. Then Maria, shaking with laughter, came to warn him that Malvolio, in yellow stockings and cross-gartered, and full of bedroom smirks and bony smiles, was coming to the Countess.

Poor Olivia! she was as mistakenly loved as she was mistakenly in love. Unable to bear his absence any longer, she sent a servant after Orsino's page, to plead with him to return.

Now as Viola was returning to the palace of the Duke, another Viola was in the town: same height, same face, same hat, same doublet and same boots. Yet not quite the same. It was Sebastian. He had not been drowned. He had been washed ashore, where, mourning his lost sister (who was, to him, as lost as he to her), he had been discovered by a gentleman by the name of Antonio. Antonio had helped him and never left his side; and now they walked together in the town.

"What's to do?" asked Sebastian, gazing with interest round the busy streets. "Shall we go see the reliques of this town?"

But Antonio would not; he had, in the past, fought against the Duke, and was still counted as an enemy. Nonetheless he urged Sebastian to walk about and view the noble buildings of the town. "Here's my purse," he said, for he knew Sebastian had no money and might see something he wished to buy. He had grown deeply fond of the youth, and thought nothing of trusting him with all his wealth. Gratefully Sebastian took his friend's purse, and promised to meet with him at a certain inn, within an hour. They parted, Sebastian one way, and Antonio another; but it was not long before Antonio, finding he needed money for his lodgings, was forced to go in search of Sebastian to ask for the return of his purse.

Olivia, gazing out of her window for the hoped-for return of Orsino's page, was sadder than her black; for the scorn of one loved was more painful by far than a brother's decease. "Where's Malvolio?" she asked. "He is sad and civil, and suits well for a servant with my fortunes."

"He is coming, madam," said Maria, "but in very strange manner."

The solemn steward had obeyed the letter to the very letter: his cross-gartered legs were as yellow as primroses, and he smiled.

"How now, Malvolio?" exclaimed Olivia, not a little surprised.

"Sweet Lady, ho, ho!" ventured Malvolio, persevering with his smile, even though his legs were painful as his garters were too tight. He winked at the Countess, kissed his fingers at her, and smirked with all his teeth.

Maria turned away; her shoulders were shaking with inward laughter.

"Why, how dost thou, man?" demanded Olivia, angrily. "What is the matter with thee?"

Malvolio, with a saucy twinkle of his feet (which gave him some discomfort and caused him to rub his constricted legs), made answer with an obscure reference to the letter he had received. The Countess, not understanding, became worried about him. "Wilt thou go to bed, Malvolio?" she suggested kindly.

"To bed?" cried Malvolio, ambition leaping within him. "Ay, sweetheart, and I'll come to thee!"

He held out his arms, but, for one reason or another, the Countess did not fly into his embrace. He pursued the matter, with further references to the letter, but before he could get his mistress to confess her love, they were interrupted with the news that the Duke's messenger had returned and was awaiting the Countess's pleasure.

"I'll come to him," said Olivia quickly; and bade Maria to fetch Sir Toby to look after her poor steward, who, she felt, had lost his wits.

Malvolio, alone, was not displeased with the way things had gone. Everything the Countess had said, fitted, or could be made to fit, with his high expectations. The very fact that she had asked for her kinsman, Sir Toby, to attend him, proved that she held him in the highest regard.

Sir Toby came, and Malvolio was condescending with him. After all, he would soon be master of the house. Then, Sir Toby and his drunken companions would be put in their proper place. "Go hang yourselves all," he said contemptuously, to his mistress's uncle, her maid, and a servant by the name of Fabian, for whom he had a particular dislike. "You are idle, shallow things; I am not of your element. You shall know more hereafter."

"Come, we'll have him in a dark room and bound," said Sir Toby when the steward had limped and stalked away. Now that the Countess thought that Malvolio was mad, he should be treated as such. He had aspired to love, and was not love madness?

Viola's audience with Olivia had been brief. Again the Countess had begged for love; and again it had been refused. "Well, come again tomorrow," had pleaded the distracted lady. Viola sighed, and left, only to be accosted at the mansion's gate by the lady's portly uncle and a servant whose looks were grave.

"Gentleman, God save thee," said Sir Toby, with much solemnity. Sir Andrew's challenge to the page had been written so foolishly that it would have provoked more laughter than fear, so Sir Toby had decided to deliver the challenge by word of mouth. Quietly he advised the page to look to his defence, for he had offended a very dangerous person.

"You mistake, sir," stammered Viola, growing pale. "I am sure no man hath any quarrel to me."

"You'll find it otherwise, I assure you," said Sir Toby grimly; and went on to present so fearsome a picture of the person who desired satisfaction, that Viola shook with terror.

"I will return again into the house," cried Viola, preferring by far to face a love-sick woman than an angry man, "and desire some conduct of the lady." But it was not to be; and Sir Toby, leaving the trembling Viola in the charge of Fabian, went to fetch her deadly adversary, Sir Andrew Aguecheek.

"Why, man, he is a very devil," confided Sir Toby to Sir Andrew, when he had found him.

"Pox on't," cried Sir Andrew, turning paler than his linen. "I'll not meddle with him."

"Ay," agreed Sir Toby, "but he will not now be pacified: Fabian can scarce hold him yonder."

This was very true, as Fabian was having the utmost difficulty in keeping Viola from bolting for her life.

"There's no remedy, sir," called out Sir Toby, coming out of the mansion and dragging Sir Andrew after him. "He will fight with you for's oath's sake!"

"Pray God defend me!" wailed Viola, struggling in the grip of Fabian, even as Sir Andrew tugged at Sir Toby's. "A little thing would make me tell them how much I lack of a man."

But the seconds were restless, and the two shaking heroes were propelled towards one another on feet that scarcely touched the ground.

"I do assure you, 'tis against my will!" sobbed Viola, as if Sir Andrew might have supposed it to be otherwise; and drew her sword.

Sir Andrew, with no more enthusiasm, drew his; and there they stood, propped up by their seconds, with their blades waving, like grass in the wind.

"Put up your sword! If this young gentleman have done offence, I take the fault on me!"

A gentleman, passing by the mansion's gate, had seen the imminent battle and had drawn his own sword to halt it. It was Antonio. He had been searching for Sebastian and now believed that he had found him, and in danger of his life. But before more could be done, a party of the

Duke's officers came by. At once, Antonio was recognized and arrested as the Duke's enemy.

"This comes with seeking you," said Antonio, somewhat bitterly to Viola, and asked for the return of his purse. "I must entreat of you some of that money," repeated Antonio, as Viola showed no sign of understanding him.

"What money, sir?" wondered Viola.

"Will you deny me now?" demanded Antonio, amazed that the youth he had befriended should prove to be so shameless a villain. He reminded the youth of the kindnesses he had done him.

"I know of none," protested Viola, her confusion increasing.

"O Heavens themselves!" cried out Antonio, more distressed by the youth's ingratitude than by the officers who held him by the arms.

"Come sir, I pray you go," commanded one of his captors; but before they dragged him away, Antonio declared to all how much he had done for the youth, and how little he was getting in recompense. He told of how he had saved him from death, how he had comforted him and supported him, and of how he had come to love him.

"What's that to us?" grunted an officer. "The time goes by. Away!"

"O how vile an idol proves this god!" shouted Antonio, pointing at Viola as he was borne away. "Thou hast, Sebastian, done good feature shame!"

Then he was gone, leaving behind him Sir Toby and Sir Andrew with a very poor opinion of Viola, who they supposed to be, not only a cowardly, but a monstrously ungrateful youth; and Viola with a tempest of feelings in her breast.

"He named Sebastian!" she breathed. Antonio had taken her for her brother; therefore Sebastian was alive! She fled back to the Duke.

If the mistake of one face for another had caused a man to despair, it soon brought a woman to rejoice. Sebastian, wandering past the Countess's mansion, was instantly accosted by Sir Toby and Sir Andrew.

"Now, sir, have I met you again?" cried Sir Andrew, made bold by all he had seen of the youth's courage. "There's for you!" And he struck him in the face.

"Why, there's for thee, and there, and there!" cried Sebastian, angrily returning Sir Andrew's blow, and with such interest as sent the knight reeling to the ground. Sir Toby drew his sword; Sebastian drew his, and blood would surely have been shed, had not the Countess herself come out to discover the cause of the commotion at her gate. Angrily she dismissed Sir Toby, and begged the young man's pardon for the antics of her drunken uncle, who aggravated her beyond measure. Then with such speaking looks and deep-felt sighs, that made her meaning as plain as she herself was lovely, begged the young man come within. Sebastian blinked. "If it be thus to dream," he marvelled, "still let me sleep!" And, unwilling to let slip what Providence had provided, followed Olivia into her house.

Sebastian, finding himself to be beloved for no reason he could think of, walked in brightness; but Malvolio, who believed himself to be loved for reasons of his own worth, was plunged into gloom. He had paid the penalty for greatness; he had risen high, and had fallen low.

Sir Toby and his companions had got their revenge. They had declared Malvolio to be mad; for what could be madder than for a steward to suppose his noble mistress was in love with him? They had locked him away in a dark chamber from which he cried out piteously to be released.

"Sir Topas," he wailed, to Feste, Olivia's jester, who had dressed himself as a curate to torment the steward to the very limits of endurance, "never was man thus wronged! Do not think I am mad. They have laid me here in hideous darkness—"

But his captors were unrelenting. It had not been enough for Malvolio to be ridiculous in the world's eyes, he had to be humbled in his own. For as long as he thought himself to be great, the world's opinion counted for little. But at length Sir Toby yielded, not to the promptings of pity, for he had none, but because he feared that his niece would lose all patience with him if he continued to abuse her solemn steward. The wretched man was allowed to write a letter to his mistress, pleading to be released.

Even as a false priest had conducted Malvolio to hell, so a true one brought Olivia to heaven. Before the young man, whom she still took to be Cesario, the Duke's page, could change his mind and run away, she took him firmly to a chapel in the town where a holy father married them without delay. Sebastian submitted gladly for, although he guessed that he was loved by mistake, he felt it would be folly to set the lady right. He loved her. Then, the wedding done, he left his bride of minutes to find Antonio and give him back his purse.

It was late afternoon. The sun had painted certain windows red and gold, and laid dark carpets along the streets. The Duke and his lords, and Viola, came strolling through the town, where they met Olivia's jester. At once the Duke paid Feste well to go and fetch his mistress for, in spite of all Olivia's refusals, Orsino had not given up hope of winning her.

Feste departed and then came calamities, so swiftly one upon another that there was scarcely reeling time between them! First Antonio, in the grip of officers and on his way to gaol, came marching by.

"Here comes the man, sir, that did rescue me," said Viola, recognizing her saviour from the duel. The Duke also recognized him, not as a saviour but as a very warlike enemy. He accused him; Viola defended him. Antonio turned upon Viola and accused her yet again of base ingratitude; and again Viola denied it.

"Here comes the Countess," cried the Duke, forgetting enemies and friends alike, as the object of his heart approached. "Gracious Olivia—"

But she would have none of him and had eyes only for his page.

"Where goes Cesario?" she cried, when, as Orsino turned to leave, Viola prepared to follow.

"After him I love . . ." returned Viola; and Olivia's worst fears were realised. The young man had changed his mind.

"Hast thou forgot thyself? Is it so long?" she demanded. "Call forth the holy father!" And then, when her pleas had no effect, she begged: "Cesario, husband, stay!"

"Husband?" exclaimed the Duke, amazed.

"Ay, husband."

"Her husband, sirrah?"

"No, my lord, not I!" swore Viola, as the Duke turned upon her in a rage.

But proof was at hand. The holy father came in answer to Olivia's summons, and confirmed that he had only just married the lady and the youth.

"O thou dissembling cub!" cried out the Duke, in anguish that his page, whom he had loved and trusted, should have so betrayed him.

"My lord, I do protest—" pleaded Viola; but before matters could be explained, yet another blow fell and added to the dreadful confusion. Sir Andrew Aguecheek, bleeding from his least useful part, which was his head, came staggering down the street, calling for a surgeon.

"Who has done this, Sir Andrew?" asked the Countess.

"The Count's gentleman, one Cesario," groaned Sir Andrew, clutching his wound. "We took him for a coward, but he's the very devil incardinate." Then he saw Viola and shrank back in terror. Next came Sir Toby, leaning on the jester's arm. He too was bleeding from a wound that was the very twin of Sir Andrew's, and which had been given him by the same fierce Cesario.

"Get him to bed," commanded the Countess, concerned for her uncle, "and let his hurt be looked to."

With moans and groans and angry belches, Sir Toby and Sir Andrew were helped away, leaving pale Viola condemned by all for an almanack of crimes: by the Duke for treachery, by Antonio for ingratitude, by Olivia for faithlessness, and by Sir Toby and Sir Andrew for assault. She trembled; she turned from one accuser to another. What could she say?

To deny treachery made her seem more treacherous; to deny ingratitude made her seem the more ungrateful; to deny faithlessness made her seem stony-hearted; and to deny assault made her a bare-faced liar when the wounds had been seen by all. Nothing less than a miracle could have absolved her, at a single stroke, from so many crimes.

"I am sorry, madam, I have hurt your kinsman," said another Cesario, stepping forward like a reflection without a glass.

"One face, one voice, one habit, and two persons!" whispered Orsino, staring from one Cesario to the other.

"How have you made division of yourself?" wondered Antonio.

"Most wonderful!" sighed Olivia, when she had determined which was her husband and which was not.

Then brother and sister embraced one another and wept with joy.

"Boy," said the Duke to his page, when at last Sebastian and Viola stood apart, "thou hast said to me a thousand times thou never shouldst love woman like to me." The sight of so much fondness had swelled his tender heart, and the untangling of so much distress into so much love had made him long to have a part in it. "Give me thy hand," he said to Viola, "and let me see thee in thy woman's weeds." She gave him her hand and he pressed it to his lips. Suddenly he loved her, for he knew that she loved him; and there's nothing so awakens love as love itself.

27

Only Malvolio still languished in darkness. The letter he had written was brought to Olivia, who, when she read it, took pity on the poor man and commanded his immediate release. He came, crumpled and dishevelled, with straw in his hair, for the chamber in which he had been locked was none of the cleanest. Bitterly he accused his mistress of having misled him, and showed her the letter that had set his madness on. She took the paper and studied it. She shook her head: the hand was not hers. "Alas, poor fool, how have they baffled thee!" she said, with a gentle shake of her head when she had divined who had been the authors of Malvolio's fall.

The steward glared about him. The general happiness of pairs and pairings warmed him into no better utterance than: "I'll be revenged on the whole pack of you!" Then he stalked away.

But Malvolio's departure cast no gloom on the company; for his injuries had been to his pride and not to his heart; and so were not fatal.

Then Viola, who had gained the love of Orsino and hung upon his arm, and Olivia, who had gained the love of Sebastian, and hung upon his arm, and Antonio who had regained his purse and his faith in the gratitude of friends, and all at a single stroke, strolled away in a golden pattern of plaited arms and inclining heads.

Feste alone remained behind. He gazed after the happy ones, and, seating himself cross-legged on the ground, sang one of his sweet sad songs:

> "When that I was and a little tiny boy,
> With hey, ho, the wind and the rain,
> A foolish thing was but a toy,
> For the rain it raineth every day."

Though he was my lady's Fool, he was the wisest of all. He was paid to play the Fool; the rest of the world did it for nothing.

King Lear

Long, long ago, before even there were churches, there ruled a king of Britain whose name was Lear. He had three daughters; and when he grew old and longed to have done with the burden of governing and enjoy only the pleasures of being a king, he resolved to divide his kingdom between his beloved children, and keep only the crown for himself. Accordingly, he summoned them to his palace, and there, in the solemn council chamber, before all the dukes and lords and knights who could be crammed inside, he asked his daughters how much they loved him; for so much should they receive.

The eldest born spoke first: Goneril, Duchess of Albany, a great lady whose marble beauty melted into fondness as she told the world how much she loved her father. She loved him better than anything in the wide universe.

"Dearer," she declared, "than eyesight, space or liberty!" Then, with a rush and a rustle of wide skirts, she mounted the steps to the throne as a dark cloud ascending, and kissed her father's hand.

The old King, in his stiff robes like Time preserved in gold, gazed down at his kissed hand. What father owned a child as dear as Goneril! Proudly he stared across the crowding coronets that dipped and bobbed admiringly, a sudden breeze rippling a sunlit sea. Smiles stretched every

29

face . . . except for one! The Earl of Kent was frowning; and his plain face, in that tapestry of smiles, made an ugly rent.

Next to speak was Regan, Duchess of Cornwall, second in birth but by no means second in beauty. Her cheeks were stained with roses and her marvellous gown was feverish with pearls. How much did she love the King, her father?

"I am made of that self metal as my sister," she cried. "I find she names my very deed of love; only she comes too short . . ." Then she too mounted to the throne and kissed her father, not on the hand but on his withered cheek.

King Lear nodded, and touched the quickly given kiss as if it might fly away; and the web of wrinkles round his eyes glimmered as if with dew. What father owned a child as precious as Regan! Again the golden tide of coronets rippled with admiration; and again the Earl of Kent looked sour. Then at last that plain blunt man smiled. It was the turn of Cordelia, the youngest born, to speak.

In plain white gown, with no gold but her hair, and no jewels but her eyes, she stood before her father as her sisters had done, to offer him love in exchange for a third of the kingdom. Her face was grave and steady; and she said nothing.

"What can you say to draw a third more opulent than your sisters?" urged the King fondly, for Cordelia was dearest to his heart; and what father ever owned a child as true as Cordelia! "Speak."

"Nothing, my lord," she said.

"Nothing?"

"Nothing."

They stared at one another, he, bewildered into anger, and she, steadily, but with a thundering heart. She knew the world was watching her, and she felt her sisters' sharply inquiring eyes. She knew what was expected of her, but she would not, could not, submit. She loved her father as a daughter should, truly and with clear eyes. She could not swear, as her sisters had done, that she adored him as a god.

King Lear stood up, and the golden tide before him whispered and shrank back. Stretched smiles withered; the elder sisters slid their looks sideways; the youngest stared straight ahead. The King put his hand to his brow. There was a place that burned and burned, as if it would scorch his brain. It was the place that Cordelia might have kissed. He saw uneasy courtiers, with frightened faces, cowering back like cattle before a threatened storm.

But there was one who stood firm, as if he cared nothing for the King's wrath: the Earl of Kent. Yet his face, too, showed fear; but it was the fear that, if the storm broke, it would destroy father, child, King and kingdom alike. When private men act in anger, only private places tremble; but with kings, the whole world is shaken into pieces.

The King's eyes blazed, and his voice was thunderous. The storm had broken and the kingdom rocked with its violence. The Earl of Kent was swept aside, flung from the kingdom by instant banishment, for daring to step between the King and the object of his rage. Cordelia herself, not knowing whether she was waking or dreaming, swayed before the thunderbolts that were hurled at her from the throne. Her inheritance, her dowry, and even her father's love were stripped from her, leaving her trembling and naked of all that should belong to the daughter of a king. Then she was cast away. Two men had courted her: the Duke of Burgundy and the King of France. Contemptuously she was offered to them, with the nothing she had offered her father. Burgundy shrugged his shoulders and turned away; but France saw differently. He took her gladly, for, to him, her true heart and her honest soul were dowry enough.

Breathing deeply, the King turned to Goneril and Regan, the daughters who had been dutiful, and divided Cordelia's inheritance between them. It was done. He had given up his power. He kept nothing back, but the crown itself and a following of a mere hundred knights. He relinquished even his palace; for with two such loving children, what need had a father of another house? Henceforward and till the end of his life, he would divide his time equally between the two he had so liberally endowed.

"Love well our father," said Cordelia, as she parted from her sisters.

"Prescribe not us our duty," came the cold reply.

Lately there had been eclipses of the sun and moon. A great darkness had fallen over the land, and beggars and wandering madmen had crept fearfully under bushes and into holes in the ground. Then had followed ruin and disorder everywhere, even in the royal palace, where the maddened King had banished Kent and cast off the good Cordelia. Surely the world was coming to an end! King against subject, father against child . . . and now, child against father! The Earl of Gloucester, another aged father in that motherless kingdom of Lear, on returning to his castle, learned that Edgar, his elder son, was plotting to kill him. Edmund, the younger, had told him, had even shown him a letter, written in Edgar's hand, in which the foul plot was as clear as day—if ever day was as dark as such a deed!

"O villain, villain!" groaned the Earl wringing his hands in dismay. "Unnatural, detested, brutish villain!"

Then Edmund, clever, handsome Edmund, laid a comforting hand upon his father's sleeve, and went in search of Edgar, to warn him, brother to brother, that their father, for some unknown cause, was in a violent passion with him, that Edgar's very life was in danger, and that, until Edmund could bring the Earl to reason, it would be best if Edgar fled.

Edgar, as noble and as foolishly honest in his way as Cordelia had been in hers, trusted his brother and believed his every word. Horribly bewildered and distressed, he ran from his father's house like a thief.

Edmund smiled as he watched him go. He despised and envied his brother, who was legitimate and so would inherit everything. He himself was merely the offspring of his father's casual lust, and would get nothing unless he shifted for himself. "Let me," he murmured softly, "if not by birth, have lands by wit." He himself had written the letter and invented the plot.

King Lear rode through the night. High upon a huge dark horse, the ancient King, cloaked and hooded in furs and heavy velvet, galloped across heath and common, through startled village and frightened hamlet, with his hundred knights streaming after, and a queer little patched figure, with face as white as paint, clinging to his back like a tattered hump. It was his Fool, his beloved Fool, who mocked at his madness, jeered at his folly, and yet was a thousand times more dear to

King Lear rode through the night

him than any child. Goneril hated him; but her hatred was as a candle beside the furnace of hatred that raged within Lear against his eldest born.

She had scorned him! She had diminished him! She had told her servants to be insolent with him! She had commanded him to halve the number of his followers! He was no more than a tedious, noisy old man, and she had driven him out with her contempt. In scarce two weeks the great love she had professed, while she stood before the throne, had dwindled into such cold ash! He had cursed her; for did ever a father own a child as vile as Goneril!

But there was always Regan, beloved Regan, who had sworn that her love for him had ever been greater than Goneril's. So it was to Regan that he was galloping so fiercely—not to her palace, for she and the Duke of Cornwall had gone from there and were now with the Earl of Gloucester. This was strange, for he had sent a messenger to warn her of his coming; and still she had gone. He found excuses for her, as a father would, good excuses . . . but why had his messenger, who had gone after her, not been sent back?

The Earl of Gloucester's castle reared up against the grim sky like a black thought in a dark mind. Outside the heavy, bolted doors, sat a man, patient and quiet, with his legs imprisoned in a stout wooden gaol. He

had been there all day. He was the King's messenger, and he had been set, as if he were a common vagabond, in the stocks.

The Duke and Duchess of Cornwall had ordered it, even though the Earl of Gloucester had protested that it was an insult to the King to treat his messenger with such disrespect. But the fellow had been brawling. He had soundly thrashed one Oswald, steward to the Duchess of Albany, who had come with a message from sister to sister. It would have been an insult to Goneril, who valued Oswald even above her husband, the mild-mannered Duke, if her servant's attacker was not severely punished. So the King's messenger had been put in the stocks; and there he sat, with nothing but philosophy for comfort and company.

He was a roughly dressed, roughly bearded, roughly spoken fellow who was new to the King's service; yet when he had seen how Goneril had treated her father, he had been as indignant as if he had served and loved the old King for all his life. He sighed and smiled ruefully. He had indeed served and loved King Lear for all his life; but, in humble clothes and with bristled cheeks, the King had never known him. He was a good man whose rough disguise showed up, rather than hid, his blunt nature. He was the banished Earl of Kent who had come back to watch over his beloved master.

He had sent letters to Cordelia in France, telling how matters stood in the kingdom, how the land was in worse disorder than ever, how the Dukes of Albany and Cornwall were at odds with one another; and that her father suffered. It gave Kent no pleasure to see how his warning had come true. His only comfort, as he sat with aching legs and aching heart, was news he had had that a French army had landed at Dover with Cordelia in its midst. He shifted in his confinement and whistled to keep up his spirits. Soon, now, King Lear's distress would be relieved.

The Earl of Gloucester had also learned of the French landing, and had guiltily hidden away the letter for fear of the Duke and Duchess of Cornwall's seeing it. The old Earl's life seemed in as ruinous a state as the kingdom itself. Edgar, his eldest son, had been proved treacherous beyond all doubt, had fled, and was being hunted down. The King's messenger was in the stocks outside his own doors; and the Earl seemed no longer to be master in his own house. Wherever he looked, he saw the Duke's armed servants; wherever he wandered, he was confronted by the sharp Duke and the sharper Duchess, till he felt like an intruder everywhere. They seemed even to have supplanted him in the affections of his last consolation, Edmund his faithful son. Edmund was a good deal more with the Duke and Duchess than with his father, the Earl.

Then, like a storm on horseback, came the King! With his wild white hair and his wild white beard flying round his flushed face, like the sun in winter, he demanded to speak with the Duke of Cornwall and his wife, who had dared to put his man in the stocks! Wretchedly, the Earl carried the King's command to his mighty guests; and still more wretchedly came back with their cool answer. The King stared at him in amazement.

"Deny to speak with me! They are sick! They are weary! They have travelled all the night!" he shouted. "Fetch me a better answer!"

"My dear Lord," ventured Gloucester, caught between the anger of his old master and the fierceness of his new, "you know the fiery quality of the Duke."

"Vengeance! Plague! Death! Confusion!" roared the King. "Fiery! What quality?" and sent Gloucester back once more, to fetch the Duke and Duchess.

At last they came, and the King's man was set at liberty; but the King scarcely noticed his going. His daughter had come to him, his beloved Regan; and what father owned a child as precious as Regan? His heart overflowed with love for her, and eagerly, he began to pour out, in tumbling words, like a hurt child to a fond mother, the cruelty he had suffered at the hands of her sister.

She stopped him. "I cannot think," she said coldly, "my sister in the least would fail her obligation."

The King faltered, swayed a little, as if the wind had caught him; and stared. Had he heard aright? And was this Regan, his warm, fond Regan, standing before him, this stony Duchess with her granite Duke? No, it could not be Regan; nor was it Regan's voice that was now so cruelly telling him that he was old and near to death, and that he was no longer fit to be master even over himself; that Goneril had been right to check and shrink him, and that he should go back and, on his knees, beg her forgiveness! It could not be Regan, and therefore he would not curse as he had cursed Goneril. It was some monster in Regan's shape, for this daughter would never have forgotten the love she'd sworn nor the gratitude she owed. She was not like Goneril.

"O Heavens, if you do love old men," he cried out, with a sudden rush of anguish, "send down and take my part!"

Goneril had come. With brilliant eyes and wind-red cheeks from travelling, she had rustled to her sister's side, and now they stood together against the old, old man. Then, while the Earl of Gloucester trembled, and the Fool turned his frightened acorn face from side to side, the two daughters, with cold, indifferent looks, and words of colder reason, crushed their father's heart and blasted his brain.

Despairingly, he rushed from one to another. He would stay with Regan, he and his hundred knights! No. Regan shook her head. Five and twenty was the utmost she would allow. Then he would stay with Goneril! Goneril had allowed him fifty, and that was twice Regan's love! No. Goneril shook her head. He had no need of five and twenty, or even ten, or five. Then Regan smiled. "What need one?" she said.

The world grew dark. Black clouds rolled and piled up in the sky, and faint lightnings began to throw up strange configurations, like monstrous, glaring faces, and huge clenched fists.

The old King was mad. He was shouting and raving and cursing his children.

"Unnatural hags, I will have such revenges on you both that all the world shall—" He clutched his head as if his brains would fly out. "I will do such things, what they are, yet I know not, but they shall be the terrors of the earth!" Suddenly he turned to his thin Fool, who was all that remained to him of his old royalty. "O Fool!" he wept, "I shall go mad!" Then, together, King and Fool rushed away into the coming storm.

Unmoved, his daughters watched him go.

"'Tis his own blame," said one.

"I'll receive him gladly," said the other, "but not one follower."

The sky turned black, and drops of rain began to fall.

"For many miles about there's scarce a bush!" pleaded Gloucester, forlornly hoping to move Lear's daughters to pity for the shelterless old man.

They shrugged their shoulders. In a world of reason, there was no room for pity. However harsh the lesson, their father must learn that he was now no more than a beggar with a crown.

"Shut up your doors, my Lord," advised the Duke of Cornwall, grasping the old Earl by the arm. "Come out o' the storm." Helplessly the Earl was drawn back into the castle, and the doors were shut with a dreadful sound. Then the sky exploded with wrath!

It was a night such as no man had ever known before. It was a night of glares and roars, of wild winds and hugely down-rushing torrents of rain, of sudden sights of a world in ruins, stark, bare and broken, thrown up blindingly fierce, then plunged into blackness again.

"Where's the King?" shouted Kent, streaming, sodden Kent; then saw him, running hither and thither, shrieking and shaking his fists at the storm for joining with his monstrous daughters to batter down his old white head.

"I am a man more sinned against than sinning!" he howled, in frantic protests against the horrible injustice of the elements, that blindly punished guilty and innocent, oppressor and victim alike. The soaked Fool, clinging to his mad master with a mouse-like grip, wailed for him to beg his daughters to let them back inside the dark castle, over which lightnings forked and glared.

Desperately Kent tried to lead them away, for the old King would have died in the storm. At first, Lear resisted; then his wits, which were flickering like a windy candle, grew steady, and he saw the shivering misery of the Fool, his only faithful child. "Come on, my boy," he urged with great tenderness, and consented to be led. "In, boy, you go first," he said, as Kent brought them to the best shelter he could find, a poor hovel, as sadly tattered as a beggar's pocket.

But it was not so empty. Within was another wanderer in the storm, another outcast from the castle. Edgar, the Earl of Gloucester's falsely accused son, had taken refuge there. But it was no longer the smiling Edgar of courts and fine clothes. Hunted and hounded and in danger of his life, he had hidden himself in a shape of wild and pitiful horror. A madman! A grinning, scowling, shouting, naked madman, such as the many who wandered the land and plagued the countryside with howls and shrieks and glarings in the night!

"Help me! help me!" cried the Fool, flying from the hovel in terror, as, after him, with staring looks and whirling words, came the madman! The wind howled, the rain pelted down, and a huge flash of lightning exposed the naked wretch, all tangled with scratches from the flaying of briars.

"Didst thou give all to thy daughters?" pondered the King, shaking his dazed and battered head. "And art thou come to this?"

"Who gives anything to poor Tom?" wondered the madman; then he and the King discoursed weirdly with one another, sense and madness coming and going, and, like the storm's flickerings, now illuminating, now plunging them into dreadful darkness.

"Look!" cried out the Fool. "Here comes a walking fire!"

A torch, hissing and smoking, was weaving through the night, and the Earl of Gloucester, fear and pity shining in his flame-lit eyes, came

stumbling towards them. Although forbidden to help the King, he had
crept secretly from the castle to find his old master and bring him to a
farm-building nearby, where food and a fire had been prepared. "What!
hath your Grace no better company?" he asked in dismay, when he found
the King in deep talk with the mad beggar. He no more knew his son
naked than he had really known him in his best attire.

But the King would not be parted from his new companion, so all
followed the Earl as he led them, secretly, to shelter. "No words, no
words," he whispered, as they drew near the castle. "Hush!"

"Child Roland to the dark tower came," mumbled the madman,
staring up at the grim bulk. "His word was still: fie, foh, and fum, I smell
the blood of a British man."

The room was humble, but there was food on the table and a fire in the
hearth; there were rough country stools and a rough country bed, on
which the Earl had laid cushions more fit for a King. "I will not be long
from you," he promised Kent, and returned to the castle to see what else
he could bring for the comfort of the broken King.

The storm was weakening; wind and rain dwindled, and the thunder
sank to a grumbling. Kent begged the King to lie down; but he would
not. He had important business first. His daughters must be brought to
trial. Their crimes? Hard hearts and ingratitude. Their judges? The
madman, the Fool and Kent. The King himself would give evidence.

"Arraign her first," he said, pointing accusingly at a stool; "'tis
Goneril. I here take my oath before this honourable assembly she kicked
the poor King, her father."

Kent turned aside, and even Edgar, the false madman, could scarce
hold back his tears for the flickering ruin of King Lear's mind. Only the
Fool, his spirits lifted by warmth and comfort, supported his master in
his madness.

"We'll go to supper i' the morning," said the King, with a gracious
gesture, as at last he lay down on the bed.

"And I'll go to bed at noon," said the Fool, fondly mocking his
master's flourish and tone.

The King was sleeping when Gloucester returned. His face was pale,
his voice trembled. Lear's daughters were planning their father's death.

The King must leave at once. There was a cart waiting that would carry him to Dover. "Come, help to bear thy master," said Kent to the Fool, as he and Gloucester between them, lifted the still sleeping King. "Thou must not stay behind."

The King had gone and the naked madman had crept away. The night was quiet and a few faint stars pricked through the tatters of the sky. There was a sudden noise of horses, galloping, then it died away. The castle was dark, and its fanged battlements seemed to strike at the sky. The Earl of Gloucester, his act of mercy done, went back inside.

They were waiting for him, the Duke and Duchess of Cornwall. The Duchess of Albany and Edmund, his son, had left him to face Regan and her terrible husband. They had discovered he had helped the King; and worse, they had found the letter telling of the French landing and Cordelia's return.

He was seized by the Duke's servants and bound tightly to a chair.

"You are my guests: do me no foul play, friends!" he pleaded, staring up into the eyes where pity had never shone. For answer, Regan leaned forward and mockingly plucked at his beard. He cried out in shocked amazement.

Then the Duke began to question him . . . about the King, about the letter. Why had he sent the King to Dover? He was a traitor and was conspiring with the enemy. Why else had he sent the King to Dover? Again and again he shook his head.

"Wherefore to Dover?" repeated Regan, with fierce insistence.

"Because I would not see thy cruel nails pluck out his poor old eyes!" cried out the Earl, driven at last to pour out all the pent-up anger in his heart against Lear's monstrous children; and he prayed that he might live to see vengeance overtake them!

"See it thou never shall!" shouted the Duke and, while servants held the old Earl firmly, he reached out, and, with sharp fingers, tore out one of his eyes!

"The other, too!" urged Regan eagerly, as if the old man's shrieks and screams of agony had made her hot for more.

"Hold your hand, my Lord!" cried out a servant, scarce able to believe what his master had done. The Duke turned on him. Swords were out. They fought. The servant wounded his master; then paid for his brave humanity by losing it. Regan stabbed him from behind.

"My Lord," breathed the dying man to Gloucester, "you have one eye left to see some mischief on him . . ." But the Duke, scowling heavily from his wound, shook his head. "Out, vile jelly!" he panted, and, with red nails, clawed out the other eye.

Gloucester was in darkness and unimagined pain. "Where is my son Edmund?" he moaned. Only to be told that it was Edmund who had betrayed him to the monsters in the castle. Then he knew what eyes had never let him see: that he, like the old King, had cast out the true child and had cherished the worst.

"Go thrust him out at gates," ordered Regan contemptuously, "and let him smell his way to Dover."

He was led away; and servants, out of sight of their mistress and master, soothed his bleeding face with whites of eggs, and gently bandaged over his horrible lack of eyes. It was morning when he stumbled out of the castle gates, though night to him. Everywhere, broken trees, weeping hedgerows and ruined fields bore witness to the fury that had been outside; the old Earl, with two red flowers for eyes, bore witness to the savagery that had been within.

An ancient countryman, a tenant of the Earl's, saw him fumbling the air, and was at once filled with pity. He took him by the hand and led him away from the castle. Gloucester begged him to go away, for he feared that any who helped him would suffer for it, even as he had suffered for helping the King.

"You cannot see your way," answered the ancient one, as if that was reason enough for setting pity above common sense. So they wandered on, the tenant carefully keeping his blind lord out of the ditches that ran, like silver sores, along the sides of the road.

Edgar was on that road, and he saw the old countryman leading his father. Then he saw his father's eyeless face, and horror seized him, and wild disbelief!

"'Tis poor mad Tom," said the countryman, recognizing the naked madman who stood, staring and trembling in their way.

"Is that the naked fellow?" asked Gloucester, remembering the King's strange companion in the storm; and when he heard that it was indeed the same fellow, he asked poor Tom to lead him to Dover. But first he begged the countryman to fetch some clothing for his naked guide.

"I'll bring the best 'parel that I have!" promised the old fellow, and hastened away to his poor cottage, as if it was a treasure-house, over-flowing with plenty. While they waited, Gloucester told his guide of a certain cliff near to Dover, that reared high above the sea. It was to the top of this cliff that he wished to be taken; for it was in his mind to end his miseries by plunging from that place.

"Give me thy arm," answered Edgar, in poor Tom's voice, for he dared not trust his own. "Poor Tom shall lead thee."

Serpents do not sicken from their own venom, but men do. Already Lear's evil daughters and Gloucester's evil son were being poisoned by the very instruments that had brought them power: greed, lust, cruelty, envy and ambition. The Duke of Cornwall was dead; he had died of the wound given him by his servant. Regan, his widow, lusted for Edmund, the handsome new Earl of Gloucester; so also did her sister Goneril, Duchess of Albany, who loathed and despised her own husband, whose mild nature shrank from his wife's merciless strength. The two sisters hated each other; and Edmund, smiling, clever Edmund, who had sworn undying affection to both of them, cared not which murdered the other for love of him, for he loved himself far better.

The Duke of Albany, a weak but honourable man, who had grieved for what had become of the King, rejoiced when he learned that the Duke of Cornwall had perished for his monstrous cruelty to Gloucester; and it was only because of the threat to the kingdom itself that he joined forces with Regan and Edmund, and marched upon Dover.

The land trembled under the tread of bony soldiers and gaunt horses; and the banners of Albany, Cornwall and Gloucester streamed out over the two Duchesses, who rode more murderously against each other, than against the invading French. Edmund rode with Regan, who, being widowed, had the better claim; so Goneril sent Oswald, her steward, with a letter to Edmund, begging him to murder the Duke of Albany: then she would be a widow, too.

But when Oswald arrived, Edmund had gone. He had ridden on ahead to seek out his father and kill him, before his wretched state moved too many to anger against those who had brought him to it.

"What might import my sister's letter?" asked Regan, staring at the sealed paper and consumed with jealous suspicions.

"I know not, my Lady," answered the steward.

She did not believe him. "I'll love thee much," she offered coaxingly. "Let me unseal the letter."

But Oswald was faithful; so Regan was forced to content herself with hiding her anger and telling the steward to warn his mistress that Edmund was not for her. Then, as Oswald rode on after Edmund, Regan called out, as a bloody afterthought, that he would be well rewarded if he found the blind Earl of Gloucester and killed him.

The blind old Earl, his wounds congealed to two black clusters, wandered in a field not far from Dover. Edgar, still unknown, led him by the hand.

"When shall I come to the top of that same hill?" he asked, wearily.

"You do climb up it now," answered Edgar.

"Methinks the ground is even," said the blind man.

"Horrible steep," promised Edgar, and, with breaking heart, persuaded his father that he stood at the very summit of a cliff so high that it made the brain sway to look down.

The blind man knelt and, giving all he had of value to his guide, took his last farewell of the world. Then he leaped, and fell, foolishly, face forward on the ground.

Edgar ran towards him, and, in a changed voice but still not his own, exclaimed in wonderment that the blind man had not been dashed to pieces! that he was unharmed! that it was not to be believed that he had fallen so far and dropped as gently as a feather! "Thy life's a miracle!" he declared; and prayed that the great shock his father had sustained would bring him out of the utter darkness of the spirit. He could not endure for his father to die in despair. Anxiously he watched the blind face turn from side to side, watching its looks change, until at last disbelief and misery softened . . .

"Henceforth," sighed Gloucester, "I'll bear affliction . . ."

"Bear free and patient thoughts," murmured Edgar, gently raising his father. "But who comes here?"

A strange fantastic figure was wandering through the high-grown corn; a mad, wild old man, stuck all over with wild flowers, and crowned with weeds. It was King Lear. He had escaped from his attendants, who, even now, were searching for him to bring him to Cordelia.

"No, they cannot touch me for coining," he announced weirdly. "I am the King himself."

"I know that voice!" cried Gloucester.

"Ha! Goneril with a white beard!" said the King, as if Gloucester's

horrible eyes reminded him of his daughter's. Then he talked reproachfully about the world, which he no longer liked; and the wind and the
rain which had made him unhappy and given him pains in his bones,
even though people had told him he was the King. Then he recognized
Gloucester and jeered at his lost sight. Then he strayed to talking about
men and women, all of whom filled him with disgust. He shuddered and
shut his eyes. They were all liars, cheats, lechers and thieves, with
nothing but lies to choose between them. Then his frantic mind, which
had buzzed like a wasp over all the wide universe, came back to his
children. His eyes blazed. "Kill, kill, kill, kill, kill, kill!" he screamed;
and began to run away, for he had seen his attendants coming for him.

This way and that way he capered, to avoid outstretched arms. "Come
and you get it!" he shouted. "You shall get it by running! Sa, sa, sa, sa!"
And away he went, weeds and flowers falling from him everywhere, and
his attendants running after.

Briefly a gentleman stayed to talk with Edgar of the poor King's state,
and of Cordelia, the daughter who truly loved him. The French army

had moved on, to do battle with the advancing British, but she was waiting for her father.

"How near's the other army?" asked Edgar, anxious for his own father's safety.

"Near, and on speedy foot," answered the gentleman. Edgar thanked him, and, when he had gone, began to lead his father away.

There was a horseman galloping along the road, a dainty horseman with plumes in his hat and a letter tucked importantly in his belt. Seeing the blind man, he reined in and dismounted. "A proclaimed prize!" he cried, his eyes bright with thoughts of advancement. "Most happy!" It was Oswald, and he drew his sword to kill the blind traitor. But Edgar opposed him. "Out, dunghill!" Oswald shouted, struggling fiercely; but the dunghill proved the better man, and Oswald fell, dying, to the ground. With his last breath he begged Edgar to bury his body and not leave it to rot in the air, and to take the letter he carried to Edmund, Earl of Gloucester. Then he died.

Edgar took the letter, and opened it. As he read it his hand trembled and his face grew pale, for the villainy in Goneril's letter to his brother showed him a world more monstrous than ever he could have imagined. As he crouched, wondering what he should do, he heard the sound of distant drums.

The running King had been caught. Gentle hands had taken him, and tended him, and washed him, and put him in fine soft clothes.

"How does my royal Lord? How fares Your Majesty?" asked a low, soft voice he thought he knew; and above him, with smiling lips and eyes bright with tears, was a countenance he remembered as from an old dream.

"Sir, do you know me?" asked the lady.

He pondered the matter deeply, then answered as truthfully as he could: "Pray do not mock me: I am a very foolish, fond old man . . . and to deal plainly, I fear I am not in my perfect mind. Methinks I should know you and know this man."

The Earl of Kent, who was standing beside Cordelia, bowed his head as his heart broke.

"Do not laugh at me," said the King anxiously, "for as I am a man, I think this lady to be my child Cordelia."

"And so I am, I am!" wept Cordelia; and King Lear's darkness lifted, and the world shone, as he embraced the child he had banished from his favour, but never from his heart.

The Duke of Albany, mild and courteous even in steel, had been given a letter. He and his Duchess, together with Regan and Edmund, had been walking among the iron forest of their joined forces, pausing here and there to talk with captains, and to glance along the corpse-faces of their soldiers, when a roughly dressed fellow, his face half hidden under a peasant's hood, beckoned to him. He stepped aside, leaving his wife and her sister, with Edmund between them, to walk on. Then the fellow had thrust a paper into his hand, begging him to read it before the battle, and alone. The Duke had asked him to wait, but he would not. He had hastened away, saying that he would return when a herald's trumpet should sound for a champion to come forward and answer for what the letter contained. When the fellow had gone, the Duke read the letter. His hand shook and his face grew pale, even as Edgar's had done. It was his wife's letter to Edmund, contriving his own murder. Edgar had given it to him. The Duke put the letter away and rejoined Edmund and the two sisters. He said nothing, for the battle drums had begun to roll and thunder.

With heavy tread, the two armies began to move against each other, at first slowly and then with increasing speed, until, with tremendous clanking and loud shouts, they met. Gaunt-eyed men fought gaunt-eyed men, struggling to and fro over the harmless land. It was a world more to die in than to live in, as crops were destroyed, cottages shattered, and men and horses screamed where birds had sung. Soon the field was a graveyard: some had died bravely, some in flight, but it made no difference as they lay, making poppies with their blood.

The French were defeated and among the prisoners were King Lear and Cordelia, who, though she might have escaped, would not leave her father's side. Edmund's men had captured them.

"Take them away," said Edmund curtly. He did not hate them, but they were in his way; and he was never so foolish as to put pity before gain.

"Come, let's away to prison," said King Lear, with his arm proudly about his daughter's shoulders, "we two alone will sing like birds i' the cage . . ." What he had lost in freedom, he had gained in love.

When the old man and his child had been led away, Edmund sent a captain after them, to kill them both.

No sooner had the officer gone, than the Duke of Albany, with Goneril and Regan, came to greet Edmund and praise him for the courage he had shown in the battle. The sisters were extravagant in their admiration; but the Duke was somewhat cooler. As Edmund swelled in importance under the glowing looks of the ladies, the Duke said coldly: "I hold you but as a subject of this war, not as a brother."

Angrily Edmund began to assert himself, when the Duke raised his hand. "Edmund," he said, "I arrest thee on capital treason; and—" (here he pointed to his wife) "this gilded serpent."

He said nothing of the letter. The time for that would come; and soon. Even he, mild Albany, had reached his limit of enduring creatures so devilish: the evil young Earl, the vile Regan, and, worst of all, the monster who was his wife.

Loudly Edmund was demanding that any man who dared to call him a traitor should come forward and prove the charge in single combat; any man, even the Duke himself. Goneril was smiling, and Albany knew that she longed for him to take up the challenge, for Edmund, fiercely confident Edmund, would have killed him in moments. Nonetheless, he was resolved.

Suddenly he saw that Regan was distressed. Her face was white and crumpled with pain. "She is not well," he said abruptly, "convey her to my tent." When the trembling Duchess had been helped away, he called a herald. "Let the trumpet sound!" he commanded. Edmund looked at him almost pityingly, and Goneril's smile broadened. If no man came forward at the trumpet's third blast, then he himself would have to fight. Already the wicked pair saw him dead. Even so, thought Albany, as the trumpet sounded, it would be better than living in their world.

Then, at the third blast, a man in armour appeared. The stranger had

. . . he stumbled, with Cordelia, dead in his arms

kept his word. He wore a helmet with the visor down. Who was he? He would say no more than that he was of noble birth, and equal with the man he challenged.

Edmund was no coward, and, though he would sooner have killed the Duke, he accepted the unknown challenger. The trumpet sounded again, and all stood back as the two men drew their swords and began to fight. Albany saw his wife's eyes glitter as she watched her lover and prayed for him. He saw her lips part with joy as Edmund seemed to have the upper hand; then he saw her grow pale with fear, and her hand fly to her mouth to stifle a cry of dismay, as Edmund fell. He had been pierced through the side by the stranger's sword! Savagely she cried out that the contest had been unjust, that Edmund had been tricked.

"Shut your mouth, dame!" commanded her husband; and he held up the letter! She stared at it, her face grey with dread. She tried to seize the letter. He thrust her away. "No tearing, lady," he warned. "I perceive you know it."

"Ask me not what I know!" she shouted; and rushed frantically away.

Edmund was dying. He lay where he had fallen and his conqueror knelt beside him. He had confessed to his crimes, and now wanted only to know whose hand had killed him. Edgar took off his helmet. Edmund gazed up at the brother he had betrayed, and sighed: "The wheel is come full circle . . ."

Then, for Edmund's life was ebbing fast, Edgar told him of their father and of how he had guided and supported the blind old man and had brought him to some sort of peace before he had died. The old Earl of Gloucester was dead. But he had not died in despair. At the very last he had learned who his guide had been. Joy had transfigured his ruined face. His heart had leaped—and then, said Edgar gently, "burst smilingly."

Edmund nodded; his brother's words had moved him deeply, perhaps, even, to do some good before it was too late. But suddenly there was a cry of, "Help, help! O help!" and a man came running, his face fearful and with a bloody knife in his hand! Goneril had killed herself; and Regan also lay dead. She had been poisoned by her sister for love of Edmund, if ever it could have been love that had inhabited that pitiless heart. The monsters had destroyed each other.

"I was contracted to them both; all three now marry in an instant," murmured Edmund, without regret. Then he remembered the good he had wished to do and, with his dying breath, begged that a messenger should go to the prison and save Cordelia and the King. He sent his sword with the messenger, so that the man should be believed.

But it was too late. There came a cry, a dreadful, desolate cry, that seemed to fill the world with its ancient misery. "Howl, howl, howl, howl!" wailed King Lear, as he stumbled over the rough ground with Cordelia, dead in his arms. He stopped and stared at those who watched him, with grief and horror in their eyes.

"A plague upon you, murderers, traitors all! I might have saved her . . ." And then, looking down on the dead face, said proudly: "I killed the slave that was a-hanging thee."

Then he seemed to forget his terrible burden, for he peered at Albany, at Edgar, and then at Kent, who had followed him through his darkest days, and now stood helpless at journey's end. He shook his head, and looked again.

"Who are you? Mine eyes are not o' the best: I'll tell you straight." He frowned. "Are you not Kent?" He nodded. "You are welcome hither," he said, as he saw, in the banished Earl, the faithful servant whose love and care had watched over him.

Then he sank to the ground, as if the small weight he carried in his arms was a world in heaviness. "And my poor fool is hanged!" he sighed, no longer knowing which child was which, Cordelia or his Fool, for both were dead. "Thou'lt come no more, never, never, never, never, never! I pray you, undo this button," he begged, as all his power and all his royal greatness dwindled down to this one last little need. "Thank you, sir . . ." Then his eyes brightened as he fancied, for a moment, that Cordelia still lived. "Look there, look there!" he cried; and then no more.

"Look up, my Lord!" cried Edgar.

"Vex not his ghost," said Kent. "O let him pass. He hates him that would upon the rack of this tough world stretch him out longer."

King Lear was dead.

The Tempest

Far, far away, upon the shore of a strange island that was forever wrapped in mists that the sun changed into moving curtains of gold, there sat an ageing man and his young, lovely daughter. They were staring out to sea. About the man's shoulders was a blue cloak, embroidered all over with silver, and beside him on the sands lay a carved staff and a book as thick and richly bound as a Bible. Sometimes his hand rested on the book, and sometimes upon his daughter's arm, as if to comfort her. His face was calm; hers was pale and frightened.

They were watching a ship that was about to be smashed into pieces. A tempest had seized it, an uncanny fury of the elements that seemed to enclose it in a swirling black bubble. As it heaved and tossed, its masts scribbled frantic messages against the blotchy sky, and its rigging all fell down like a madman's hair. Tiny figures, black as fleas, and with patched white faces, clung where they could; and shrieks and screams, small as the squealing of mice, drifted to the watchers on the shore. Then it was over. Fire, liquid as blazing ink, ran along the yards. The timbers snarled and cracked, the ship split, and was lost. The tempest subsided, the dark bubble dispersed, and the sea was calm.

"Be collected," comforted the father, his arm about his daughter's trembling shoulders: "no more amazement: tell your piteous heart there's no harm done."

He spoke the truth. He himself, Prospero the enchanter, had raised the storm and, as he promised his daughter Miranda, not a soul had been lost. He had, by his strange power, brought them all safe to the island.

He stood up, and, frowning, began to pace to and fro, making little yellow tempests in the sand, which his long, heavy cloak smoothed away, so that he seemed to have walked, invisibly, on air. Silently Miranda watched . . .

Presently he halted. He smiled at her inquiring looks and then, putting off his cloak, that mysteriously glittering garment into which had been woven, by his own deep skill, all his magical powers, he seated himself beside her. At last the time had come for him to tell her how they had come to this strange isle, what they had been before, and why he had raised the tempest that had wrecked the ship.

"Canst thou remember a time before we came?" he asked, but more as master to pupil than father to child. She faltered upon some dim recollection of shadowy serving women. He brushed it aside, and then began to tell her a tale of such grim happenings that his eyes burned with anger at the memory of them, even though they had taken place far away and long ago.

She had indeed had serving women, and many of them, for she was the only child of a Duke. He, Prospero, her humble, solitary father, had once been a rich and mighty prince; the Duke of Milan, no less. But he had been such a ruler that the outward show of greatness and the exercise of princely power had mattered less to him than the kingdom of the mind. "My library," he confided to Miranda, "was dukedom large enough . . ." So, to free himself for the study that he loved, he had given over the tediousness of government to one he had trusted with all his heart: his brother Antonio.

But alas! he had been more wise in books than in hearts, and as he uttered his brother's name, his brow darkened and Miranda grew frightened as, for the first time, the chill of human wickedness touched her bright world.

Antonio, not content with the use of power, wanted the reality and the semblance of it, too. In exchange for the promise of the dukedom, he conspired with the King of Naples, sworn enemy of Milan; and, one night, he opened the city's gates and let the enemy in. Milan fell, and Duke Prospero was overthrown.

"Wherefore did they not that hour destroy us?" asked Miranda, for her father's brother seemed limitless in his evil.

Prospero shook his head. He and his infant daughter had not been spared out of pity, but because Antonio had feared the consequence of public crime. Instead, he had cast them adrift, in a rotting craft, with neither mast nor sail, and trusted in the blind elements to do his murders secretly. And so it would have happened, had not a kindly Neapolitan, by name of Gonzalo, furnished them with food and drink, with clothing and with those precious volumes from Prospero's library from which the enchanter had learned his power.

Long, long they had drifted, the father and his crying child, until at last they had come to this uncanny isle, where, for twelve years now, they had lived together with none but each other for human company.

"And now, I pray you, sir," murmured Miranda, her mind heavy with bewilderment, "your reason for raising this sea-storm?"

Prospero's eyes gleamed with triumph. The vessel had contained his enemies. Now they were all ashore and within his grasp. "Here cease more questions," he commanded. "Thou art inclined to sleep . . ." He laid a hand on her head. She smiled and sighed, and closed her eyes; and, in a moment, was asleep. Gently Prospero smoothed her golden hair and brushed away the sand that might have troubled her face.

He stood up and put on his cloak once more. He looked up at the sky, then to the sea, then to the island's haunted woods. "Come away, servant, come," he called softly. "I am ready now. Approach, my Ariel, come."

There was a thin noise, as of wind across lute strings, and with a flash and a whirl and a quick unwinding of air, Prospero's servant appeared.

An odd servant: a slight, weird, dancing, darting servant, very bright to look at, never still save for trembling dragonfly moments, forever trying on faces, as if at the tailor's . . .

"All hail, great master! Grave sir, hail!" cried Ariel, with a thousand courtly bows, all performed in the twinkling of an eye.

"Hast thou, spirit," asked the enchanter, "performed to point the tempest that I bade thee?"

"To every article," promised the spirit, with another bright parcel of bows; and told, with eager and child-like delight, of the frantic terror aboard the ship, of how the passengers had flung themselves, shrieking, into the sea, and Ferdinand, the King of Naples' son, had cried out: "Hell is empty, and all the devils are here!"

Prospero smiled and Ariel, encouraged by such a mark of approval, went on to tell how all had been brought ashore, miraculously fresh and dry, as if the tempest had never been. They had been dispersed in groups about the island, none knowing of any other's having survived. Even the vessel itself had been restored in every particular and now lay in a harbour with the sailors safely under hatches and locked fast in a dreamless sleep.

"The King's son have I landed by himself," said Ariel, with a queer, sideways smile . . .

Prospero nodded, and then proposed still more work for his servant; between now and nightfall, much needed to be done. But Ariel scowled.

"How now, moody?" demanded Prospero, angered by the spirit's peevish looks. "What is't thou canst demand?"

"My liberty."

But Ariel's service still had two days more to run; and Prospero, frowning at the spirit's presumption, so that Ariel shrank before him, reminded his servant of how that servitude had first begun. Had Ariel forgotten how things were when Prospero and Miranda had first come to the isle?

Ariel had not; nonetheless, despite wild shakings of the head and imploring looks, Prospero reminded the spirit that the isle had been filled, not with airy music, but with desolate howls and moans that proceeded from deep in a cleft in a pine tree. There Ariel had been imprisoned by Sycorax, a foul witch, for refusing to obey her worst commands. Sycorax had died, leaving her misshapen son, Caliban, to rule the isle, and Ariel in hopeless wailing misery.

From this misery Prospero had freed the spirit, and, in return, had demanded twelve years of absolute obedience.

"If thou more murmur'st," threatened Prospero, "I will rend an oak and peg thee in his knotty entrails . . ."

At once the frightened spirit was all willingness to obey and do anything to please the great enchanter.

"Do so," said Prospero; "and after two days I will discharge thee."

"That's my noble master! What shall I do? Say what; what shall I do?"

Prospero smiled at his servant's anxiety and then bade Ariel take on the shape of a sea-nymph, and to be visible to none but himself. Once more there was a noise as of wind across lute strings, and Ariel was gone.

The enchanter gazed after his servant with a deep fondness. Not for more worlds than Ariel could have given him would he have punished that wayward spirit. He bent down and awakened his still sleeping daughter.

"Come on," he proposed, as she rubbed her eyes and smiled at him; "we'll visit Caliban, my slave."

"'Tis a villain, sir," protested Miranda. Prospero shook his head. Even villains had their uses, and Caliban's was to fetch wood and do all manner of menial toil.

"Caliban!" he called, as they approached a dwelling made of rough stones and rock. "Thou earth, thou! speak!"

"There's wood enough within," came a voice as thick and harsh as tangled briers; but before Prospero could command again, a fragile sea-nymph, with Ariel's eager eyes, and Ariel's bows and dartings, whirled to his side, hovered, took softly breathed instruction, and sped away upon a mysterious errand. Then Prospero turned back to his other servant on the isle. "Thou poisonous slave!" he shouted. "Come forth!" and Caliban, unable to defy his great master any longer, came cursing out of his hovel.

A slow, heavy, lumbering creature, all scowls and bristles, with his ugly nakedness scarcely covered by skins as rough and hairy as his own; a creature of darkness, like the foul witch who had borne him, and of curses, like the devil who had fathered him.

"This island's mine, by Sycorax my mother," he snarled, but crouching low before the enchanter whom he feared even more than he hated. For Prospero had the power to fill him from top to toe with a thousand aches and dazzling pains that made him roar out in the night.

But it had not always been so, Caliban remembered. When Prospero had first come to the isle he had soothed and comforted Caliban, and taught him many marvellous things, so that Caliban had shown him all the secrets and wonders of the isle. It was then that Prospero had turned against him and had seized the island for himself . . .

"Thou most lying slave!" cried Prospero, pale with anger. His kindness to the misshapen creature that crouched, hatefully, at his feet, had only ceased when that creature, filled with lust, had sought to violate Miranda.

Caliban's sunken eyes gleamed at the memory. He turned his heavy head towards Miranda. She drew back in horror. "I pitied thee," she said, with bitter regret, "took pains to make thee speak . . ."

"You taught me language," answered Caliban, savagely, "and my profit on't is, I know how to curse!"

But because it had been gentle Miranda who had taught him to use the words, his very curses were musical; and because he knew no other way, helplessly he clothed the darkest and most brutish thoughts in the language of light.

"Hag-seed, hence!" commanded Prospero abruptly and, under threat of sharp aches and bone-grinding cramps, despatched the monster of the isle to fetch more fuel, for he had heard faint music in the air.

The sea-nymph returned, and with a strange catch from the sea. Playing upon a small, delicate stringed instrument, and singing very high and silvery, the spirit drew along, as if by invisible cords, a youth, richly dressed and noble in appearance.

"Come unto these yellow sands . . ." tempted the invisible Ariel; and the youth stumbled after, haunted and tantalized by the music in the air. It was Ferdinand, the King of Naples' son. He had been mourning the father he believed drowned, when he had heard the music and had followed it helplessly. For a moment the singing ceased, and the youth looked about him in bewilderment; then it began again:

"Full fathom five thy father lies;
Of his bones are coral made,
Those are pearls that were his eyes . . ."

He sank down in despair as the song remembered his loss.

"Say what thou seest . . ." murmured Prospero to Miranda, for the youth was too wrapped in grief and the mysteries of the isle to see the watching enchanter and his daughter.

"What is't? a spirit?" breathed Miranda, lost in wonderment, for she had never seen a young man before.

"No, wench," smiled her father; "it eats and sleeps and hath such senses as we have."

Then Ferdinand saw Miranda.

"At the first sight they have changed eyes," breathed Prospero. "Delicate Ariel, I'll set thee free for this." Fondly he looked on as the youth and his daughter stood in amazed admiration of one another. Though Ferdinand, unlike the girl, was no stranger to his own kind, he had never seen such a one as she. Surely the magic of the isle had made its masterpiece, and whatever wonders were to come, none could out-dazzle Miranda! Eagerly he explained that he was now the King of Naples as he feared his father had perished in the storm; and, in a wild burst of adoration, offered to make Miranda the Queen.

Here Prospero intervened, and stepped between his daughter and the youth, cutting off the ardour of their looks. Their love had been so quick and sudden that he feared it could not last. Some testing time, some hardship, some obstacle to be overcome was needed to judge its strength.

Sternly he confronted Ferdinand. He was lying. He was not the King of Naples. He was a spy, set upon the island to seize it.

"No, as I am a man!" protested Ferdinand, peering from side to side round the grim father for a sight of his entrancing daughter; and Miranda, her head wandering likewise, like a waving flower, strongly supported him.

"Speak not you for him!" Prospero commanded, spreading his mantle to obscure her view. "He's a traitor. Come; I'll manacle thy neck and feet together . . ."

Angrily Ferdinand drew his sword. A foolish move. Prospero raised his staff, and Ferdinand felt the air turn to iron and fix him from head to toe.

"Beseech you, father!" implored Miranda, on behalf of the marble Ferdinand.

"Silence!" commanded Prospero, turning upon his daughter. What did she know of the world of men? "Having seen but him and Caliban," he said contemptuously. "Foolish wench! To the most of men this is a Caliban, and they to him are angels!"

"My affections are then most humble," cried Miranda, still striving, round her father, for another glimpse of Ferdinand; "I have no ambition to see a goodlier man!"

And Ferdinand too, released enough from enchantment to speak, pleaded his love. Let great Prospero chain and enslave him, he would willingly endure all, if, but once a day, even through prison bars, he might see Miranda.

Prospero, hiding his smiles, withdrew and, briefly, let their craning looks meet. Rapidly he murmured more instructions to the invisibly hovering Ariel, who nodded, bowed half a hundred times, and sped away. Then, resuming his sternness, he returned. "Come, follow!" he commanded Ferdinand harshly; and then to Miranda, who begged, pleaded and clung obstinately to his mantle, "Speak not for him!"

Though he was a mighty enchanter, with power over lightning, thunder, wind and rain, though he could turn men to stone, fill them with pains, and drowse them to sleep, though he could call up visions and bewitch the air, he had no power over love. There his authority stopped. All he could do was, by harsh pretence, to test the strength of it.

In another part of the island, in a green glade thickly curtained with trees, there was heaped up the richest treasure of the wrecked ship. A gathering of gorgeous castaways, velvet gentlemen, embroidered all over with crowns and coronets sat and strolled and debated their situation. Alonzo, the King of Naples, sat on the stump of a tree, his tragic head in his tragic hands, and mourned the loss of his son.

"Beseech you, sir, be merry," comforted an old councillor, by name of Gonzalo, and pointed out that the King had much to be thankful for. After all, he and his companions were saved and on dry land . . .

"Prithee, peace," said the King, in no mood for philosophy.

"He receives comfort like cold porridge," remarked the King's brother Sebastian, to Antonio, the Duke of Milan. They were a sharp, knowing, ambitious pair of gentlemen, men of the real world. Though they were pleased enough to find themselves alive, they were none too pleased to find themselves on such an island, far from courts and affairs. Nor were they better pleased with their company. The King was feeble and Gonzalo was a tedious old fool, fit for nothing but to laugh at.

"Here is everything advantageous to life," said Gonzalo, examining the grass, fingering the soil and peering at the trees through spectacles that enlarged all virtues to his kindly eyes.

"True," said Antonio mockingly; "save means to live."

They would not let him be. Whatever he praised, from the miracle of their salvation to the wonder of their clothing seeming fresh and new, they jeered at. Until, at last, the old man gave up.

"You are gentlemen of brave mettle," he said wearily. He yawned. Suddenly he was overcome by a strong desire for sleep. It was strange: there seemed to be a sound of music in the air, very sweet and heavy. And stranger still, some heard it and some did not. Of those who heard it, first Gonzalo, then two other lords, and then the grieving King himself, were overcome by its drowsy charm, and closed their eyes in sleep. Then the music ceased, and Ariel, the unseen musician, silently left the glade. The two who had heard nothing, remained awake, wide awake.

"What a strange drowsiness possesses them," wondered Sebastian, gazing round at the figures on the grass, who lay, quiet as painted people.

"It is the quality o' the climate," murmured Antonio, his eyes fixed upon the sleeping King. The two gentlemen stared at one another; and each saw in the other an image of himself. Each was brother to greatness; one had taken his chance and succeeded; the other's was still to come.

Antonio, still staring at the sleeping King, began to say something, as if to himself, then stopped, then sighed, then looked Sebastian quickly in the face, and murmured: "My strong imagination sees a crown dropping upon thy head."

Sebastian looked puzzled, and pretended not to catch the drift of Antonio's remark; but very quietly. It would be foolish to wake the sleepers. The two gentlemen began to stroll about, on tiptoe, and to peer and stare among the trees.

"Will you grant with me," proposed Antonio, reassuring himself that a shadow was not a watcher, "that Ferdinand is drowned?"

"He's gone," agreed Sebastian, confirming that a bush was not a spy.

"Then tell me," pursued Antonio, approaching the breathing King, "who's the next heir of Naples?"

The King's daughter. But she was Queen of Tunis, pointed out Antonio, and that was far from Naples. Carefully he measured with his eyes the distance between the helpless King and the helpless Gonzalo. Then he looked hard at Sebastian. Being damned himself in the destruction of a brother, he wanted company in his damnation. Sebastian nodded, and Antonio knew that the idea he had put into Sebastian's head had found a ready kennel.

"Draw thy sword," whispered Sebastian, nodding towards his sleeping brother.

"Draw together," breathed Antonio, not wanting to be the only murderer and so in another's power. He nodded towards Gonzalo. Then he drew his sword, but not until he had seen Sebastian do the same. Together they stood, poised for double murder.

Suddenly Gonzalo awoke! "Now good angels," he cried out, "preserve the King!" As if in a dream he had heard a high, silvery voice singing in his ear: "Shake off slumber and beware! Awake, awake!"

In a moment, all were awake and on their feet, and staring with amazement at the two who stood, with glaring eyes and dangerous swords.

"Why are you drawn?" demanded the King, his hand upon his own weapon.

Confusedly, first Sebastian and then Antonio, said they had heard the roaring of lions nearby.

"Heard you this, Gonzalo?" asked the King. The old man frowned and admitted that he had indeed heard a strange sound that had awakened him. The King was satisfied; nonetheless, they must all leave the glade and continue the search, even though it was hopeless, for his lost son.

Mouse-eyed Ariel watched them go. There was nothing on the isle that could be unknown to the lord of it. Prospero, through the eyes of his servant, watched over all.

There was a growling of thunder and the sky was overcast. On a desolate part of the shore, where a leaden sea lapped upon leaden sands, Caliban toiled under his burden of wood. Savagely he cursed his master, who, for the smallest offence, visited him with biting terrors and with hissing snakes.

"Lo, now lo!" he cried out suddenly. "Here comes a spirit of his, and to torment me for bringing wood in slowly! I'll fall flat . . ."

And down the monster fell, flinging his stinking cloak over his stinking head, and leaving nothing visible but his hairy legs and feet.

The spirit approached; a queer spirit in patched colours with tiny bells sewn to points on his sleeves and cap, so that he jingled like a town of distant churches. It was Trinculo, the King of Naples' jester, an ageing fool who lived only on the echo of old jokes. Saved from the shipwreck by a Providence that plainly did not know right from wrong, he wandered across the shore until he spied the cloak and the ugly legs and feet.

"What have we here?" wondered Trinculo, peering at the strange object and poking at it with his toe. "A man, or a fish? Dead or alive? A fish; he smells like a fish; a very ancient and fish-like smell . . ." Thunder growled and threatened again. Trinculo stared about him. There was no shelter anywhere. "Misery acquaints a man with strange bedfellows," he said, and, shutting his eyes and holding his nose, crept under the creature's cloak. Caliban, in mortal terror of the strange spirit, neither spoke nor moved.

Came sounds of a song: not magical in the island's sense, but weavy and peppered with hiccups. A portly fellow in important breeches, waving a bottle like a weapon against flies, came tottering and staggering along the shore. It was Stephano, the King's butler, who had floated to land on a barrel of wine. He kicked against the cloak, not in anger, but because he was too drunk to see it.

"Do not torment me:—O!" came a voice that was thick and harsh. Cautiously Stephano examined the speaking bundle; found it had four legs and no head. Was not surprised. Prodded it.

"Do not torment me, prithee," moaned Caliban, putting out his head. "I'll bring my wood home faster."

Stephano pondered. "He shall taste of my bottle," he said, and thrust it, vaguely, into the hazy, bristly monster's mouth.

"Stephano!" came another voice from the cloak. This was truly uncanny. Stephano flew into a panic. Then Trinculo came out, and the two friends embraced and danced about in their joy at finding each other alive.

Caliban looked on, awed beyond measure by the splendour of the new spirits, and in particular by the one who had given him wine. It seemed to hold a greater enchantment than even Prospero's. "I will kneel to him," whispered Caliban, and crawled humbly towards the ponderous, swaying drunkard. "Hast thou not dropped from heaven?" he asked, staring up at the bottle.

"Out o' the moon," said Stephano; and Caliban believed him.

The drunkard was charmed by his worshipper, and gave him more to drink; but the jester was not pleased. "A most ridiculous monster," he sneered enviously, "to make a wonder of a poor drunkard!"

Nonetheless, off they went together in a staggering bundle, to find where Stephano had hidden his barrel of wine: the butler hiccuping, the jester jeering, and the monster singing and promising his new master all the wonders of the isle. "'Ban, 'Ban, Ca-Caliban," he roared, "has a new master—get a new man!"

A little way from Prospero's dwelling—a rough house of wood, sufficient to keep out the weather and keep in comfort and warmth—the King of Naples' son was carrying logs. Back and forth he toiled, pausing only to wipe the sweat from his brow. He had sworn that he would gladly endure enslavement if only he could see Miranda once a day; and Prospero had put him to the test. Suddenly the house door opened and Miranda, with a quick, backward glance, came running out. "Alas!" she cried, seeing Ferdinand bent, like a beckoning finger, under his heavy

. . . off they went together in a staggering bundle

burden, "pray you, work not so hard!" She begged him to rest. "My father is hard at study," she promised, with another backward glance. "He's safe for these three hours."

A shadow stirred in the doorway. Prospero was indeed at study, but it was hearts, not books. He smiled at the innocence of his daughter's conspiracy.

"If you'll sit down," urged Miranda, "I'll bear your logs the while."

Ferdinand shook his head. Though the work was heavy, there was pleasure in it: it was not for a harsh master that he laboured, but for a mistress, fair as the sun.

Again Prospero smiled. He had given the young man Caliban's task so that he might seem a Caliban in Miranda's eyes; but Ferdinand laboured willingly and the harsh toil, far from debasing him, had made him seem more noble than before.

"The very instant that I saw you," panted Ferdinand, between logs, "did my heart fly to your service . . ."

"Do you love me?" asked Miranda, more used to plainer speech and hoping she had understood. He did indeed, and told her so again and again; and she, weeping with happiness, confessed the same. Then she left him, for the endless space of half an hour; and he went on heaving logs that seemed as light and airy as dandelion clocks. And Prospero, the hidden observer, shook his head, and sighed, and smiled.

Stephano's wine barrel had been found. He had hidden it beside a stream, under trees. Now he sat astride it, like the king of grapes, while his two subjects squabbled among themselves. Caliban hated Trinculo, who was too familiar with the god of the bottle; and Trinculo despised Caliban because he did not think Stephano worth worshipping.

"Why thou deboshed fish!" jeered Trinculo, as Caliban kissed Stephano's foot.

"Bite him to death, I prithee!" implored Caliban, longing for his new master to dispose of the jester. But Stephano, like a wise ruler, kept the peace; and bent an ear to Caliban who told him of the sorcerer who had stolen the isle.

"Thou liest!" said a voice like Trinculo's. Savagely Caliban turned upon him. Trinculo denied all knowledge of having opened his mouth. Caliban grunted and went on to propose how the isle might be captured by murdering Prospero as he slept.

"Thou liest: thou canst not," said Trinculo's voice again; and again Trinculo denied having spoken. Caliban raged at him, and Stephano warned Trinculo to hold his tongue; and for good measure, and to Caliban's delight, he punched his head.

Even though they were all drunk enough for marvels, it was a strange confusion that had fallen on them, hearing voices when no one spoke; and matters grew stranger still when Stephano began to sing, and was accompanied by mysterious music in the air. The butler and the jester stared at one another aghast. This was more uncanny than anything out of a bottle!

"Be not afeard," urged Caliban, anxious to calm them; "the isle is full of noises, sounds, and sweet airs, that give delight and hurt not . . ."

They took his word for it, and, indeed, as they listened, found a strange pleasure in the music. So much so that, when it began to move away, they rose and, floating on clouds of wine, followed after. This way and that, they went, clinging one to another, as Ariel, the invisible imitator of Trinculo, and the invisible musician to Stephano, led them on. Their conspiracy was as open to Prospero as was the conspiring of Sebastian and Antonio. Plots and murders, greed and cunning were but as waking dreams.

"I can go no further, sir," groaned Gonzalo as the King's party came into a glade that seemed the very image of a glade they had not long left. "I must needs rest me."

The King sighed and took pity on the weary old man, and consented to rest awhile.

"The next advantage will we take thoroughly," breathed Sebastian to Antonio, as their companions sank down exhausted on the grass. His resolve was as firm as ever Antonio could have wished; both men were now eye-deep in thoughts of blood. "I say tonight—"

He fell silent and clutched Antonio by the sleeve; and amazement seized the glade. A rich music had invaded the air. The trees wavered,

like trees painted on a veil, became unreal, then seemed to be drawn aside, as if to reveal, briefly, the true face of the haunted isle. Filmy shapes appeared in the air, as if they had always been present, and wanted only clearer sight to be seen. Some had heads like birds, others like wolves, or bears or stags. They were grim in aspect, but gentle in movement. They carried a great table, laden with fruits and meat and tall flagons of wine, which they placed upon the ground; and, with courteous bows and gestures, invited those present to partake of the feast. Then they dissolved, leaving the table behind.

"What were these?" marvelled the King; and he spoke in admiring tones of the gentleness of the spirits.

"Praise in departing," murmured Prospero, the invisible watcher of the scene. For as the hungry lords approached the feast, there was a roar of thunder and a glare of lighting! The glade darkened, there was a thudding of huge wings, and down flew a hideous bird, with the head of a hag and with talons like grappling irons! It perched on the table, clapped its wings, and the feast vanished! Then it turned its red-pouched eyes accusingly on Alonzo, the King of Naples, Sebastian, his brother, and Antonio, Duke of Milan, and shrieked: "You are three men of sin!"

In terror, they drew their swords. Prospero raised his staff. They cried out, staggered, their arms nearly breaking, for their swords were suddenly as heavy as churches! A wild wind began to blow; the trees bent, and the glade seemed enclosed in a dark bubble of tempest. Then

the Harpy on the table, in tones that rode the uproar, damned the three men of sin for their old crime against Prospero. It was for this that they were now being punished.

Then lightning blazed again, thunder bellowed, and the Harpy spread its wings and flew away. At once the tempest faded, and the filmy shapes, with the same gentle courtesy as before, returned and bore the table away. Prospero's enemies stared at one another; their faces were grey with guilt.

Prospero nodded. His enemies were within his power. Ariel, in the shape of the Harpy, had done well. Then he remembered Ferdinand, that patient log-bearer, whose back was likely to break before his spirit, and Miranda, 'who loved him. Swiftly Prospero departed, leaving the glade distracted as the guilty men fled in desperation, and the frightened lords followed anxiously after.

"If I have too austerely punished you," said Prospero, smiling faintly as Miranda nodded and Ferdinand, bruised and aching, stoutly disclaimed, "Your compensation makes amends . . ." Then he revealed that his harshness had been only to test their love and constancy; upon which they smiled modestly, like children who have done well at school. "Sit then," said Prospero, gesturing towards Ferdinand's last log; and, while they sat, side by side, with no eyes but for each other, he summoned Ariel. The great enchanter was not without vanity. Seeing the enchantment in which the lovers held one another, he was stirred to show them that his own power was still greater. Quietly he instructed his servant, who bowed and bowed and sped away. The lovers murmured on. Suddenly there was music in the air, as soft and sweet as any the isle had known. But the lovers murmured on. A strange golden light began to suffuse the grass before them; but the lovers saw only the light in each other's eyes, and still they murmured on.

"No tongue!" commanded Prospero, not without irritation; "all eyes! be silent!"

Guiltily the lovers obeyed; and their eyes grew round with wonderment. Three strange, unearthly women, had stepped out of the air and on to the green stage. They were tall, shining and gracious and robed, it seemed, in softly-coloured vapours. One was Iris, goddess of the rainbow; one was Ceres, goddess of the harvest; and one was Juno, goddess of them all. Ceremoniously they bowed to the lovers and blessed their coming marriage in stately song.

"This is a most majestic vision!" breathed Ferdinand, amazed; and Prospero, gratified by so respectful a response, raised his staff. At once, it was as if the whole world had been an invisible playhouse that had opened its store and tumbled out its richest treasures! A gorgeous crowd of spirits came swirling, dancing out of nowhere, and filled the green: spirits of stream and woodland, of flocks and pastures, smiling nymphs and weird fantastic reapers . . .

Suddenly Prospero stood up. His face was dark with anger! The music faltered and broke up into harsh noises, and the spirits, with looks of dismay, vanished back into the air.

In the midst of his magic, Prospero had remembered Caliban and his murderous plot. The time for it was almost ripe. Then he saw that his sudden anger and the abrupt departure of the vision had distressed the lovers.

"Be cheerful, sir," he urged, taking pity on the confused Ferdinand. "Our revels now are ended . . ." He begged the lovers to leave him for a while. He was disturbed, and wished, as he put it, "to still the beating of my mind."

When they had retired, with many a backward glance, into the house, he called Ariel to his side and bade him lay out on a line certain bright and showy garments that were in his possession. He had enchanted a King with an imaginary feast; lovers with imaginary goddesses; for drunkards there was no more need than to lay out fine clothes.

There was a crashing and a stumbling and a blind blundering among the trees as the butler, the jester and the monster drew near the enchanter's house. They had followed the unseen musician through clinging bush and spiteful briar, through filthy ditch and stinking pool, they had lost their bottles, their tempers and their wits, and were as foul and reeking as their thoughts.

"Prithee, my King, be quiet!" warned Caliban, for they were almost at Prospero's dwelling, where murder was to be done. "Give me thy hand," belched Stephano, swaying horribly. "I do begin to have bloody thoughts!" The conspirators put their fingers to their lips, and tottered on.

Suddenly Trinculo saw finery hanging, like executed courtiers, on a line: saw robes and gowns, hats like velvet puddings and wondrous cloaks fit for a duke or a bishop, and instantly saw, in his muddy mind's eye, a Trinculo new-made and marvellous beyond belief.

"Let it alone, thou fool; it is but trash!" cried Caliban, alarmed; but it was too late. Stephano also had been captivated, and was seeing a new Stephano, a glittering, magnificent and even kingly Stephano . . .

"Put off that gown, Trinculo!" he shouted, for the lowly jester had seized on the best one. "Let it alone!" howled Caliban, as his companions began to squabble over the treasures. "Do the murder first!" But they were too busy fighting and struggling and thrusting heads into armholes and making gaudy ghosts with their waving arms, to heed the monster's warning.

Then came a sudden noise of horns and barking dogs. At once, heads came out of sleeves, like conjuror's eggs, and glared palely. Where was the hunt, and who was the quarry? In a moment they knew. Out of the trees there came bounding, with savage eyes and hungry jaws, a pack of huge phantom hounds! The conspirators howled with terror and fled!

Contemptuously, the huntsmen, Prospero and Ariel, urged on the dogs and watched the quarry run.

His enemies were at his mercy, and the time for vengeance was at hand. Soon all would be over, and Ariel would have to be set free. "How fares the King and 's followers?" he asked his impatient, yet ever-obedient servant. Ariel told him that they had been divided and held in separate enchantments: the King, his brother and Antonio in one place, and the other lords elsewhere. "Him you termed, sir, 'the good old lord Gonzalo'; his tears run down his beard like winter's drops," said the spirit gently. "If you now beheld them, your affections would become tender."

"Dost thou think so, spirit?" asked Prospero, looking strangely at the quick, unearthly creature at his side.

"Mine would, sir, were I human," answered Ariel.

The enchanter bowed his head. The spirit had taught him. Though he had acted like a god, had raised a tempest and brought men to darkest

despair, he himself was still human; and vengeance was for the worst, not the best of his kind. "Go release them, Ariel," he commanded. "My charms I'll break, their senses I'll restore."

When his servant had gone, Prospero drew a circle on the ground with his staff. This was to be the last of his magic, his last enchantment. Though he had, in the past, performed huge wonders, had commanded the sun, the sea, and even the dead to obey him, though he had made kings of spirits and ghosts of kings, he had now reached the furthest limits of his power.

He stood aside and concealed himself as Ariel returned, leading the King and all his lords. To the accompaniment of solemn music, the spirit led them into the circle, where at once they were held, like a wooden King and wooden lords, unable to move or to speak. One by one Prospero contemplated them and, as the calming music played, his enemies, fixed in look and attitude, some with arms raised, some with mouths open as if about to speak, seemed less real than dreams.

He sighed and shook his head, and sent Ariel to fetch the sword and hat and robes that he had worn when he was Duke of Milan. Swiftly Ariel returned, and, singing merrily, helped to attire the enchanter until he was exactly that Prospero, Duke of Milan, whom Alonzo, Sebastian and Antonio had treacherously overthrown and believed long dead.

"Why, that's my dainty Ariel!" murmured Prospero, when the task was done. "I shall miss thee!" Then he despatched the spirit to the King's ship, to awaken the sailors from their charmed sleep. As Ariel departed, the solemn music ceased, and the still figures in the circle began to move. They looked about them, rubbed their eyes; then amazement fixed them again. The dead had risen! Before them, in all his familiar dignity, stood Prospero, the rightful Duke of Milan!

Most amiably, even affectionately, the betrayed Duke bade them all welcome. But this was too much for the King, who had long suffered inwardly from the wickedness towards Prospero that he himself had helped to bring about. "Pardon me my wrongs!" he begged, and with all the anguish of true repentance.

But to Prospero, love and gratitude came before forgiveness, and he warmly embraced old Gonzalo, whose kindness towards himself and his helpless child he had never forogtten. The old man stammered out his astonishment and joy; but before he could continue, doubtless into lengthy philosophy, Prospero turned to Sebastian and Antonio. "That brace of lords", as he called them, stood with dread in their eyes. They knew full well that Prospero had seen them through and through, that he had seen not only their villainy towards himself, but also their plot to kill the King. Then Prospero said quietly: "At this time I will tell no tales," and they breathed again. They had been forgiven by silence, which made light of themselves, and left their crimes to weigh upon their hearts.

Last of all, Prospero turned to the King, who still wept for his lost son. Prospero nodded, and confided that he himself had lost a daughter. "O heavens!" cried the King, and wished that he could have died instead, and that his son and Prospero's daughter were alive and King and Queen of Naples. "When did you lose your daughter?"

"In this last tempest," answered Prospero, turning aside to hide his smile. Then he begged the King to enter his house, which, though humble, held a wonder that might well please the King as much as the return of his dukedom pleased Prospero. Doubtfully the King approached. Prospero opened wide the door; and the King cried out! There within sat Ferdinand and Miranda, at play for kingdoms over a game of chess!

"O wonder!" cried Miranda, seeing so many lords and all at once, and each far fairer than Caliban. "How beauteous mankind is! O brave new world, that has such people in it!"

"'Tis new to thee," murmured Prospero, with a suddenly sad smile.

Then the lost son embraced the lost father, and the King discovered that his son and Prospero's daughter were indeed to be married, and his own hopeless hope had been fulfilled, without his having to die for it! Then Ariel brought the sleepy sailors, and there was more amazement, as all had believed each other drowned. "This is as strange a maze as e'er men trod," wondered the King. Prospero begged the King not to trouble his thoughts with the mysteries of the day. Presently he would tell all. He looked about him, as if counting up the number present. He frowned. "There are yet missing of your company," he said, "some few odd lads that you remember not."

The few odd lads, in number, two, and in person, one Stephano, a butler, and one Trinculo, a jester, together with a lumbering, brutish creature that seemed neither fish nor flesh, but stank of both, were driven in by Ariel.

They still wore their stolen finery, but such was the scratched, cramped misery it hung upon, that each seemed a mockery of the other. "Two of these fellows you must know and own," said Prospero. Then, pointing to Caliban, confessed: "This thing of darkness I acknowledge mine."

"How fine my master is!" cried Caliban, seeing Prospero in ducal robes; and straightway transferred his allegiance to the better man. "What a thrice-double ass was I, to take this drunkard for a god, and worship this dull fool!" No hint of contradiction came from his companions; they were too sore to do anything but admit the truth.

Prospero dismissed them, and with no worse punishment than to put back what they had stolen. Then Prospero renewed his invitation to the King to enter his house, where he would tell him all, and, in the morning, sail with him to Naples, for the wedding of their children; after which, he himself would retire to his dukedom of Milan.

"I'll deliver all," he assured the King; "and promise you calm seas, auspicious gales . . . My Ariel, chick," he murmured to his hovering, beloved servant, "that is thy charge; then to the elements be free, and fare thou well!" Ariel laughed; and then, with a thousand thousand bows that made a shining circle round the enchanter, the spirit fled.

That night, when all had retired to bed, Prospero stood by the sea, a tall and lonely figure, silvered by starlight. First his magic mantle, then his magic book, and last of all his staff, broken in two, he cast into the waves. He had no more need of them, nor of the enchanted isle. By his art he had made men see themselves, and, through make-believe, come to truth. Now he, too, like Ariel and Caliban, longed to be free.

The Merchant of Venice

In the watery city of Venice, where high-necked boats, like children's painted horses, nod and curtsey along the flowing streets, and the bright air is full of the winks and chinks of smiling money, there lived a merchant by the name of Antonio. He was as good and upright a man as ever merchant was, and all his wealth was laid out in tall, billowing vessels that ventured for trade far and wide.

He had everything a merchant might have wished for; but he was melancholy and knew not why. It was as if there was a shadow over the sun, cooling his pleasures and darkening his days. As he strolled along the busy Rialto, where rich men gathered in their velvet caps and brocaded gowns and talked of affairs, two friends tried to discover the cause of his sadness, and so cure it. Was he troubled about the safety of his vessels? Or was he in love, which was a mournful business if ever there was one? He shook his head.

As they walked, they were joined by three young men, dressed in the height of silken fashion. Their names were Bassanio, Lorenzo and Gratiano, and at first sight there seemed little else to choose between them. They were three young men with nothing better to do than to stroll, and talk, and laugh and enjoy being young.

"You look not well, Signior Antonio," observed Gratiano, who was the liveliest of the three, "you have too much respect upon the world . . ."

The merchant disclaimed; and Gratiano rattled on, nineteen to the dozen, if not twenty, until even he became wearied of his own chatter. Linking arms with Lorenzo, he drifted away after the others, who had already gone. The merchant and Bassanio were left alone.

"Gratiano speaks an infinite deal of nothing," said Bassanio, falling into seriousness as if out of respect for his companion's grave looks.

Antonio smiled. He was deeply fond of Bassanio and looked upon him almost as a son. It often happens with older men, whose sober lives are lined and straitened in with affairs of business, that they look fondly on the happy carelessness of youth, as they might take pleasure in the spring time's birds.

There was a lady that Bassanio had talked of, and had promised to speak of again. Antonio inquired about her but Bassanio shook his head. He carried too heavy a cargo of present troubles to spread his sails for love. He had spent all his rich inheritance and was drowning in a sea of debts.

"To you, Antonio," he confessed, "I owe the most in money and in love . . ."

Antonio bade him not think of it. It grieved the good merchant to see the carefree young man grow grey and pinched for the want of so mean a thing as money.

"My purse, my person," he offered impulsively, "my extremest means lie all unlocked to your occasions."

Bassanio needed no more invitation. If but Antonio would lend him what he needed for a certain enterprise, then Bassanio was confident all would be repaid. The merchant smiled at the young man's enthusiasm, and asked what the certain enterprise might be? Bassanio hesitated; and sighed.

"In Belmont," said he, with an ardent look, "is a lady richly left . . ." Not only was this lady as lovely as she was rich, but she was jewelled with every virtue; and suitors came from far and wide to gain her heart and hand. "Her name is Portia," said Bassanio, as if in that name was enshrined all the beauty of the world. He had seen her once and had received such encouragement from her eyes that he was sure he would succeed in winning her. That is, if only he had the money to present himself before her as a suitor of equal worth among his rivals.

Antonio nodded. Maybe it was not an enterprise that a sober merchant would have embarked upon, but it seemed proper for a youth like Bassanio, who was made, not for trade, but for love.

"Thou know'st," he began, "that all my fortunes are at sea; neither have I money nor commodity to raise a present sum." Here, Bassanio began to look dismayed. Antonio continued: "Therefore go forth, try what my credit can in Venice do. Go presently inquire (and so will I) where money is . . ."

Bassanio beamed. His eyes shone with tears of gratitude. Antonio was his good angel. He shook him warmly by the hand and sped away to find some worthy man from whom he might borrow money against Antonio's good name. Antonio gazed affectionately after him as he hastened, like a bright dream, among the sombrely robed men of business who thronged the Rialto. Presently he was gone, and the merchant's strange melancholy returned . . .

Far across the sea in Belmont, the Lady Portia's palace was besieged by sighs. Suitors drooped and languished, sad as urn draperies, in her doorways, in her gardens, in her stables, and in her wine vaults.

"By my troth, Nerissa," she confided to her maid, being weighed down by all this forlorn furniture, and shadowed by a strange condition laid upon her by her dead father that she should never choose a husband but must instead be chosen, "my little body is aweary of this great world."

Portia's hair was fair as sunshine and her countenance was fairer still. In stature she was, perhaps, a finger's breadth below the middle height; but such was the grace of her form that, beside her, those of the middle height seemed too tall. Whoever gained her love would never want for sunny days, nor a dearer summer than hers. Yet this fair lady could only be won by lottery. By her dying father's decree her fate was locked in one of three caskets, of gold, of silver, and of lead. One choice was allowed each suitor. If he chose wrongly, that was the end of his hopes.

"What warmth is there in your affection towards any one of these princely suitors that are already come?" asked Nerissa, curious to learn if her mistress's heart inclined any one way more than another.

"I pray thee over-name them," said Portia with a yawn.

"First there is the Neapolitan prince."

The lady wrinkled her nose.

"He doth nothing but talk of his horse, and he makes it a great appropriation to his own good parts that he can shoe him himself; I am much afeard my lady his mother played false with a smith."

Nerissa laughed.

"Then there is the County Palatine."

"He doth nothing but frown," complained Portia, "he hears merry tales and smiles not. I had rather be married to a death's head with a bone in his mouth."

Nerissa agreed with her young mistress. Belmont was a house of smiles.

"How say you by the French lord, Monsieur Le Bon?"

"God made him," pronounced Portia, "and therefore let him pass for a man." Nothing more, it seemed, could be said in favour of Monsieur Le Bon.

"What say you then to Falconbridge, the young baron of England?"

"You know I say nothing to him, for he understands not me, nor I him . . . alas! who can converse with a dumb-show?"

The other suitors fared no better in Portia's esteem; there was a Scottish lord who did nothing but quarrel and brawl, and a German duke who did nothing but drink. "I will do anything, Nerissa," wailed Portia, quite overcome by the thought of the wine-swilling duke, "ere I will be married to a sponge."

But Portia's fears proved groundless. Her present crop of suitors was departing and there was none who cared to risk his fortune on the lottery of the caskets.

"Do you not remember lady," said Nerissa suddenly, "in your father's time, a Venetian (a scholar and a soldier) that came hither in company of the Marquis of Montferrat?"

Portia frowned; then her eyes gleamed brightly.

"Yes, yes, it was Bassanio, as I think so was he called."

"True madam, he of all the men that ever my foolish eyes looked upon was the best deserving a fair lady."

"I remember him well," murmured Portia, smiling to herself, "and I remember him worthy of thy praise."

In Venice, Bassanio had laid his hands on money. He had found a man who might be willing to lend him money against the word and bond of his friend Antonio. In a narrow street, where the water ran dark and crooked between high weeping walls, and little barred windows, like imprisoned eyes, stared dully down, he had met with a lean, bearded man in black, who smiled and frowned and smiled and frowned, and rubbed his hands together as if he would get to the bone of them. Shylock was his name, and he was a Jew.

He was not a man to Bassanio's liking, nor to the liking of any Venetian, for he seemed to crawl across the fair fabric of the city like a spider, spoiling it. But he lent money.

"Three thousand ducats, well," mused the Jew, rubbing his hands and frowning in his beard.

"Aye, sir, for three months," urged Bassanio, hovering brightly in attendance on the dark, ugly Jew.

"Three thousand ducats for three months, and Antonio bound," brooded the Jew, beginning to pace back and forth with such nervous rapidity that Bassanio was hard put to keep up with him.

Shylock was doubtful. He allowed that Antonio was a good man, meaning that the merchant's credit was good—that being the only way by which a merchant's goodness was to be measured—but all his wealth was laid out in ships at sea, and, as the Jew put it, "ships are but boards, sailors but men . . . there is the peril of waters, winds and rocks."

He shook his head; and poor Bassanio looked dismayed. He sighed; and Bassanio's heart dropped fathoms deep. Then he chuckled; and Bassanio walked on air!

"Three thousand ducats," said the Jew, most cheerfully. "I think I may take his bond . . . May I speak with Antonio?"

"If it please you to dine with us," offered Bassanio eagerly.

The Jew took a pace back. He stared at Bassanio as if he was mad.

"Yes, to smell pork," he answered savagely. "I will buy with you, sell with you, talk with you, walk with you, and so following; but I will not eat with you, drink with you, nor pray with you . . ."

A figure approached.

"This is Signior Antonio," said Bassanio quickly. He was fearful that he might have, unwittingly, offended the lender of money. With an anxious watch upon the Jew (lest he lose him), the young man went a few paces to meet the merchant, who was plainly pleased to have found his friend. Shylock, shrinking back against the wall till he seemed no more than an ugly stain upon it, stared at the merchant.

"How like a fawning publican he looks!" he snarled into his beard. "I hate him for he is a Christian." Nor was this the only reason for the Jew's hate. The merchant lent money without interest, and so brought down the cost of borrowing in Venice. Money was the Jew's only commodity, and the Christian undermined him. The Christian could make money out of trade; the Jew, by Venetian law, could only make money out of money. Take away his money and you take away his life. For these reasons the dark Jew hated the bright Christians of Venice; and, strongest of all, he hated them because they hated him. Hate breeds hate as fast as summer flies.

But nothing of this hatred showed as he greeted the merchant with smiles and bows and outstretched palms. All was satin courtesy. Antonio, on the other hand, regarded the cringing Jew with unconcealed contempt. He loathed and despised the Jew and, had it not been for the purpose of supplying the need of his young friend, who looked anxiously from one to the other, he would have scorned to walk upon the same side of the street as Shylock.

"Three thousand ducats," said Shylock, "'tis a good round sum. Three months from twelve, then let me see the rate."

"Well, Shylock," demanded the merchant coldly, "shall we be beholding to you?"

The Jew smiled humbly; and sighed.

"Signior Antonio, many a time and oft in the Rialto you have rated me about my moneys and my usances; still have I borne it with a patient

. . . he seemed to crawl across the fair fabric of the city

shrug, for suff'rance is the badge of all our tribe. You call me misbeliever, cut-throat dog, and spat upon my Jewish gaberdine . . . Well then, it now appears you need my help . . . 'Shylock, we would have moneys,' you say so . . . What should I say to you? Should I not say 'Hath a dog money? Is it possible a cur can lend three thousand ducats?' or shall I bend low, and in a bondman's key . . . say this: 'Fair sir, you spat on me on Wednesday last . . . another time you called me dog: and for these courtesies I'll lend you thus much moneys'?"

"I am as like to call thee so again," said Antonio contemptuously; for the Jew's long drawn out complainings had seemed to the upright merchant—whose affairs were open to the world—no better than the needless whining of a cur. Angrily, for he could see that his young friend was worried, he went on to demand a plain answer. Would the Jew, or would he not, lend the money? If the money was to be lent, then let it be done according to a bond. If the bond was broken, then the penalty must be exacted. Antonio desired no favours from the Jew.

"Why look how you storm!" cried Shylock, shrinking before the merchant's anger as before a taskmaster's whip. "I would be friends with you," he pleaded; and then, to prove his good faith, offered to lend the money and demand not a jot of interest.

"This were kindness!" cried Bassanio, as the prospect of going to Belmont with servants in attendance and fine clothes on his back seemed within his grasp.

Shylock, now friends with everybody (though none was friends with him), nodded and nodded and rubbed his skinny hands. They must go at once to a notary and draw up the bond. Though there was to be no interest, it was proper that there should be a bond, to be exacted only if the money lent was not repaid. And what should that bond be? Not property, not furnishings, not jewels, but—here the Jew laughed merrily, and the high-pitched sound made the barred windows seem to look sharply down—but a pound of the merchant's living flesh! And why not? Was not money flesh and life to the Jew? Why not then to the merchant? Shylock smiled at the humour of it with all the openness at his command. But smiles and snarls were kissing cousins to his lips. Antonio stared. Then he shrugged his shoulders and smiled. The Jew's humour was as strange as the Jew. He was content to seal the bargain which seemed, to him, far-fetched in the extreme.

"You shall not seal to such a bond for me," muttered Bassanio, suddenly uneasy for his friend.

But Antonio brushed aside his friend's concern: his ships and his money would all be home again a month before the bond was due. Shylock also was eager to quiet Bassanio's fears.

"If he should break his day what should I gain by exaction of the forfeiture?" he demanded. "A pound of man's flesh taken from a man, is not so estimable, profitable neither as flesh of muttons, beefs or goats." No, no, it was only to oblige Antonio and be his friend that he had proposed so unthrifty a bond.

The merchant believed him—and why not? What manner of man could really desire flesh instead of ducats?

"Hie thee gentle Jew," he laughed, as Shylock scuttled away to gather in the ducats, "the Hebrew will turn Christian, he grows kind."

But Bassanio shook his head. "I like not fair terms and a villain's mind."

Antonio smiled, and once more brushed aside his young friend's fears and forebodings.

Now Shylock had a daughter called Jessica, and she was as lovely as the night in Spring. Her mother must have been most wondrous for the daughter to have come by so much beauty, though mixed with Shylock's blood. She longed with all her heart to fly from the Jew's dark house, not to freedom, but to the prettier prison of love. She loved Lorenzo, Bassanio's friend, and he loved her, though all that had passed between them had been sighs from a window and sighs from the street. Nor was she alone in longing to escape from Shylock. The Jew had a servant by name of Launcelot Gobbo who likewise pined. He was a lively youth, and could no longer endure the miserly life of locks and bolts, and keys and strong-boxes, and rooms that never saw the light of day.

He was the first to fly away. He took his chance when it came, which was when Bassanio called to leave a letter, bidding the Jew come to supper with Antonio. Launcelot begged to be taken into Bassanio's service, which Bassanio gladly did, for he had need of a servant now that he was to go to Belmont and try his fortune with the lady there. Gratiano, that idle talker, strolling by took it into his head (where there was room enough and to spare), to ask if he, too, might go to Belmont with Bassanio. Bassanio sighed. It was hard to refuse a friend, but harder still to oblige such a one. He pleaded that, if Gratiano came, he would behave with proper modesty, for the fair lady of Belmont would surely not look kindly on a suitor who came with a chattering idiot in his train.

Sweet Jessica was as miserable as a widowed jackdaw when Launcelot told her of his good luck. She grieved that her father's hated house would now be robbed of its only cheerfulness.

"But fare thee well," she wished him, "there is a ducat for thee . . ."

She gave him the gold and, in addition, with much secrecy gave him a letter for his new master's friend, the handsome Lorenzo. When Launcelot had gone she sighed most bitterly, for she was ashamed that she was her father's child. "O Lorenzo," she whispered, "if thou keep promise I shall end this strife, become a Christian and thy loving wife!"

Young Launcelot, who loved and pitied his old master's daughter with all his heart, delivered the letter as swiftly as he could. Eagerly Lorenzo read it. His eyes shone, his heart soared. The letter was such a letter as lovers dream of. His Jessica was waiting for him. She had gathered together a dowry of gold and jewels, and was waiting for him to come and take her from her father's house.

It was a night of carnival. Flutes and songs and drums enriched the warm air. Slow gondolas, heavy with lovers, like baskets crammed with

grapes, drifted between the mansions, looped and necklaced with little lights. Strange, fantastic figures, led by torch bearers, danced and capered along the water-streets, and mocked at their mirror images as they kept rippled pace. Masks and laughter were the order of the night, save in one dark street and in one dark house where the Jew, Shylock, lived.

The door opened, and Shylock came out. His eyes glittered angrily as he heard the sounds of distant music and light laughter. He called for his daughter and she came, gleaming softly, like a candle.

"I am bid forth to supper Jessica," he said. "There are my keys . . ." She took the heavy ring, which, with its dull iron garnishings, hung on her white arm like a manacle on a moonbeam. "Jessica my girl," said the father, caught by a sudden dread, "look to my house. I am right loath to go, there is some ill a-brewing towards my rest, for I did dream of money-bags tonight."

He shivered in his long black gown; then a louder burst of music made him angry again. "Lock up my doors," he commanded, as sounds of singing and dancing feet drew near. "Clamber not you up to the casements then nor thrust your head into the public street to gaze on Christian fools with varnished faces." He shook his head. "I have no mind of feasting forth tonight: but I will go . . ."

Breathing deeply with relief, Jessica watched her father go, his dark shape putting out the distant lights, like a cloud among stars. Then she went back within doors.

Presently two friends of Lorenzo came by. They paused, looked up at the house, and nodded. This was the place where they were to meet. They waited, murmuring mockingly of lovers being late. Then Lorenzo came. All three wore painted masks with painted smiles that hid . . . more smiles. So that one might have wondered which were faces, which were masks. Lorenzo gazed up towards a casement that was stoutly shuttered. He called softly:

"Ho! Who's within?"

The shutters opened and a light shone out, and in that light was Jessica. Pretty Jessica, anxiously disguised in costume of a boy. She looked down, saw the painted smiler looking up.

"Who are you?"

"Lorenzo and thy love!"

She laughed for joy and then, bidding him catch , cast down, like a bright tear from her father's house, a casket of jewels and gold. Then she vanished from the window to lock the doors and fill her purse and boy's pockets with all the ducats she could carry away. So she left her father's scowls for love's smiles, and her father's darkness for love's light, taking with her his treasure and herself, who was the dearest treasure of all.

That very night, in a close and secret gondola, Lorenzo and Jessica fled from the city and Shylock's wrath. At the same time, or very near it, Bassanio with his friend Gratiano, and attended by Launcelot Gobbo his new servant, embarked for Belmont and its lady. He carried with him the love and fond hopes of Antonio the merchant who, for Bassanio's sake, had pledged his very life to the Jew.

Even as the casket that Jessica had thrown down from Shylock's window had contained her father's treasure, so one of the three closed caskets in Belmont contained another father's treasure: not gold, not jewels, but his daughter herself. In one of them was locked fair Portia's likeness, and he who chose it would gain her hand and heart. But in which casket? The gold, the silver, or the lead? That was the question. To choose right meant happiness beyond measure; to choose wrong meant, by the harsh condition imposed on the chooser, to go forever without a wife.

Soft lutes played delicate airs in the silken chamber where the caskets were, for a new suitor had come to Belmont to try for the lady. The Prince of Morocco, a turbaned Moor whose dark face sprang from his rich attire like ebony from snow. That he loved fair Portia was not to be doubted, for he was willing to risk all on the chance of winning her. While Portia and her maids looked uncertainly on, wondering where he would choose, he studied the three caskets, each in turn, as if his fierce eyes would probe the metal and spy the treasure within.

"This first of gold," murmured the dark Prince, "who this inscription bears, 'Who chooseth me shall gain what many men desire.' The second silver, which this promise carries, 'Who chooseth me shall get as much as he deserves.' This third, dull lead, with warning all as blunt, 'Who chooseth me must give and hazard all he hath.'" He shook his head.

"The one of them contains my picture, Prince," said Portia softly, "if you choose that then I am yours withal."

He flashed upon her a smile like dark fruit sliced; then returned to his contemplation of the caskets. Not lead, never lead. "Is't like that lead contains her?" he wondered. "'Twere damnation to think so base a thought!" But what of silver? "O sinful thought!" he exclaimed, "never so rich a gem was set in worse than gold!" He picked up the golden casket. "Deliver me the key!" he demanded, his deep voice shaking with expectation. "Here do I choose . . ."

"There take it Prince," said Portia quietly, "and if my form lies there then I am yours!"

He took the key and unlocked the casket. He looked within. A grey pallor over-washed his dark complexion. Not fair Portia but a Death's head glared up at him. He had lost all. He took his sad departure with dignity and some nobility.

"A gentle riddance," breathed Portia, much relieved, for, though she had admired the Prince, she had not loved him. "Draw the curtains, go."

In Venice, in busy, monied Venice, all was confusion. The Jew had discovered the loss of his daughter and the loss of his gold. He was mad with dismay, not knowing which loss had plunged the sharper dagger in his heart.

"I never heard a passion so confused," marvelled a friend of Antonio's to another, "as the dog Jew did utter in the streets—'My daughter! O my ducats! O my daughter! Fled with a Christian! O my Christian ducats! Justice, the law . . .'"

As the other listened to the tale of the Jew's wild distraction, he shook his head gravely. "Let good Antonio look he keep his day," he murmured, "or he shall pay for this."

Upon which his companion remembered, as people often do when there's a chance of disaster for others, that he'd heard a rumour that one of Antonio's ships had been wrecked. The two gentlemen stared at one another, and then with words, if not with hearts, expressed their deep concern for what might befall their friend Antonio if he failed to keep his bond.

In Belmont, where the concerns of Venice were as distant as the moon, another suitor had come to try for Portia's hand. A Spanish gentleman, gorgeous in velvet and with a hand and wrist as proud as a swan's neck. The Prince of Arragon, no less. While Portia and Nerissa and the bowing servants of the Prince looked on, the nobleman himself surveyed the caskets and the prize. Modestly Portia lowered her eyes, and hid a smile.

The leaden basket detained him not an instant: so princely a hand was never formed to touch so base a metal. Gold he toyed with, then put it by, for the good reason that it promised "what many men desire". "I will not choose what many men desire," he said, with a curl of his lip and a wave of his hand, "because I will not jump with common spirits, and rank me with the barbarous multitudes." The servants bowed and murmured admiringly, while Portia and Nerissa cast their eyes to heaven. So to the silver casket he turned. "'Who chooseth me shall get as much as he deserves'." He smiled knowingly and his servants nodded at their master's sagacity. What could such a prince as he deserve, but the very best? "Give me a key for this," he commanded, with a snap of his fingers and a waiting hand, "and instantly unlock my fortunes here."

The casket was opened, and the Prince looked within. He was silent. At such a moment the Moor's complexion had turned to grey; this Prince's colour darkened to red, and all his servants trembled.

"What's here?" he demanded at length, "the portrait of a blinking idiot." Anger gave way to grief. "Did I deserve no more than a fool's head?" he asked of the lady who most unkindly smiled. "Is that my prize?"

"To offend and judge are distinct offices," said Portia, a little sorry for the downcast Prince, "and of opposed natures."

He sighed heavily; but before he took his departure, he mustered up his spirits sufficiently to admit, "With one fool's head I came to woo, but I go away with two."

When the Prince and all his servants had departed, there came news that yet another suitor was approaching. His messenger, a young Venetian was already at the gate. Portia and Nerissa looked at one another. Who could this messenger's master be?

"Bassanio," prayed Nerissa, "Lord Love, if thy will it be!"

The water ran choppily by the Rialto, as an invisible wind, like strong rumour, sent it scurrying. Two good friends of Antonio talked solemnly, amid the bustle and business of brokers and merchants. Again they'd heard tales that one of Antonio's ships had been wrecked and all its cargo lost. They shook their heads sadly over their friend's ill-luck, and prayed there would be no more of it.

"How now Shylock!" exclaimed one, as the Jew drew near, "what news among the merchants?"

The Jew, his eyes all red from weeping, glared at the Christian gentlemen, in whose contemptuous smiles he read, all too easily, mockery for his loss. His daughter was gone, and they laughed at him.

Such a daughter, they jeered, was too good for such a father to keep. "But tell us," they asked, brushing aside the Jew's misfortunes, "do you hear whether Antonio have had any loss at sea or no?"

Another knife in his heart, for Antonio was in distress and near to being bankrupt. More ducats thrown to the dogs! "Let him look to his bond," snarled Shylock, "let him look to his bond!"

"Why," cried one of the gentlemen, in some surprise, "I am sure if he forfeit thou wilt not take his flesh—what's that good for?"

"To bait fish withal," screamed the Jew, beside himself with grief and rage, "if it will feed nothing else, it will feed my revenge."

The two gentlemen stepped back; passers-by paused; velvet lords and ladies turned, stared, exchanged glances of scorn (but discreetly for none wanted to be noticed and publicly pounced upon by the inflamed Jew), as the black-gowned Shylock raved on: "He hath disgraced me and hindered me half a million, laughed at my losses, mocked at my gains,

89

scorned my nation, thwarted my bargains, cooled my friends, heated mine enemies. And what's his reason? I am a Jew." Here, the money-lender glared about him with such ferocious distress and such ancient anguish, that the brightly hovering world of Venice seemed to shrink and tremble, like butterflies' wings at the cooling of summer. Shylock went on, his voice as raw as the shrieking of sea birds: "Hath not a Jew eyes? Hath not a Jew hands, organs, dimensions, senses, affections, passions? fed with the same food, hurt by the same weapons, subject to the same diseases, healed by the same means, warmed and cooled by the same winter and summer as a Christian is? If you prick us do we not bleed? If you tickle us do we not laugh? If you poison us do we not die? And if you wrong us shall we not revenge? If a Jew wrong a Christian, what is his humility? revenge! If a Christian wrong a Jew, what should his sufferance be by Christian example? Why revenge! The villainy you teach me I will execute, and it shall go hard but I will better the instruction."

Shylock stopped, panting from his exertions. To the relief of Antonio's friends, a messenger came, bidding them come to the merchant's house. The lookers-on shrugged their shoulders and strolled away. Shylock stood alone, until another of his tribe, one Tubal, joined him.

"What news from Genoa?" demanded Shylock. "Hast thou found my daughter?"

The news was bad. Tubal had heard of her but not seen her. Shylock was plunged into the blackest misery. All his riches gone. Would that his daughter was dead! "The curse never fell upon our nation till now," he groaned, "I never felt it till now . . ."

But, on the other hand, there was news in Genoa that one of Antonio's ships had been cast away. Ah! That was better! Yet then again, Tubal had heard, in talkative Genoa, that Shylock's daughter had spent, at one sitting, four score ducats.

"Thou stick'st a dagger in me," moaned Shylock.

But, said Tubal, Antonio's creditors were gathering, and the Jew was pacified—until he heard that one of them had had a ring off Jessica for a monkey.

"Out upon her!" wept Shylock, wringing his hands and tearing at the shiny ringlets of his hair, "it was my turquoise, I had it of Leah when I was a bachelor; I would not have given it for a wilderness of monkeys!"

But, thank God, Antonio was ruined, and Shylock sent Tubal for an officer to enforce his terrible claim upon the proud merchant who had spurned him.

In Belmont, in smiling Belmont, the new suitor had appeared; and to Portia's joy and fear he was that very Bassanio she remembered from long ago: to her joy because her heart danced to see him, and to her fear because, if he failed in his choice of casket, she would never see him more. In vain she begged him put off the fateful choice, and take pleasure in her house and gardens, and the soft air of Belmont, which was always filled with music; but Bassanio, having come thus far, and at such a cost, could not endure to delay. So now he stood before the caskets, with Gratiano (strangely quiet Gratiano), by his side; and the fair lady of Belmont, with all her maids like pale daisies bending towards her warmth and light, watched him intently. Softly, though in a voice that trembled, Portia bade a page boy, who sat cross-legged and fondled a lute almost as large as himself, to sing. The child frowned down at his instrument, and gravely began: "Tell me where is Fancy bred, or in the heart or in the head?"

Some say it was the song that guided Bassanio in his choice, for Portia already loved him well enough to give his fortune a proper turn; but she was ever honourable in her dealings, and well Bassanio knew it. No! If he was guided at all, it was not by rhyme, but by the bright sudden looks of Portia's sea-blue eyes, which warned him that true beauty dwells within. It was his own love and hers that taught him the wisdom to know where his best hope lay: not in gold, not in silver, but in quiet, unassuming lead. "And here choose I," he breathed. "Joy be the consequence!"

And so it was. Within the leaden casket was fair Portia's portrait. Bassanio had won the lady of his heart. The joy of the chosen was no less than the joy of the chooser; they were a pair fairly matched. To solemnize their promised marriage, Portia gave Bassanio a ring, and made him swear that he would never, so long as he loved her, part with it. (Such a ring Leah had given to Shylock, and Jessica had stolen it away.) Willingly Bassanio promised. And then Gratiano spoke up: he too had found a bride, whose promise had depended on the choice of casket. She was Portia's maid, Nerissa, whose loveliness was only exceeded by her mistress's as the lily by the rose. It would seem that, by holding his tongue in accordance with his promise, Gratiano had made a better conquest by silence than by talk.

Then, in the midst of this high summer of happiness, a cloud came over the sun. There arrived from Venice Lorenzo and Jessica, and a friend of Antonio's. They brought a letter from the merchant to his young friend.

"Sweet Bassanio," wrote the merchant, in the extremity of his distress, "my ships have all miscarried, my creditors grow cruel, my estate is very low, my bond to the Jew is forfeit, and, since in paying it, it is impossible I should all live, debts are cleared between you and I, if I might but see you at my death; notwithstanding, use your pleasure; if your love do not persuade you to come, let not my letter."

Belmont was fallen into dullness. The house was quiet and the gardens emptied. Lutes and guitars were coffined in their cases, for the two new brides had been widowed by the need of a friend. Their husbands, Bassanio and Gratiano, had hastened to Venice to try to save the good Antonio. But there was little hope. Even though Portia had urged Bassanio to offer the Jew many times the value of the bond, it was feared he would not take it. His daughter Jessica declared that she had heard her father swear that there was no money that could buy back the bond. His love of ducats had been quite swallowed up in his desire for revenge. He would have his pound of flesh. He knew full well that not even the Duke could deny him this; for the bond had been drawn up in accordance with the law of Venice, and to skirt that law would be to undermine it, and so undermine the chief strength of the state.

Portia thought deeply about these matters, and wondered how she might help her husband's friend with her wit if her wealth proved to be of no avail. It was a matter of law, and, though no lawyer herself, she had a cousin in Padua, by name of Doctor Bellario, who was most learned in the science. To Bellario, then, she sent her servant with a letter requiring certain notes and articles of clothing to be dispatched to the Venice ferry, where she and her maid would receive them. Then, confiding to Lorenzo and Jessica the charge of her house, she gave out that she and Nerissa were retiring to a monastery while their husbands were away. This done, she and Nerissa left Belmont on their strange adventure.

"Come on, Nerissa," she murmured, with brightly gleaming eyes, "I have work in hand that you yet know not of; we'll see our husbands before they think of us!"

The waters of Venice ran dark and deep beside the Hall of Justice, reflecting stone walls and no more than a knife of the sky. Within, among gilded pillars and richly tapestried walls, from which long-dead law-givers gazed faintly down, there was much murmuring as the Duke and

all the dignitaries of the State entered to hear the cause and give judgement. They sat, with a sigh of crimson velvets and a quiet chiming of their chains of gold. Antonio was summoned and duly fetched. Poor man! his face was already as pale as death. He saw Bassanio among the onlookers, and seemed to gain a little courage from the presence of his young friend.

"Go one and call the Jew into the court," commanded the Duke, Shylock was called; and Shylock came. In Sabbath gown, as black as night, he stood before the court, rubbing and rubbing his thin white hands, as the Duke urged him to be merciful and not demand the terrible payment of the bond. Shylock shook his head, and his oiled locks gleamed redly in the crowding candlelight, as if his bloody thoughts had stained them. He would have his bond. He stared defiantly at the assembled lords in all their pride. "If you deny it," he warned, "let the danger light upon your charter and your city's freedom!"

Impulsively Bassanio stepped forward and pleaded with the Jew. Shylock answered him coldly, curtly, and scarce deigning to look at him. Antonio interposed and begged Bassanio not waste his breath. "Make no more offers," he pleaded, weary with distress, "let me have judgement and the Jew his will."

"For thy three thousand ducats here is six!" cried Bassanio, throwing down a heavy purse on to the table of judgement. Again Shylock shook his head. He would have nothing but his bond.

"How shalt thou hope for mercy rend'ring none?" wondered the Duke, shocked beyond measure by the force of the Jew's hatred.

"What judgement shall I dread doing no wrong?" demanded Shylock angry with this Christian court that sought to escape its own laws. "If you deny me," he cried, "fie upon your law! There is no force in the decrees of Venice: I stand for judgement; answer, shall I have it?"

The Duke and his lords gravely conferred. There was no doubt that the Jew had law upon his side. If only the learned Doctor Bellario, for whom the Duke had sent, would come and unperplex the court! Then, even as that doctor's name was spoken, it was learned that he had sent a messenger with letters . . .

"Bring us the letters!" exclaimed the Duke, "call the messenger!"

The messenger was called, and the messenger came: a most curious small clerk, in clerk's gown, and clerk's hat, with clerk's wig and clerk's spectacles, so that nothing showed but what was proper to a clerk, who did not look like Nerissa at all. In a voice that struggled to keep low, but kept rising, like a swimmer for air, the clerk presented the Duke with Doctor Bellario's greetings, and his letters. As the Duke read the letters, the court buzzed with expectation; then sharply drew in its breath as it was seen that Shylock, merciless Shylock, had taken out his knife and was steadily sharpening it against the sole of his shoe.

Doctor Bellario's letters told that he was sick and unable to attend; but that, in his place, he had sent a young lawyer in whom he had the greatest faith. The Duke looked up, and there before him stood the young lawyer: a most curious small young lawyer, in lawyer's gown and lawyer's hat, with lawyer's wig and lawyer's thick spectacles so that nothing showed but what was proper to a lawyer, who did not look like fair Portia at all. The Duke looked doubtfully at the little advocate, whose chin, nestling in lawyer's bands, was as beardless as silk. Was the young lawyer acquainted with the cause before the court? The young lawyer was; and the young lawyer's voice was not unlike the clerk's,

being low in parts. The Duke shrugged his shoulders and, with a wave of his many-ringed hand, indicated that the trial between the Jew and the merchant of Venice should proceed.

"Of a strange nature is the suit you follow," said the lawyer to the Jew, "yet in such rule that the Venetian law cannot impugn you as you do proceed . . ." The Jew's beard revealed, rather than hid, the grimness of his smile. "Do you confess the bond?" asked the lawyer of the merchant. Helplessly the merchant confessed it. "Then must the Jew be merciful," decided the lawyer.

"On what compulsion must I?" demanded the Jew. "Tell me that!" The court murmured. What compulsion could this small lawyer bring upon the dark, threatening Jew to make him merciful? The lawyer faced the Jew; took a pace towards him; held out hands in a gesture of pleading—hands that were whiter and gentler than lawyer's hands ever were; and spoke to him:

"The quality of mercy is not strained, it droppeth as the gentle rain from heaven upon the place beneath; it is twice blessed, it blesseth him that gives, and him that takes, 'tis mightiest in the mightiest, it becomes the throned monarch better than his crown . . ." Thus the lawyer pleaded with Shylock to temper justice with mercy. But Shylock, savage Shylock, would have nothing of it. He demanded his pound of the merchant's flesh.

"Is he not able to discharge the money?" inquired the lawyer of the court.

"Yes, here I tender it for him in the court!" cried Bassanio, and offered twice the sum, or even ten times (upon which the small lawyer looked sharply at the young man who was so prodigal with ducats), to redeem the bond. "If that will not suffice," went on Bassanio, "it must appear that malice bears down truth. Wrest once the law to your authority; to do a great right, do a little wrong, and curb this cruel devil of his will."

"It must not be," said the lawyer, "there is no power in Venice can alter a decree established: 'twill be recorded for a precedent . . ."

"A Daniel come to judgement: yea, a Daniel!" cried Shylock, capering with delight to find the justice of his cause upheld. "O wise young judge how I do honour thee!"

The knife faltered

The small lawyer nodded, and asked to see the bond. It was given and, when read, proved to be as the Jew had said.

"Take thrice thy money, bid me tear the bond," urged the lawyer. But Shylock would not relent. He stood by the law, and the law upheld him. Antonio must pay the forfeit: a pound of his living flesh, to be cut nearest his heart.

"The law allows it, and the court awards it," decreed the lawyer. So Antonio, condemned Antonio, took his last farewell of Bassanio and prepared himself for Shylock's upraised knife. The court leaned forward, pale with dread at what the law could do.

"Tarry a little," said the lawyer suddenly, even as the knife was at Antonio's breast, "there is something else. This bond doth give thee here no jot of blood, the words expressly are 'a pound of flesh': take then thy bond, take thou thy pound of flesh, but in cutting it, if thou dost shed one drop of Christian blood, thy lands and goods are, by the laws of Venice, confiscate unto the state of Venice."

The knife faltered; the hand that held it shook and trembled and a dreadful bitterness curdled the Jew's fierce face. The very law he had invoked had defeated him. The mocking laughter of the court rang in his ears like the worst of Sunday's bells. He put away his knife; he rubbed and rubbed his hands, and muttered that he would take the offer of thrice the bond.

"Here is the money!" cried Bassanio, gladly.

But the small lawyer would not allow it; and, with a look of mingled affection and reproof at the extravagant young man, pressed Shylock still harder with the weight of the law. He was to have only what he had demanded, neither less nor more. Not even his principal was to be restored; only the pound of flesh without one drop of blood. He staggered, stared about him, saw only a sea of Christian faces and a sea of Christian smiles. He longed only to be gone. But even this was denied him. He, an alien, had undoubtedly sought the life of a citizen, therefore all his wealth was to be taken, half for the merchant, half for the state. His life itself was now in the hand of the Duke.

"Down therefore," cried the lawyer who had once urged him to show mercy, "and beg mercy of the Duke."

"That thou shall see the difference of our spirit," pronounced the Duke, "I pardon thee thy life before thou ask it . . ."

Shylock shook his head. He smiled bitterly. Of what use was his life now?

"Take my life and all," he whispered, "pardon not that. You take my house, when you do take the prop that doth sustain my house: you take my life when you do take the means whereby I live."

The small lawyer, who had, perhaps, been carried away by the ingeniousness of argument, was struck by the Jew's tragic words, and remembered. He turned to the merchant and asked:

"What mercy can you render him Antonio?"

Antonio proved no less merciful than the Duke. Half of Shylock's wealth should be restored, if he would, at his death, leave it to his daughter and her husband; the other half Antonio himself would use, and likewise bequeath to Jessica and Lorenzo. All this should be allowed upon one condition, that the Jew should turn Christian.

"Art thou contented Jew?" asked the lawyer, with the most gentle regard. "What dost thou say?"

"I am content," muttered the Jew; and, with bowed head, left the court to embrace a gentler God than the one that had brought him. As he went, the thronged candles tugged after him, as if to lend him a little of the radiance of a court in which, not justice, not the law, but mercy had triumphed.

When all were dispersed and the Duke departed, Bassanio embraced his saved friend; and together they thanked the small lawyer whose wit and skill had so marvellously succeeded. What gift could they give him? At first the lawyer would take nothing; but then, when pressed, asked no more than Bassanio's ring. Alas! it was the very ring that Portia had given him and which he'd sworn to keep so long as he should live. He made excuses, said it was not good enough, and offered, instead, to find the dearest ring in all Venice. But the lawyer would take nothing else, and so took nothing. Together with his small clerk, he left the court, making scornful comment upon those who offer and then turn niggardly when put to the performance.

"My lord Bassanio," urged Antonio, "let him have the ring . . ."

Bassanio sighed. He took the ring from his finger and sent Gratiano with it to overtake the small lawyer and his small clerk. So Bassanio parted with Portia's ring; and, at the same time, Gratiano parted with Nerissa's, for she, too, had given her husband a ring in love's pledge; which ring the lawyer's small clerk had begged.

The moon was high in Belmont and the dark gardens flowed with silver, like a Venice built in dreams.

"In such a night," sighed Lorenzo, as he strolled entwined with Jessica, and gave an instance of lovers long ago.

"In such a night," sighed Jessica, and gave another, no less apt.

"In such a night," proposed Lorenzo . . . and so they continued, night for night, until they were distracted by music that heralded the return of Portia and Nerissa, who were followed, soon after, by Bassanio and Gratiano, with the saved merchant Antonio, newly come from Venice. Lutes, guitars and viols sweet as honey swelled the tender meeting of wives and husbands . . . until a discord broke up the harmony. This discord concerned the giving of a ring. Gratiano, so it seemed, had given Nerissa's ring to a lawyer's clerk in Venice. Nerissa was outraged; and so was fair Portia when she learned that her husband, the ardent Bassanio, had given her ring to the lawyer. So much for love, so much for promises, so much for husbands' vows breathed in the first heat of passion! Antonio, much dismayed by the distress his own distress had brought about, sought to intercede. Portia sighed, and relented.

"Give him this," she sighed, "and bid him keep it better than the other." She gave the merchant a ring which he, in turn, gave to the apologising Bassanio. He took it, he glanced at it, he stared. It was the very ring he had given to the lawyer. Likewise, and at the same time, Gratiano was given the very ring he had bestowed upon the clerk. At once, base suspicions entered the minds of the husbands of how their wives might have come by the rings. But soon all was told, of how Portia had been the lawyer and Nerissa the clerk. So all ended in music, smiles and happiness; and fair Portia, practising the mercy she had preached, embraced her husband with all her heart.

The Taming of the Shrew

In the county of Warwickshire there lived a tinker, who, in his time, had followed many trades, and caught up with none. He was Christopher Sly by name, and coarse, drunken and brutish by nature.

"You will not pay for the glasses you have burst?" demanded the hostess of the inn he patronised.

For answer, he shook his fat head, belched, and lay down on the floor. The hostess, a female as sweet as a lemon, threatened him with a constable.

"Let him come," mumbled Sly, and, endeavouring to pull a stool over him as if it was a blanket, fell like a corpse into a tomb of snores. The hostess shook her fist and departed.

But before she could return, a most extraordinary thing happened to Christopher Sly. There was a sound of horns (which he heard not) and a barking of dogs. Then, flushed from galloping the countryside, a plumed and booted lord accompanied by huntsmen and servants, strode into the inn. They looked about them and saw, under a table, the drunken tinker, his pig-like countenance wreathed in smiles of ale. The lord shuddered, "Grim death, how foul and loathsome is thine image!" he exclaimed, somewhat fancifully although it must be admitted that

Christopher Sly might as well have been dead for all he knew of lords and huntsmen and the world about him.

Then the lord, whose head was well-stocked with old tales of gods changing humans into swine, thought it an excellent idea to change this swinish tinker into a lord. Accordingly he told his servants to carry the snoring Sly to his mansion, wash him, improve him with perfumes, lay him in the richest chamber, and, when he woke, to bow to him, call him 'lord', offer him the best of food and drink and clothing, show him a simpering, girlish page-boy dressed up as his lady wife, and to explain to him that he had just awakened from a long lunacy during which he had only imagined that he was a tinker called Christopher Sly. Then, to fuddle him further, he was to be shown a play, and it was to be performed so straight and serious that he would no longer know what was true and what was make-believe. Then the lord went off, like one of the gods of old, to watch the transformation of the tinker into something rich and strange.

Christopher Sly woke up. He blinked, through eyes like stained-glass windows. He was in a room as gorgeous as a palace and was sitting on a mountain of cushions; and there were servants bowing all round him. He was not surprised. The world often looked queer when he woke up but after he'd had a drink or two, it turned ordinary again. "For God's sake, a pot of small ale!" he cried urgently. This time the vision did not fade; instead it grew more visionary and unreal. He was offered all manner of delicate things, quite unsuited to a tinker's tastes; and, when he objected, he was told that there was no such person as Christopher Sly, that Christopher Sly had only been a long bad dream, and that he was really a lord who had only just awakened from it.

He blinked again and thumped his head. Then music began to twink and scrape and a smiling gentleman talked of Apollos and Daphnes and suchlike, which was all Greek to Sly; and then a female appeared, pretty as a page-boy with a bosom as neat as a pair of oranges, and, most wonderful, she was his lady wife! This was plain good English to the tinker, who straightway wanted to take her to bed. But alas! this was not to be. He had been sick for so long, that he must husband his husband-

strength awhile, lest his malady return. He and his lady-wife were to sit modestly side by side and watch a play. A play? He had never seen a play in his life before and did not know in the least what to expect; but he was ready to put up with anything rather than risk falling back into the horrible dream of being Christopher Sly.

Of a sudden, there was a loud flourish on a trumpet, that made the tinker jump; and the chamber grew as quiet as an empty church. Then, before the tinker's very eyes, the strangest transformation took place, so strange that he could not be clear in his head whether he was Christopher Sly, thumping-bag of hostesses and butt of angry females, asleep; a lord awake—or a piece of transparent air, and the dream of other watchers. The tapestried walls, the encrusted ceiling, the lady-wife and servants seemed to dissolve, and the great mansion itself to vanish; and in their place was magically the clear blue sky and rosy painted streets of an old Italian town!

It was sunny, bustling Padua, where rich old Baptista Minola had two daughters, one like an angel from heaven, and one from the other place.

The last was Katherine, who had a tongue like burnt bacon, and a temper like mustard without beef. Bianca, the angel, had two suitors, which was not to be wondered at; Katherine, the elder, had none, which was not to be wondered at either. Their father would have given half his fortune to have got Katherine off his hands; and Bianca would have given the other half, because her father had determined that she could not marry unless someone married Katherine first. And that seemed as likely a happening as snow in hell. So they all walked along a street in Padua, Baptista between Bianca's two suitors, and his two daughters behind: Katherine looking daggers at the gentle and well-loved Bianca, and Bianca, who was more seemly and domestic, looking needles back.

Hopelessly old Baptista suggested that, if the suitors transferred their attentions to his eldest child, he would make it well worth their while. Vigorously the gentlemen shook their heads; which, though she would not have had either of them save on a roasting-dish with an apple in his mouth, did not please Katherine at all. Addressing herself to the younger (for the other was no better than an ancient money-bag in wrinkled stockings), she offered to "comb his noddle with a three-legged stool." Her father glared at her, and she glared back; and most decidedly got the better of the exchange.

"Go in, Bianca," said her father gently to his angel, for they stood outside his house. Bianca curtsied modestly, and, with a mildly reproachful look at her sister, withdrew to her books and music and suchlike maidenly pursuits. The suitors sighed; and Baptista asked if they knew of schoolmasters who might further improve Bianca, if such a thing were possible. While they thought about it, Baptista hurried into the house, saying, over his shoulder: "Katherina, you may stay," either in the hope that she and the gentleman would soften towards one another, or else just to make good his escape.

"Why, and I trust I may go too, may I not?" demanded Katherine, with a look that would have curdled ale. "Ha!" she cried; and went in after her father like a whirlwind, and slammed the door.

The suitors looked at one another. It was plain that, if they wished to prosper with Bianca, they would have to find a husband for Katherine first.

"There be good fellows in the world," said Hortensio, the younger, "would take her with all faults, and money enough."

They nodded, but with little conviction. Could there really be such a man?

"Would I had given him the best horse in Padua to begin his wooing," sighed the ancient money-bag, whose name was Gremio, "that would thoroughly woo her, wed her, and bed her, and rid the house of her!"

They shook their heads and departed, leaving the street quiet, save for in Baptista's house where doors kept going off like exploding chestnuts as Katherine stormed from room to room.

Two figures came out from a neighbouring doorway, where they had been silent lookers-on. They were from Pisa and strangers to Padua, and they marvelled greatly at what they had seen and heard. One was Lucentio, a young gentleman in colours so bright you might have cooked by them; the other was his servant Tranio, who wore long striped stockings, like barbers' poles, and a cap like a brace of pheasant. The servant looked at his master, and the master looked into air. His eyes were as round and bright as sixpences. He was spellbound! He had seen an angel, a gentle angel of loveliness! He had fallen in love with Bianca! Everything else fled from his brain. He quite forgot that he had come to Padua on business for his father. He could think of nothing but Bianca and how he might get to her.

He would disguise himself as a schoolmaster! He had heard her father say that he wanted masters for her.

"Not possible," said Tranio firmly: "for who shall bear your part and be in Padua here Vicentio's son?"

This was true. He was to have taken lodgings to entertain rich merchants for his father, Vicentio. He could not be in two places at once. He pondered; but not for long, for love lends wings to thought. He and Tranio would change about! Tranio would be Lucentio and entertain his father's friends, while he, Lucentio, would be a humble schoolmaster, teaching the fair Bianca Latin, Greek, and whatever more her modesty would allow. Tranio agreed, for deception ran in his veins like blood; so without more ado, man and master changed cloaks and hats, and were instantly transformed.

Hortensio, wracking his brains to think of some presentable fellow whose spirit was stout enough, and whose purse was lean enough, to try his fortunes with Katherine, walked slowly back to his house. He stopped. There was an argument in progress outside his gate. A sturdy young man was heartily thumping his companion, who was roaring for help. Hortensio smiled. One was Petruchio, a friend of his from Verona; the other was his friend's servant Grumio, who doubtless deserved what he was getting. He hastened to greet them and to ask Petruchio what he was doing in Padua.

"Such wind as scatters young men through the world," began Petruchio, in a fine and lofty style, for he was an excellent fellow and the best of comrades in an ale-house brawl; but then his face grew solemn, and an anxious look haunted his eyes. His father had died and had left him, to put it plainly, somewhat short of money. "Crowns in my purse I have, and goods at home," he said hastily, as if to reassure Hortensio that he had not come to borrow money. "I come," he said with utter honesty, "to wive it wealthily in Padua . . ."

Hortensio's heart quickened. Could his prayers have been answered so pat? Cautiously he mentioned that he knew of a lady who was very rich. Then he shook his head. She had disadvantages. "Thou'rt too much my friend," he said regretfully, "I'll not wish thee to her."

But Petruchio was not so easily put off. What was wrong with the lady? A sharp tongue and a bad temper? "Think you a little din can daunt mine ears?" he demanded bravely. "Have I not in my time heard lions roar?"

Hortensio shook his head. "I would not wed her," he said, "for a mine of gold."

"Thou know'st not gold's effect," said Petruchio bitterly, having discovered the evil of need and thinking peace a small price to pay to be rid of it. "Tell me her father's name and 'tis enough . . ."

"Her father is Baptista Minola," said Hortensio, seeing that nothing would shake his friend's resolve; and went on to tell him everything, even that he himself hoped to marry the younger daughter when Katherine had been taken off her father's hands.

"I know her father," nodded Petruchio; and this turned out to be a great convenience to Hortensio, who promptly asked a favour. When Petruchio called on old Baptista he should take with him a certain schoolmaster and recommend him warmly as an instructor to Bianca. This schoolmaster would, of course, be Hortensio himself in an impenetrable disguise.

Readily, Petruchio agreed; but before anything could be done, Bianca's other suitor, the ancient Gremio appeared. And he was not alone. By the strangest chance, he had found a schoolmaster for Bianca, a pleasant enough looking fellow, but no better dressed than a tinker on Sunday. He said his name was Cambio, but anyone who knew him could have seen, with half an eye, that he was Lucentio in disguise.

Hortensio, annoyed that his rival should have forestalled him in the business of schoolmasters, remarked that he, too, had found a learned person; but, what was more to the point, he had also found someone willing to court Katherine. He pointed to Petruchio. Gremio peered at him incredulously.

"Hortensio," he asked quietly, "have you told him all her faults?"

"I know she is an irksome brawling scold," said Petruchio.

Gremio shrugged his shoulders. "If you have a stomach," he said, "to it a God's name! you shall have me assisting you in all."

Then Hortensio, finding himself lagging behind Gremio yet again, made the same offer; and Petruchio sighed with relief. He had been wondering where the money would come from to pay the cost of wooing.

They were preparing to set off for Baptista's house, when matters took yet another turn. A personage in a brightly coloured cloak and hat, came mincing down the street like a sunburst. He greeted them ceremoniously, and announced himself as yet another suitor to the fair Bianca. The two rivals were indignant. Who was this impudent newcomer? He declared that he was one Lucentio of Pisa, and very rich; though anyone with half an eye could have seen that he was Tranio in his master's clothes, and guessed that his master had put him up to it; but they believed him.

"Did you yet ever see Baptista's daughter?" demanded Hortensio.

"No, sir," replied Tranio; but he had heard that she was beautiful and wealthy, and that was enough for him.

The rivals looked at one another. They sighed. Honey-sweet Bianca was gathering suitors like bees. They had no right to send the new one away, but, nonetheless, he ought to pay his share towards the cost of getting rid of that fierce impediment, Katherine. "You must," said Hortensio, gesturing towards Petruchio, "as we do, gratify this gentleman . . ."

Tranio, cheerfully making free with his master's money, agreed. Petruchio beamed. He felt a new man. But those who knew better, felt that Katherine would soon make an old one of him.

The door of Baptista's house flew open, and out came Bianca, weeping like April with the fury of March close behind. Her sister, by means of horrible threats and superior strength, had tied her hands together and pushed her out into the street. Loudly she jeered at Bianca for her suitors, while gentle Bianca wept and meekly pleaded to be set free.

"You have but jested with me all this while," she ventured, smiling bravely through her tears. "I prithee, sister Kate, untie my hands."

Katherine hit her, bringing down her hair like a tumbled sheaf of corn. Bianca shrieked; and out of the house came Baptista. He saw his angel bound and weeping, and was outraged. Tenderly he untied her and

demanded of her cruel persecutor: "When did she cross thee with a bitter word?"

"Her silence flouts me!" answered Katherine, and, with upraised fists, flew at her sister yet again.

"Bianca, get thee in!" urged Baptista, stepping hastily between his children and allowing Bianca to escape.

"I see she is your treasure!" shouted Katherine; and, her breast heaving with indignation, she rushed away to weep and plot revenge.

"Was ever gentleman thus grieved as I?" groaned Baptista; and then hurriedly composed himself for visitors were approaching.

They were Signior Gremio, Bianca's elderly suitor, smiling like a crumpled face in a tapestry, with some half dozen strangers, all of whom were smiling too. But then, why not? The sun was bright and, doubtless, none of them had daughters. Then the morning, which had begun so stormily for Baptista, turned radiant!

Not only had that good Signior Gremio brought him a schoolmaster for Bianca, wise in Latin and Greek, but also, and most marvellously, a suitor for Katherine! He was a fine-looking young fellow by name of Petruchio of Verona. Baptista had known his father, so he was no idle scrap of nonsense off the streets. On the contrary, he was well-dressed and courteous, and had inquired most civilly: "Pray have you not a daughter called Katherina, fair and virtuous?"

"I have a daughter, sir," Baptista had responded, "called Katherina," and had left it at that. He did not wish to misrepresent his eldest child; particularly as none could fail to hear her stormy passage through the house. But Petruchio was not put off; and he, too, had brought a schoolmaster, skilled in music and mathematics, whom he offered like an academic bouquet. Baptista stared. He had never seen a more learned looking man in all his life. Solemnly gowned in black, he peered out at the world through spectacles as thick as bottles and he was whiskered like a broom. A man like that must have had a whole university in his head!

Baptista was delighted; but his morning's good fortune was not over yet. Another of the strangers, a young gentleman in a brightly coloured hat and cloak, bowed low and presented himself as Lucentio of Pisa, who was enormously rich. It was his earnest desire to be numbered among the suitors to the fair Bianca, and he pressed upon Baptista, with his best wishes, a pudding-faced boy bearing a pile of Greek and Latin volumes, and a lute.

What a morning! Baptista, who had never before got anything by having daughters, save aggravation and distress, now found himself the happy possessor of two more suitors—one for each child—two schoolmasters, and the instruments of their craft! And all in a matter of minutes! Beaming, he despatched lute, books and scholars into his house, so that his daughters' improvement might begin without delay. Then he turned eagerly to Petruchio to settle the matter of Katherine's dowry, before the young man could change his mind.

"Well mayst thou woo," said Baptista, warmly shaking Petruchio by the hand when matters were settled, "and happy be thy speed . . ." Then his hope of seeing his eldest daughter married and in Verona, received a set-back.

The door burst open and out staggered Petruchio's learned gift. He was clutching his brow, which was decorated with a lute-string and splinters of wood. Katherine had broken his lute over his head.

Baptista sighed; and, comforting the dazed scholar as best he could, prepared to lead him back into the house to try for better things with the gentle Bianca. "Signor Petruchio," he asked uncomfortably, "will you go with us, or shall I send my daughter Kate to you?"

"I pray you do," said Petruchio; and off went the father, marvelling greatly.

Kate came out. She was divided between anger at having been sent for, and curiosity to see why. She had never had a suitor before, and she did not like the look of him. He smirked at her as if she was a joint of lamb.

"Good morrow, Kate, for that's your name, I hear," he said.

"Well have you heard, but something hard of hearing," she answered coldly; "they call me Katherine that do talk of me."

"You lie, in faith," said he, returning her cold look with a warm one, "for you are called plain Kate, and bonny Kate, and sometimes Kate the curst; but Kate, the prettiest Kate in Christendom!" He spoke the truth, for she was indeed beautiful; and when he concluded by saying: "Myself am moved to woo thee for my wife," he meant it.

She replied, contemptuously. He countered amiably. She frowned; he smiled. She called him an ass; he called her a woman. She told him to be off.

"Nay, come again," said he, "good Kate, I am a gentleman—"

"That I'll try!" she cried, and hit him as hard as she could.

"I swear I'll cuff you," said Petruchio, rubbing his burning cheek and keeping his temper with difficulty, "if you strike again."

She scowled; and lowered her hand.

"Nay, come, Kate, come," said he, coaxingly, "you must not look so sour."

"It is my fashion when I see a crab," she answered; and so the courtship proceeded, sweet as vinegar, and gentle as a raging sea: she the wind, and he the mariner fighting to contain her blasts.

"Now, Kate, I am a husband for your turn!" he panted, pinioning her arms and struggling to avoid her kicks. "I am he am born to tame you, Kate, and bring you from a wild Kate to a Kate conformable as other household Kates!"

Suddenly he set her free; her father was coming, together with Bianca's suitors.

"Now, Signor Petruchio," inquired Baptista, looking uneasily from flushed face to flushed and glaring face, "how speed you with my daughter?"

"How but well, sir?" responded Petruchio, to the father's relief. "How but well?"

"Why, how now, daughter Katherine?" asked Baptista tenderly, perceiving that his eldest child looked somewhat despondent. "In your dumps?"

"Call you me daughter?" shrieked Katherine, and went on to abuse the poor man for daring to thrust her upon, as she put it, "one half lunatic, a madcap ruffian and a swearing Jack!" She pointed a trembling finger at Petruchio, so there should be no mistake about who she meant.

Father and suitors looked dismayed; but Petruchio, with the utmost cheerfulness assured them that all was well. He and Kate had agreed that, in company she should be perverse, while in private they were the best of lovers. Furthermore, matters had proceeded so swiftly between them, that he was off to Venice to buy wedding clothes, for they were to be married on Sunday!

"And kiss me, Kate!" he cried, seizing the speechless Katherine round the waist and holding her tightly: "We will be married o' Sunday!" Then he whirled her away, leaving father and suitors overwhelmed with joy.

"Faith, gentlemen, now I play a merchant's part," said Baptista, addressing himself to Bianca's suitors; for now it remained only for him to dispose of his other child.

Gremio, by reason of having been first in the field, claimed the prior right; but Tranio, in his master's hat and cloak, claimed a better love. Gremio sneered at his rival for being too young; and Tranio jeered at Gremio for being too old. So Baptista, exercising his rights of judgement, declared that Bianca's love was a prize to be won, not by words but by deeds. Whoever offered most should have her. Gleefully Gremio rushed in with a list of his considerable property, all of which he was willing to make over to Bianca. Tranio, with the reckless generosity of one who promises in another's name, outbid him to the tune of two more houses and two thousand ducats a year. Gremio staggered, but bravely came up with more land and an argosy in Marseilles. Then Tranio sank

Petruchio came to his wedding in rags and rubbish

him with three argosies, and a whole fleet besides. Gremio was finished, and the father shook the victor by the hand. "Your offer is the best," he said, affectionately; "and let your father make her the assurance, she is your own."

Bianca was learning Latin. While the sage of music and mathematics watched suspiciously from the other side of the room, and twangled on his new lute, Bianca's head was bent so close to the other sage's, that she might have got knowledge through seepage. They murmured low; and it was wonderful, Bianca discovered, what interesting meanings might be got from Ovid. For instance, when Penelope wrote to Ulysses, she saw fit to tell him that her name was Lucentio, son of Vicentio of Pisa, that he had disguised himself to make love to her, and that his man Tranio was disguised as himself in order to get rid of old Gremio.

Bianca nodded, and, learning fast, translated the same passage again, when it appeared that Penelope wrote to tell Ulysses that . . . she knew him not, that she trusted him not, that he was to speak soft lest the musical sage overheard them; and that he was not to give up hope. She smiled, and he smiled, and Ovid, had he known the use to which his work had been put, would not have been displeased.

Next came the turn of the music master; and he did not lag far behind. He instructed his fair pupil in the scale, which, in accordance with a new system of fingering, invented by himself, revealed that her whiskered and bottled-eyed teacher was Hortensio in disguise, that he loved her, and that he would surely perish if she refused him.

"Tut! I like it not!" said Bianca, pushing aside the mysteriously legible lute. "Old fashions please me best. I am not so nice, to change true rules for odd inventions." She gazed fondly at the Latinist, and Hortensio scowled.

Kate's wedding Sunday had come, and was nearly gone; and it had been a day that neither bride, nor bride's people, nor priest nor sexton nor church itself was ever likely to forget. And not on account of joy.

The groom was late, so late that it was feared he would not come. Kate was thrown into an agony of mortification, for the shame of being abandoned was worse than the shame of being married. Then he came, and it would have been better if he hadn't; for the shame of being married turned out to be ten times worse than shame of being left. Petruchio came to his wedding in rags and rubbish, in old patched clothes, odd boots and a broken sword, and he rode upon a horse that could scarcely stagger.

"Good sooth," said he in surprise, when his attire was called into question, "to me she's married, not unto my clothes."

But all this was no more than a mild prologue to the wedding itself. When asked if he would take Katherine for his wife, he answered so loud and with such swearing, that the priest dropped the book in amazement; and Petruchio cuffed him soundly as he bent to pick it up! After which, he called for wine, drank some, and threw the rest over the sexton. "This done," related the shocked Gremio, who had been witness to everything, "he took the bride about the neck, and kissed her lips with such a clamorous smack that at the parting all the church did echo!"

It had indeed been a wedding to remember, with a mad bridegroom and a bride so terrified that she dared not speak for fear of what might happen next. Then came the wedding feast, which was over before it had begun. Petruchio would not stay, and Katherine would not go. "Do what thou canst," she said, "I will not go today." She turned to the wedding guests. "Gentlemen, forward to the bridal dinner . . ."

"They shall go forward, Kate, at thy command," agreed Petruchio. "But for my bonny Kate, she must with me!" Then, seizing her round the waist, and waving his battered sword as if to defy all the world, he heaved her out of the house!

The wedding guests stared at the violently swinging door. Some smiled, some laughed, some rose to follow. "Nay, let them go," said old Baptista, more frightened of his daughter than for her; "a couple of quiet ones."

The journey to Petruchio's house was long, hard and muddy; and, when bride and bridegroom arrived, Kate was faint and quiet from weariness and hunger. But Petruchio was in the best of spirits. He sang, and cuffed his servants and swore at them, and, in general, behaved as if he was back in church.

"Sit down, Kate," he roared, "and welcome! Food, food, food, food!"

Kate regarded her shabby husband and his shabby house with hatred; nonetheless, she sat, for hunger was a strict master, even over the most turbulent of spirits.

Food came, and Kate brightened; but alas! the food was not to Petruchio's liking. It was ill-prepared and burnt; and he flung it back in his servants' faces. "Be patient," he said to his enraged and starving bride. "Tomorrow't shall be mended, and for this night we'll fast for company. Come, I will bring thee to thy bridal chamber." She went as mildly as a tiger, and with such a look that those who saw it might have supposed she meant to dine upon her husband as he slept.

Petruchio smiled. He had got Kate's dowry, but now he was greedy and wanted more. He wanted her heart as well. But Kate's heart, like gold or any precious thing, was buried deep, and needed mining for, with strength and resolution, and loud explosions. Accordingly he kept her awake all night, with lectures and complaints about the ill-made bed.

Hortensio was disgusted. Bianca, in spite of her claim to be pleased by old fashions, had turned from him, the seasoned admirer, and bestowed her favours on the wretched young teacher of Latin. Bitterly he had watched them exchange looks and sighs, and steal sly kisses, like furtive apples. At length, he could endure it no longer; and his deathless love, for want of fuel, flickered and died. There was a rich widow he knew, and he would marry her; but first he would go to see how his friend Petruchio was faring, with his fierce Kate. As whiskers, spectacles and lutes had done him no good, he felt he had much to learn before he tried again.

Petruchio's wife was not well pleased.

"Mistress, what cheer?" inquired Hortensio, cautiously.

"Faith, as cold as can be," came the bitter reply. She was hungry. Her husband, all concern, brought her food he had prepared himself. She looked at it, as if it might vanish before her eyes.

"What, not a word?" asked Petruchio, disappointed by the reception of his efforts. "Nay then, thou love'st it not. Here, take away this dish."

"I pray you, let it stand," cried Katherine quickly, her bright tongue moistening her eager lips.

"The poorest service is repaid with thanks," said Petruchio.

"I thank you, sir," said Katherine; and Hortensio stared.

She began to eat, as one who has not eaten for many days; but was stopped, it seemed, almost as soon as she had begun. A tailor came in, laden with rich gowns for the lady. Kate eyed them with interest; but Petruchio was enraged. Everything the tailor showed was at fault. There was nothing, in all his stock, that was good enough for Kate.

"I never saw a better fashioned gown," pleaded Katherine, as the tailor displayed the choicest garment she had seen.

"He means to make a puppet of thee!" said Petruchio contemptuously; and dismissed the tailor and all his wares. "Well, come, my Kate," he said, comfortingly, "we will unto your father's even in these honest mean habiliments. 'Tis the mind that makes the body rich."

Kate's eyes filled with tears. Her gown was the gown she had come in,

and was somewhat the worse for wear. Petruchio called for horses, for it was in his mind to set out directly for Padua and old Baptista's house.

"Let's see," he said, "I think 'tis now some seven o'clock . . ."

"I dare assure you, sir," corrected Kate, " 'tis almost two . . ."

Petruchio frowned. "It shall be what o'clock I say it is."

"Why," murmured Hortensio, shaking his head, "so this gallant will command the sun!"

And so he did, upon the long and tedious journey back to Padua.

"Good Lord!" he cried out suddenly. "How bright and goodly shines the moon!"

"The moon? The sun!" protested Kate. "It is not moonlight now."

"I say it is the moon!"

"I know it is the sun."

"It shall be moon, or star, or what I list," said Petruchio firmly; "Or e'er I journey to your father's house."

"Say as he says," pleaded Hortensio, "or we shall never go."

Kate sighed. She was aching and weary; and she had suffered much, she reflected, as she had made others suffer. It would be folly to suffer more. It was the moon if he wanted it to be the moon, or a candle if he preferred. It was the wiser course, she thought, to deny the evidence of her senses, than her good sense.

"What you will have it named," she said, "even that it is, and so it shall be so for Katherine." She looked at him. He was a plain, rough fellow who had weathered her storms. He was, she felt, a mariner to be admired. She smiled at him; and he tried hard not to smile back.

"Petruchio," said Hortensio softly, "go thy ways, the field is won."

There was a great celebration in old Baptista's house, a wedding feast of huge proportions. It was a feast to celebrate a triple marriage: Lucentio, as himself at last, and books and scholarship thrown to the winds, had got Baptista's blessing and gentle Bianca's hand. Hortensio had briskly courted and married the widow, who sat beside him, as ripe and tempting as an orchard of plums. And Kate and Petruchio, who, though married once, seemed now married again, heart to heart.

"Nothing but sit and sit, and eat and eat!" cried Petruchio, with a cheerful and knowing look to his wife. The talk was free and merry, and presently the ladies withdrew. Then the gentlemen talked of the good fortune they had in their wives; until old Baptista, overcome with wine and sympathy, leaned over and laid his arm consolingly upon the shoulder of the husband of his eldest child. "Now, in good sadness, son Petruchio," he wept, "I think thou hast the veriest shrew of all."

Gently Petruchio set his father-in-law upright. "Well, I say no," he said; for he would not rate his Katherine below her sister or Hortensio's plump bride. Indeed, he rated her far above them; so much so that he was willing to wager a hundred crowns on Kate's proving superior in courtesy and duty. Each husband was to send for his wife; and whichever came first should take the prize.

"Who shall begin?" cried Hortensio.

"That will I," said Lucentio, whose bride was an angel of gentleness. He sent his boy to fetch her, and smiled confidently as he waited.

The boy returned. "My mistress sends you word," he said uncomfortably, "she is busy and she cannot come."

"Is that an answer?" asked Petruchio, gravely.

"Pray God," said old Gremio, between mouthfuls, "your wife send you not a worse."

Petruchio shrugged his shoulders, and waited while Hortensio sent the boy to fetch the widow. He returned almost as soon as he'd gone.

"She will not come," was the message. "She bids you come to her."

"Worse and worse!" cried Petruchio, shocked beyond measure. "Go to your mistress," he bade his servant. "Say I command her come to me."

"I know her answer," said Hortensio, when the servant had gone.

"What?"

"She will not."

The table nodded sagely, when old Baptista cried out: "Now, by my holidame, here comes Katherina!"

Kate came in, looked about her, saw amazement on every face, save on her husband's. "What is your will, sir, that you send for me?" she asked.

"Where is your sister and Hortensio's wife?"

"They sit conferring by the parlour fire," answered Kate, trying not to smile.

"Go fetch them hither," commanded Petruchio; and waited for the errant ladies to appear.

"Now fair befall thee, good Petruchio!" cried old Baptista, through rosy clouds of wine; and he offered a second dowry with Katherina, for surely she was a new Kate.

The new Kate came, and, smiling, made a pleasant contrast with the peevish looks of the ladies she had fetched.

"Katherine, I charge thee," said Petrucio, "tell these headstrong women what duty they do owe their lords and husbands."

"Come, come, you're mocking," protested Hortensio's wife, "we will have no telling!"

But they did; and most eloquently. Kate bade them consider what they owed their husbands, for safety, security and comfort; and then to consider how little they were asked in return. Or was obedience to another's wishes so demeaning a thing? "My mind hath been as big as one of yours," she said, "my heart as great, my reason haply more, to bandy word for word and frown for frown." She shook her head. Such warfare profited none. Then, with a sudden gesture, she knelt and placed her hand beneath her husband's foot.

All were silent. The gesture had not humbled Kate; but had raised her husband because it showed that he was high in her esteem.

"Why, there's a wench!" cried Petruchio, in admiration. "Come on, and kiss me, Kate!" He had begun his courting with a love of coin; but now he knew no greater riches than the coins of love.

"Come, Kate, we'll to bed," he said, and led her gently away. One by one the others followed, until the feasting chamber was empty and in darkness.

All was silent, save for a sound of soft snores. Was it a sleeping reveller; or was it a sleeping tinker, all alone?

King Richard the Second

Enter King Richard the Second of England: in gold and figured velvet and flashing jewels, with a following of nobles, like a spilling of bright coins, eager to be spent upon the glittering King.

He had been King since he was a little boy; his grandfather had been a great king, his father a mighty prince, and all his uncles were dukes. There was nothing about him that was not royal; and he walked and nodded and smiled as if the air was full of unseen flatterers, murmuring in his ear.

"Old John of Gaunt, time-honoured Lancaster," he began, and the assembled multitude of lords made way for the Duke of Lancaster, the greatest of the King's uncles. He was an old, old man, venerable as a mountain, and with much snow on top. He bowed; and it was strange to see so old and dignified a man bowing to one so gay and young.

"Hast thou," inquired the King, "according to thy oath and bond, brought hither Harry Herford, thy bold son?"

The court grew quiet, expectant faces turned. There was a deadly dispute between Henry Bolingbroke, Duke of Herford, and Thomas Mowbray, Duke of Norfolk. Bolingbroke had publicly accused Mowbray of treason and murder; and the two Dukes had been summoned to stand before the King.

"Call them to our presence," commanded the King. He waved his hand, as if to pluck Bolingbroke and Mowbray from the air. The lords stirred; and the two Dukes appeared.

They took up places opposing one another. The air between them trembled with anger. But neither spoke nor even moved, for they were in the presence of the King. First Bolingbroke was released from silence. He put his case while Mowbray was required to stand, stiff as a carving, and hear himself accused of the vilest crimes. Then Bolingbroke, scowling like a thundercloud, had to stand likewise, and hold his tongue, while Mowbray called him, "slanderous coward and a villain . . ."

Then Bolingbroke again, then Mowbray—each hurling at the other words like cannonballs—as well they might have been, for these two Dukes were more than private men. They represented, in their powerful persons, castles, lands and troops of armed soldiers. So that the quarrel between them, if unchecked, might have shaken down stone walls, burned villages and soaked many a fair field with English blood.

But to the golden King, like a second sun in the sky, this fury between his Dukes was no more than a squabbling of sparrows over a crumb.

"Wrath-kindled gentlemen," he interposed, raising his hand for silence, "be rul'd by me, let's purge this choler without letting blood. Forget, forgive, conclude and be agreed," he advised, with a cheerful smile as if to unruly children. "Our doctors say this is no month to bleed."

This was his wish and the King's wish was every man's command. His word stood next to the Word of God; it had been so since he was a little boy. But the two Dukes had gone too far in anger to be soothed by words and they set their private honour above the wishes of the King. Though King Richard might talk till Doomsday, the Dukes demanded satisfaction of each other in single combat to the death.

"We were not born to sue but to command," frowned the King, striving to conceal his displeasure at this flouting of his will. "Be ready, as your lives shall answer it, at Coventry upon Saint Lambert's day . . ."

So the King decreed, not as he had wished, but as his Dukes had desired.

The field of combat was prepared. The day was bright; painted tents swayed and bloomed, and lords and ladies crowded the green. King Richard and his court, like banked-up gorgeous images, sat upon a gilded balcony, awaiting the entry of the Dukes.

Presently they came, huge and stiff in jointed steel, each holding his plumed helmet to his armoured breast, like a flower of death. The King nodded; and each Duke, in accordance with the ceremony of combat, repeated the cause of his quarrel and affirmed his readiness to uphold it in mortal fight.

"Harry of Herford," proclaimed the marshal-at-arms, in roaring tones so that all might hear, "receive thy lance and God defend the right!"

The tall thin weapon was awarded to Bolingbroke; then another to Thomas Mowbray, Duke of Norfolk. All was in strict accordance with the ceremony of combat.

"Sound trumpets!" bellowed the marshal, "and set forward, combatants!"

The trumpets sounded, high, harsh and brilliant in the morning air. The Dukes made ready and the multitude strained forward, eager to see which Duke would live, and which would shortly die.

Suddenly all was stopped. Before a single blow had been struck, before a single drop of blood had been shed, the King had put an end to it. His royal gesture had been enough.

"Let them lay by their helmets," he commanded, "and both return back to their chairs again . . ."

The King had not forgotten how the two proud men had scorned his wishes. Now they would pay for their disobedience. Because the quarrel between them was dangerous, and might lead to civil war, they must leave the kingdom. King Richard banished Bolingbroke for ten long years, and Thomas Mowbray for the remainder of his days. The golden King had spoken; and his word was next to God's.

The punishment was heavy, but as it fell on both, they had no choice but to submit. Nonetheless, Bolingbroke would have the last word.

"Confess thy treasons," he demanded of Mowbray, "ere thou fly the realm!" He was still eager to prove himself to have been in the right.

Mowbray, immeasurably sad at the timeless loss of his native land, shook his head.

"No, Bolingbroke," he answered. "If ever I were traitor, my name be blotted from the book of life. But what thou art," he went on slowly, and staring hard at Bolingbroke as to see his soul, "God, thou, and I do know . . . and all too soon, I fear, the King shall rue."

But the King was indifferent and had already turned away to speak with his uncle, old John of Gaunt. The old man was grieving. The ten long years of Harry Bolingbroke's banishment would prove too long. The old man would never see his son again. At once King Richard, filled with tenderness for his uncle, shortened the punishment by four years. Bolingbroke, hearing this, half-smiled.

"Four lagging winters and four wanton springs end in a word," he sighed; "such is the breath of kings."

But the old man still shook his head. Even the six years remaining would prove too long.

"Why, uncle," cried King Richard, anxious to comfort old John of Gaunt, "thou hast many years to live!"

"But not a minute, King," said the old man grimly, "that thou canst give."

King Richard shrugged his shoulders. Whatever might be said, the day had gone well. He had behaved wisely and justly; and had ridded himself of two dangerous and powerful men.

King Richard was in his court, a bright and lively place, where the very air was dressed in perfumes before it was admitted into the presence of the King. It was like a high-walled summer garden, shutting out the winter of the world, where his favourites—chief among whom were three knights, Bushy, Bagot and Greene—like painted butterflies, played and fed.

Bagot and Greene were with him when the news came that Bolingbroke had gone. Richard was delighted. He could not abide his stern and careful cousin. He detested Bolingbroke's way of courting the common people—a commodity that Richard himself regarded with remote distaste.

"Off goes his bonnet to an oyster wench," jeered Richard. "A brace of draymen bid God speed him well, and had the tribute of his supple knee with, 'Thanks my countrymen, my loving friends!'" (delivered, to his companions' entertainment, in shrewd imitation of Bolingbroke's harsh voice), "as were our England in reversion his . . ."

"Well, he is gone," said Greene happily; and the talk turned to the ever-present need for money and how best it might be squeezed from the land. Money for this, money for that, and money for soldiers to fight the Irish wars.

Bushy came in and was greeted by one and all. Bushy was excited; he had news. Old John of Gaunt had fallen sick and was near to death. The friends looked at one another. Their eyes sparkled. Rich old John of Gaunt!

"Now put it God," cried King Richard, heartlessly eager as a child upon his birthday, "in the physician's mind to help him to his grave immediately! The lining of his coffers shall make coats to deck our soldiers for these Irish wars. Come, gentlemen, let's all go visit him, and pray God we may make haste and come too late!"

The stern old man, in his stern old house, was dying. Sober lords and black-gowned attendants looked on as he conversed with his brother, the Duke of York. These last two sons of a great dead king spoke sadly of the young King who danced and laughed and postured and frittered the great inheritance away.

"Will the King come," wondered the dying man, "that I may breathe my last in wholesome counsel to his unstaid youth?"

But York could give no comfort. Wise counsel would never touch this king. Poisoned flattery alone had his ear. John of Gaunt grew restless and angry. He struggled to rise from his chair. His brother, with scarcely more strength than he, made haste to support him.

"Methinks I am a prophet new-inspired," cried out the dying man; and indeed there was, to those who watched, something wild and prophetic about the white-haired old man, whose eyes blazed in his bloodless face as he gave frantic utterance to his aching love and his aching fears for England.

"This little world," he cried out, and his voice cracked with the cracking of his full heart, "this precious stone set in the silver sea . . . this blessed plot, this earth, this realm, this England . . . this dear, dear land," he wept, "is now leased out—I die pronouncing it—like to a tenement or pelting farm . . . England . . . is now bound in with shame, with inky blots and rotten parchment bonds . . . ah would the scandal vanish with my life . . ."

Tears, like bitter rivers, streamed down his dried-up cheeks, as he stood swaying in his brother's arms.

"The King is come," muttered the Duke of York, "deal kindly with his youth . . ."

King Richard entered, accompanied by his favourites and his pretty Queen. Attired more like a gorgeous bridegroom than a visitor to the

;ick, he moved fastidiously about the darkened room, eyeing the rich hangings, appraising the silver cups, exchanging glances with his companions, and stepping round and round his dying uncle, so that it seemed that the bright candle was attracted to the dusty trembling moth.

"What comfort, man? How is't with aged Gaunt?" he inquired with casual concern; while aged Gaunt, sinking back into his chair, stared hollowly at the hollow King.

"Old Gaunt indeed, and gaunt in being old," he muttered; and then, presuming on the respect due to an old man dying, reproached the King for the senseless evils of his spendthrift reign.

"Landlord of England art thou now," he accused, "not King—"

"A lunatic lean-witted fool!" shouted the King, losing all patience with his tedious uncle who had shamed him before his friends. "Presuming on an ague's privilege—"

"O spare me not!" raged the old man, beating his futile fists on the arms of his chair, while those present looked on, aghast and ashamed at this unseemly quarrel between the dying man and the vigorous one, the uncle and the nephew, the subject and his king. "Convey me to my bed," panted the old man at length; for he felt that darkness was closing in upon him; "then to my grave . . ."

"And let them die that age and sullens have!" flung out the King contemptuously, as attendants came to help his uncle away, "for both hast thou—"

Many kind hands assisted the old Duke, who seemed, amid strong shoulders and strong arms, no more than a shabby bundle of gown. When he had gone, there followed an awkwardness. Gently the Duke of York tried to make his brother's peace with the King. Then all too soon news came that John of Gaunt had made his own peace, and with a higher power than Richard's. He was dead.

"The ripest fruit first falls," said King Richard impulsively; "and so doth he."

He spoke from the heart. His uncle's death had saddened him; for old John of Gaunt had been his boyhood's father. But then it was over. He had paid his tribute and that was that. He was King Richard again and was concerned with matters of state. The Irish wars. Money.

With princely calm he announced that he was possessing himself of his dead uncle's property in order to pay for his Irish war. The Duke of York stared at him. He was outraged. He could scarcely credit this bare-faced robbery, this pillage of the newly dead man's house.

"Why, uncle, what's the matter?" asked Richard, honestly surprised that his actions should be questioned.

Swallowing down his indignation, the Duke explained that the dead man's title and property now belonged, by right of succession, to Bolingbroke, the banished son . . .

"Think what you will," exclaimed the King impatiently, "we seize into our hands his plate, his goods, his money and his lands!"

The Duke retired, bowing low as much under the weight of grief as in respect for the arbitrary young King.

"Tomorrow next we will for Ireland," announced King Richard, shrugging off his doddering old uncle's disapproval; and then, as if regretting the harsh words that had passed, and wishing to make amends, he declared that he would make the Duke of York Lord Governor of England while he, the King, was absent from the realm. "For he is just," he added, with something of wistfulness in his air, like a child suddenly left in a great mansion all alone, "and always loved us well . . ."

The Queen was in the castle at Windsor, while her husband was far away in Ireland, with all the soldiers his dead uncle's wealth could buy. She was melancholy, but from no cause she could determine. Bushy and Bagot, who attended her, supposed she was sad on account of parting from the King.

"It may be so," sighed the Queen, thinking of her Richard, her gentle, charming Richard, "but yet my inward soul persuades me it is other-wise . . ."

"'Tis nothing but conceit, my gracious lady," said Bushy; but the Queen shook her head. Her premonition of sorrow was too strong to be reasoned away.

Suddenly Greene entered the chamber; and, from his pale and fright-ened looks, the Queen knew that he had come to give her fear its name.

Before him was Bolingbroke . . . and a forest of steel

Bolingbroke! He had returned! Already he was in England with many men under arms. Already the great Duke of Northumberland had joined him; and others, too. If the news was to be believed, half of England had gone over to Bolingbroke.

"Here comes the Duke of York!" cried Greene, as the aged Lord Governor of England came bustling in to the presence of the Queen.

"Uncle, for God's sake," she pleaded, "speak comfortable words!"

"Comfort's in heaven," he replied, "and we are on the earth . . ." and he went on to confirm the worst of the news.

The poor old man was confused and distracted, and knew not which way to turn. His duty was to his nephew, King Richard; yet he could not help feeling deeply for his nephew Bolingbroke, whom the King had wronged and robbed.

"If I know how or which way to order these affairs, thus thrust disorderly into my hands," he wailed, fidgeting about the chamber, peering unhappily behind furnishings and out of the tall thin windows, as if there was a Bolingbroke in every corner and in every cloud.

"Come, cousin," he cried, extending a frail arm to the frightened Queen, "I'll dispose of you." Then, bidding the King's favourites muster what arms they could he led the Queen away.

The three looked at one another. They knew the time had come to part.

"Farewell at once," said Greene, "for once, for all, and ever."

"Well, we may meet again," said Bushy, though with little hope.

"I fear me, never," said Bagot; and the three friends stared at one another with smiles as pale as bone.

The aged Duke, the Lord Governor of England, journeyed to Gloucestershire to hold Berkeley Castle against the onward march of his nephew Bolingbroke. Fierce as an old lion, he would do his duty and defend the realm. Then, with clanking of steel and gasping of horses, came Bolingbroke; and the Lord Governor of England tottered out to confront him. In warlike armour, so that his wrinkled head poking out looked like a withered kernel in a sound shell, the old man frowned at his rebellious nephew.

Bolingbroke, with all eyes upon him, knelt before his uncle. It was his duty to do so; and Bolingbroke was a man who always wanted to seem to be in the right.

"Show me thy humble heart and not thy knee," demanded the old man, a little confused by his great nephew's show of humility.

"My gracious uncle—"

"Tut, tut, grace me no grace, nor uncle me no uncle!"

"My gracious uncle," protested Bolingbroke, "let me know my fault—"

"Thou art a banished man, and here art come before the expiration of thy time . . ."

But Bolingbroke, still kneeling, explained matters otherwise. He had been banished as Duke of Herford; he returned as Duke of Lancaster. He came only to claim his rightful inheritance . . . The old man faltered.

"You are my father," urged Bolingbroke, "for methinks in you I see old Gaunt alive . . ."

The old lion sighed. He had scarce enough teeth remaining to chew gruel. Before him was Bolingbroke, the Duke of Northumberland, and a forest of steel. Behind him, there was nothing.

"I do not remain as neuter," he said; and gave up the castle and himself to Bolingbroke.

Bolingbroke marched on. Strongholds fell, castles opened their gates, and the common people, whom he had always courted, came running from cottage, farm and town, to join him. All England was for Boling-broke; then England's King came back.

The crossing from Ireland had been rough; but the fury of the elements had done no more than make him bright with anger. That Bolingbroke should so much as set his foot upon the kingdom was a crime; and that he should come in arms was treason against God. But he would fall, as all bad men must fall, before the divine splendour of the King. Bolingbroke could never succeed. Though all the world might fight for him, God and His angels were for Richard, and theirs was the power that must conquer all. King Richard knew, as he had always known, since he was a little boy, that there was a sacred mystery in kingship before which all men must bow.

Then the blows began to fall; and when they fell they were like thunderbolts upon King Richard's defenceless head. Twenty thousand Welshmen, on whose help he had counted, had dispersed and fled; his beloved friends, Bushy and Greene, had been dragged from Bristol Castle and put to death; and the old Duke of York—that uncle who had loved him well—had abandoned him and joined with Bolingbroke.

As, one by one, these cruel calamities were told to him, he faltered and staggered, in bewilderment and pain. He could not believe that such things could happen to a king. His friends—he still had friends who loved him—tried to comfort him, and rouse him back to glory. For a time, they seemed to succeed, and he was royal Richard again; but all too briefly. In the twinkling of an eye, the golden King had turned to lead, and he sank, fathoms deep, into a grave of dreams.

"For God's sake," he pleaded, "let us sit upon the ground and tell sad stories of the death of kings . . ."

The mansion of majesty in which he'd always dwelt, secure and happy, had cracked at last, and no matter where he hid, cold winds kept blowing in. Together with his companions—now pitifully few—he fled to Flint Castle; for the very earth on which he stood, seemed to shake and tremble under the advancing tread of Bolingbroke.

A trumpet sounded. Its thin sharp note pierced the castle's crumbling walls, echoed in its ancient courtyards, and fled, shrieking, down its winding stairs and along its stony veins. The few friends within, whirled hither and thither, like cornered autumn leaves. The trumpet was Bolingbroke's. His herald was at the gate.

King Richard, pale as ivory, attired himself in cloth of gold and every last device of royalty. He set his crown upon his head; and when he looked into a mirror, he seemed to blaze with majesty. And yet he wondered, was it enough? It must be enough, because there was nothing else. Together with his companions, he stepped out on to the battlements. The ground before the castle had grown a crop of armed men. As far as the eye could see, there stretched and swayed a huge iron harvest, speckled with pennants and banners, like poppies, under the morning sun.

Bolingbroke, grim with rebel barons, looked up and noted that the bright King faltered.

"Yet looks he like a king," sighed the old Duke of York, who had been carried along on the tide of Bolingbroke's success like a battered piece of furnishing from some wrecked ship. "Behold his eye, as bright as is the eagle's . . ."

King Richard became aware that Bolingbroke's messenger, the Duke of Northumberland, was waiting below. He saw, through a veil of tears, that the messenger was standing. He should have knelt. Bitter anger seized the King. He raged against the Duke below for not granting him due respect. He could see Bolingbroke himself, and misty sight refracted him into a thousand Bolingbrokes. Anger fed upon anger.

"Tell Bolingbroke," he shouted shrilly, "for yon methinks he stands, that every stride he makes upon my land is dangerous treason."

The Duke below protested that Bolingbroke had come only to claim what was lawfully his own. If this was granted then Bolingbroke would be content.

Could it really be so? The King's anger wavered; and he clutched at a straw.

"Northumberland," he called down, "say thus the King returns: his noble cousin is right welcome hither."

Northumberland went back to his master, bearing the King's meek reply. The King stared after him; saw him speak with Bolingbroke; saw Bolingbroke grimly nod . . . At once King Richard wished with all his heart that he had sent fierce defiance instead of feeble submission. He should have played the fiery dragon in his wrath, instead of the shining dragonfly, with broken wings. But it was too late. Northumberland was coming back. He could see Bolingbroke and all his barons staring up. He tried to read what was in their harsh faces, before the harsh message was delivered.

"What must the King do now?" he wondered, having cast away his greatness. He shrugged his shoulders. "The King shall do it. Must he be deposed? The King shall be contented. Must he lose the name of King? a

God's name let it go! I'll give my jewels for a set of beads, my gorgeous palace for a hermitage . . ."

So he plunged, with the sinking of his heart, from the top of the world, to the very bottom. If he could not be the highest in the land, he would be the lowest. He could not endure the middle way.

"What says King Bolingbroke?" demanded King Richard, as the messenger waited once more below. "Will His Majesty give Richard leave to live till Richard die?"

"My lord," returned the Duke of Northumberland coolly, "may it please you to come down?"

"Down, down I come," sighed King Richard, overcome by the meek sadness of his end. "Down, King."

He descended into the court below, where Bolingbroke already awaited him. Always careful to seem to be in the right, Bolingbroke knelt before his sovereign.

"Up, cousin, up," said King Richard wearily; "your heart is up, I know, thus high at least."

He touched his golden crown. Bolingbroke disclaimed. But King Richard knew better. He smiled and shook his head.

"Set on towards London, cousin, is it so?" he asked.

Bolingbroke nodded.

"Then I must not say no," sighed the King.

Bolingbroke had come only to seek redress for his wrongs. But his wrongs were more than the loss of his title and estates; they were the wrongs of all England. They were the wrongs his father, old John of Gaunt, had died lamenting; they were the wrongs inflicted upon the kingdom by a bad king and his bad favourites—those gilded butterflies of Richard's, which, to Bolingbroke, were "the caterpillars of the commonwealth".

He plucked them out and destroyed them, he subdued quarrels between lords, and was, in all respects but one, the King. He was wise, patient and lawful; he had every quality that Richard lacked, but one. He lacked the name of King.

Then, in Westminster Hall, where Bolingbroke sat in half majesty, with a treasury of Dukes and barons in attendance, the old Duke of York came with welcome news. Richard was willing and ready to give up the crown, to his cousin Bolingbroke. Bolingbroke rose to his feet. He was profoundly relieved. His victory had been achieved by consent.

"In God's name I'll ascend the regal throne!" he cried out in ringing tones, so that all might know he acted in agreement and accordance with the law.

"Fetch hither Richard," he commanded, "that in common view he may surrender; so we shall proceed without suspicion."

King Richard came, and Bolingbroke was shocked to see him. The fallen King was dressed in a plain coarse gown, like a beggar, or a monk. Everything about him, his bewilderment, his dismal complaints, proclaimed his abject ruin. The gay and glittering Richard was no more.

Why had he done this, when he might have come with the dignity of the high office he still held? To shame Bolingbroke? To excite pity? To show the world how cruel was his fall? To play out his last scene before a mighty audience with pathos, because he lacked grandeur?

Not unkindly, Bolingbroke let him have his say, which was long and full of sad philosophy, with small resentments, like the nips and pinches of a punished child, creeping in. To Bolingbroke, Richard was indeed a child, who had been fetched into the harsh world of men; and his loss was more than the loss of kingship; it was the loss of childhood, too.

At last it was over, and Richard was no longer King. "I'll beg one boon," he said in parting, "and then be gone."

"Name it, fair cousin."

"And shall I have?"

"You shall."

"Then give me leave to go."

"Whither?"

"Whither you will, so I were from your sights."

Bolingbroke sighed. Though there was nothing in Richard himself to be feared, he could not permit him to wander the highways and appear in the streets. An uncrowned King, even such a King as Richard, might all too easily be crowned again in discontented hearts. Sombrely he ordered

Richard to be taken to the Tower; then had second thoughts, and sent him further off, to be hidden away and forgotten in far-off Pomfret Castle.

But though kings may be hidden from men's eyes, they cannot be hidden from men's minds. No sooner was Bolingbroke crowned, than Richard's friends conspired to kill the new King and restore the old. The Duke of York's only son was one of the conspirators, and should, by rights, have died for it. But Bolingbroke was merciful and pardoned him. He was king enough to know that mercy secures the crown more surely than does the axe. Yet he was also man enough to know—and mortal man at that—that as long as harmless Richard lived, he, King Bolingbroke, wore a borrowed crown. He longed for Richard's death, but would do nothing to bring it about. To stain his hands with royal blood would be to stain his soul, and tarnish the brightness of his reign. Yet he longed for Richard's death . . .

There was a man in Windsor Castle, a grim, lean fellow always in dark attire. His name was Exton, and he lingered about the King, attended his every word, and watched his every look, as if to read his innermost thoughts. He was like the King's shadow, or the dark side of his soul. Then, one fatal day, the King let fall an unguarded word; and his shadow stooped to catch it up . . .

"Didst thou not mark the King, what words he spake?" muttered Exton to his servants. "Have I no friend will rid me ᴄ ꜰthis living fear?" he whispered, repeating the King's words. "Was it not so?"

"Those were his very words."

"He spake it twice," said Exton, eagerly.

"He did."

"I am the King's friend," murmured the shadow, "and I will rid his foe."

Death came to King Richard in Pomfret Castle, in a dark room, barely furnished, with stone walls, a barred door and a narrow bed. Such a place he had imagined, when he had been about to fall from his high estate.

136

Now he had fallen, and was as low and unconsidered as the least of his subjects, he tried to draw some comfort from his state. But there was no one to see him, no one to hear him; and time ticked away his life.

"I wasted time," he sighed forlornly, "and now doth time waste me . . ."

A strange man entered and bowed low.

"Thanks, noble peer," smiled Richard, grateful for the show of respect. "What art thou?"

"I was a poor groom of thy stable, King," answered the man, "when thou wert King . . ." And he went on to tell of Bolingbroke's coronation and how Bolingbroke had ridden King Richard's favourite horse.

"Rode he on Barbary?" wondered the King sadly. "How went he under him?"

"So proudly as if he disdain'd the ground," answered the groom reluctantly; and King Richard cursed the horse for ingratitude and mindless treachery.

Great matters—the loss of his kingdom, the loss of his crown, the loss of his freedom, even—moved him only to melancholy philosophy; but little things, such as his horse obeying Bolingbroke, bored into his heart like needles, and made it sting.

The prison keeper entered with a plate of meat. The groom departed.

"Taste of it first as thou art wont to do," commanded King Richard. But the keeper would not. He had been ordered otherwise by one Sir Pierce of Exton, who had come from the King.

This trifling denial of his royalty was yet another needle in King Richard's heart.

"The devil take Henry of Lancaster, and thee!" shouted King Richard, with all the pent-up fury and bitterness of his soul. "Patience is stale and I am weary of it!"

He struck the man; then, black as night save for a glinting of daggers and eyes, Death rushed into the room. For the first and the last time in his life, King Richard defended himself like a king. He killed two of his attackers before he himself was struck down.

"Exton," he whispered, as he lay dying, "thy fierce hand hath with the King's blood stained the King's own land . . ."

The murderer looked down upon the dead King, and, for a moment, was filled with horror at the deed he had done.

Bolingbroke, the King, was at Windsor, occupied in affairs of state, when shadowy Exton, pale of face and with burning eyes, came before him, with servants bearing a nameless, black draped coffin. Even before Exton spoke, Bolingbroke knew that the coffin contained a murdered king.

"Exton, I thank thee not," he muttered.

"From your own mouth, my lord," said the murderer, "I did this deed."

"They love not poison," whispered Bolingbroke, pale with dread, "that do poison need . . ."

Though he had always striven, and would always strive, to be in the right, he knew that his soul was stained and his reign was tarnished with the blood of the murdered King.

King Henry IV. Part One

Though murdered kings, like all dead men, lie quiet and unoffending in the ground, they rot and spread contagion in men's minds. King Richard was in the earth, and nibbled clean by worms; but the kingdom festered with the consequences of his violent end.

In a sombre, cheerless chamber in the royal palace in London, the new King and his dukes and earls debated the troubled state of the land. There was war in Wales, there was war in Scotland, and there was war in the new King's heart. Bolingbroke—now King Henry the Fourth—longed to go to the Holy Land and fight for Christ, so that he might wash his soul free from the stain of murdered Richard's blood; but stern necessity compelled him to stay at home and fight for himself.

Guilt and kingship had aged him; those who had helped him to the throne, now resented him, and even good news was spiked with bad. Harry Percy, the Duke of Northumberland's brilliant son, known to all as Hotspur, had won a great victory in Scotland, which should have been cause for rejoicing—and would have been, had it not now seemed that the young man had been fighting more for himself than for his King. He had taken many rich Scottish prisoners, and would not give them up.

This impudent refusal, this bare-faced robbery of royal ransoms, greatly angered the King; but, at the same time, he could not help admiring the fierce young man's boldness and daring. Whatever Hotspur did, was done with courage and pride.

In his heart of hearts, King Henry envied the Duke of Northumberland and his glorious son. His own first-born, his own Harry, had turned out to be a hero only of the stews and taverns, and crown prince of riot and disorder.

"O that it could be proved," he sighed, "that some night-tripping fairy had exchanged in cradle-clothes our children where they lay . . . Then I would have his Harry and he mine . . ."

War and rebellion were heavy burdens on his shoulders, but his son's behaviour was an arrow in his heart. He shook his head and, with an effort, put aside his private distress. Hotspur, no matter how brightly he shone, had disobeyed him; and must answer for it.

While the King, with his dukes and earls, was thus engaged, considering matters of great moment, his son, Prince Hal, was likewise considering a matter of moment. Or, more particularly, the matter of *a* moment. In short, the time of day.

The Prince's apartment, in another part of the town, was somewhat more genial than his father's. In place of state papers were playbills and ballads; in place of serious earls were empty bottles; and in place of sober dukes was a portly knight, by name of Sir John Falstaff, asleep and snoring on a couch. His belt, huge enough to encompass a horse, was unbuckled, and his belly rose and fell like the sea.

For a moment, the Prince gazed down upon him, partly in humorous affection, and partly in wonderment, as if the day had wiped out all recollection of the night. They made a curious pair: the slender, handsome young Prince and the fat old man. They would seem to have had little in common but humanity—of which the sleeping knight, by reason of his enormous bulk, must have had the lion's share. The prince smiled; and, picking up a bottle, anointed the knight's bald head with some unaccountably forgotten drops of wine.

"Now, Hal," complained Falstaff, rising like a whale from his dreams, "what time of day is it, lad?"

"What a devil hast thou to do with the time of the day?" marvelled the

Prince. "Unless hours were cups of sack," he went on, regarding the empty bottles and the blowsy, unbuttoned state of the knight, "and minutes capons, and clocks the tongues of bawds, and dials the signs of leaping-houses, and the blessed sun himself a fair hot wench in flame-coloured taffeta, I see no reason why thou should be so superfluous as to demand the time of the day."

"Indeed, you come near me now, Hal," admitted the fat old man, wiping the wine from his stained pate and delicately tasting his finger-ends, "for we that take purses go by the moon . . ."

So they fell to a cheerful bickering about stealing purses and repentance for such sins, with the young man making fun of his old companion —sometimes sharply enough to wound—and the knight affecting remorse and blaming the King's son for leading him astray.

"Thou hast done much harm upon me, Hal," he protested piously, "God forgive thee for it."

But in the very next moment, when the Prince slyly put the possibility before him, he was ready and eager to steal a purse wherever one might be had.

"From praying to purse-taking!" wondered the Prince, quite overcome by Falstaff's affable disregard for all law but his own.

"Why, Hal," explained Falstaff, quite unabashed, "'tis my vocation, Hal, 'tis no sin for a man to labour in his vocation!"

No sooner had he uttered this sentiment, in a high-pitched, churchly chant, and with an expression of fat religious devotion, than his best hopes were answered. Poins, a young friend of the Prince's, entered the apartment with an air of some excitement.

"Tomorrow morning," he announced, "by four o'clock early at Gad's Hill, there are pilgrims going to Canterbury with rich offerings, and traders riding to London with fat purses." It would be child's play—and it was play to such children—to waylay the travellers and rob them of all they had.

Falstaff beamed happily. He turned to the Prince.

"Hal, wilt thou make one?"

"Who, I rob?" returned the Prince indignantly. "I, a thief? Not I, by my faith!"

"There's neither honesty, manhood, nor good fellowship in thee," said Falstaff, disgusted by the unlooked-for honesty of his companion. But the Prince was unmoved; so Falstaff departed, leaving Poins to do what he could to change the Prince's mind.

No sooner had the fat knight flourished his bulk out of the room, than Poins laid his arm familiarly round the Prince's shoulders.

"Now my good, sweet honey lord," he murmured coaxingly, "ride with us tomorrow. I have a jest to execute that I cannot manage alone."

The jest was this: he and the Prince, together with Falstaff and his ruffianly associates, namely, Bardolph, Peto and Gadshill, should waylay the travellers; then Poins and the Prince should leave the others to rob them. "And when they have the booty," chuckled Poins, "if you and I do not rob them, cut this head from off my shoulders!"

The valour of Falstaff and his men being notorious, there was no doubt that Poins and the Prince would be more than a match for them.

"The virtue of this jest," Poins assured the Prince, "will be the incomprehensible lies that this same fat rogue will tell us when we meet at supper; of how thirty at least he fought with."

"Well, I'll go with thee," laughed the Prince. "Meet me tomorrow night in Eastcheap."

When Poins had gone, Prince Hal shrugged his shoulders, almost as if he wanted to shake off the memory of a too-familiar arm that had so lately rested upon them. He frowned. He both loved his companions, with their idle, lawless way, and despised them. Sooner or later, he knew, he would have to take on the heavy burden of kingship, and have done with Falstaff and his friends. And he would be the better for it. Yet, in his heart of hearts, he grieved. His present way of life was part of the folly of youth, which must be outgrown. Yet to outgrow the folly would be to outgrow youth. He sighed; and tried to comfort himself with the thought of how brightly he would shine when the time came for him to throw off his loose behaviour and stand before the world as the admired and glorious king.

While one Harry was idly dreaming of the glory that would be his, the other Harry was much concerned with the glory that *was* his. And he was going to keep it. Hotspur, the fiery son of the Duke of Northumberland, together with his father and his uncle, the Earl of Worcester, was at Windsor. He had come in answer to the King's summons and was prepared to defend his actions by attacking those of everybody else. They met in the council chamber where the King voiced his sharp displeasure, particularly against the Earl of Worcester, whom he blamed chiefly for Hotspur's defiance.

"Worcester, get thee gone," he commanded, "for I do see danger and disobedience in thine eye."

The Earl, thinly hiding his anger under a cloak of courtesy, withdrew. The King frowned after him; then, turning to Northumberland and his son, demanded to know why Hotspur had refused to deliver up his Scottish prisoners.

"My liege, I did deny no prisoners," responded Hotspur indignantly, forgetful of the fact that he had. It had been a misunderstanding, on account of the messenger the King had sent. Hotspur had not liked him. In fact, he was a person to whom Hotspur had taken the strongest exception. He had arrived on the battlefield at a bad time, when, as Hotspur put it, "I was dry with rage and extreme toil, breathless and faint, leaning upon my sword."

143

It seemed that the royal messenger had been one of those elegant gentlemen who had minced his way across the battlefield, and had complained faintly of the smell of corpses and the disagreeable nature of battlefields in general.

"He made me mad," exploded Hotspur at length, pacing the room in his agitation, now sitting, now standing, now confiding in the King's very ear, now addressing the ceiling, now the wall, "to see him shine so brisk and smell so sweet and talk so like a waiting-gentlewoman of guns and drums and wounds, God save the mark!"

In a word, Hotspur had lost his temper and had sent the King's messenger about his business without properly understanding what that business was.

The scene, as represented by the fierce young man, brought a smile even to the King's lips, and it was hard not to sympathise with him, for plainly he set valour and honour above everything; but he had done wrong. He had disobeyed his King and the conditions he had proposed for giving up his prisoners had only made matters worse. He had had the impudence to demand that his brother-in-law, Mortimer, who had been captured in Wales and was now held by the ferocious Owen Glendower, should be ransomed.

Now the King had no love for Mortimer, who had lately married Glendower's daughter and so become an ally of the enemy.

"I shall never hold that man my friend," pronounced the King, staring sombrely at Hotspur, "whose tongue shall ask me for one penny cost to ransom home revolted Mortimer."

"Revolted Mortimer!" shouted Hotspur, forgetful of respect in the royal presence. He was incensed by the unjust accusation and he rushed to his brother-in-law's defence. But the King would have nothing of it.

"Send us your prisoners," he said coldly, "or you will hear of it."

He and his attendant lords swept from the chamber, leaving Hotspur to burn with helpless rage. His father tried to calm him, but Hotspur's fire was not so easily put out. His uncle Worcester came quietly back into the chamber; and still Hotspur raged on about his brother-in-law, whose very name the King had forbidden him to pronounce.

As he raved, and strode, and banged the table, the father and the uncle exchanged interested looks. Surely all this wild energy could be put to a more profitable use? Imperceptibly they nodded; and the Earl of Worcester, almost by the way, remarked that the King could hardly be blamed for disliking Mortimer, for had not Mortimer been proclaimed, by dead King Richard, as his heir?

"He was," agreed Northumberland instantly, "I heard the proclamation."

Hotspur paused. He stared from his father to his uncle, and from his uncle to his father, as if scarcely able to believe what he had heard.

"But soft, I pray you," he demanded, breathing deeply, "did King Richard then proclaim my brother Edmund Mortimer heir to the crown?"

"He did," confirmed Northumberland, "myself did hear it."

Then he and Worcester, the two seasoned men of power, stood back, as it were, to warm their dangerous hearts and dangerous hands at Hotspur's wild blaze. They hated the King and sought only to uncrown him. But to do it, they needed Hotspur. They would be the shaft of rebellion's spear, but he, admired by all for his high honour, must be the brightly shining tip. They knew that Hotspur would not stir unless honour was at stake, so they had given him cause to join with them against the thankless, dishonourable King.

Patiently they waited for him to have done raging against, "this thorn, this canker, Bolingbroke . . . this vile politician, Bolingbroke," then they put it to him that there were others of a like mind. Eagerly the young man listened; and then and there, in the King's own council chamber, the rebellion against the throne began.

While the Harry of the north was thus preparing for his great enterprise, which was to be no less than hurling a dishonourable king from a doubtful throne, in other words, robbing a robber, Harry of the south was already out and about upon a similar enterprise . . . although on a more modest scale.

Four o'clock of a black morning on the highway at Gad's Hill. Fearful hissings and creepings in the bushy dark, and a huge lurking robber quaking with anger.

"A plague upon it when thieves cannot be true one to another!" cursed Falstaff, abandoned by his companions and left alone.

There came a faint whistling from the darkness, as of soused and bleary nightingales. "A plague upon you all," raged Falstaff, brandishing his sword to the terror of the bushes, "give me my horse, you rogues, give me my horse and be hanged!"

"Peace, ye fat guts," whispered Prince Hal, creeping out of the shadows, "lie down, lay thine ear close to the ground and list if thou canst hear the tread of travellers."

"Have you any levers to lift me up again," demanded the fat knight, "being down? I prithee, good Prince Hal, help me to my horse, good King's son."

Indignantly the Prince declined.

"Hang thyself in thine own heir-apparent garters!" snarled Falstaff, and threatened that, if he should be taken, he would inform on his friends without hesitation.

Shadows stirred, grass rustled and twigs snapped. Each from his hole of darkness, the robbers appeared. They whispered together. Falstaff and his men—four in all, and armed to the blackened teeth with pistols, cudgels, swords, daggers and determination—were to lie in wait for the travellers in the narrow lane. Poins and the Prince were to hide further down the hill, so that any who escaped the first ambush would be caught by the second. Much nodding and grinning and glinting of eyes . . . Be quiet! Travellers were coming! How many? Some eight or ten . . .

"Zounds, will they not rob us?" wondered Falstaff uneasily.

The travellers drew near, toiling wearily up the hill. Hastily Poins and the Prince vanished into the night.

"Now, my masters," breathed Falstaff, valiantly grasping his sword, which seemed no bigger than a tooth-pick beside his vast bulk, "every man to his business."

The travellers appeared, no more than four round-faced innocents, jingling with purses and property.

"Stand!" bellowed the thieves.

"Jesus bless us!" shrieked the merchants; and there followed a fearful scene of curses, thumps and grunts as the ravening wolves fell upon the

hapless lambs and robbed them of all they possessed. It was over in moments, and the thieves made off, leaving the merchants trussed up in a bundle of shaking legs and rolling eyes.

Poins and the Prince came out of concealment, nodded to one another, and silently followed Falstaff and his men. Presently they came upon them as they were about to share out their gains. The young men, cloaked and hooded, hid behind trees, and listened.

". . . and the Prince and Poins be not two arrant cowards," grunted Falstaff, who had seen nothing of the young men during the desperate duel with the merchants. "There's no equity stirring; there's no more valour in that Poins than in a wild duck."

The young men drew their swords.

"Your money!" roared the Prince, in a voice of thunder.

"Villains!" bellowed Poins in a voice as terrible; and the pair of them rushed out upon the startled four.

The bold thieves turned faces white as milk; and then, without pausing to reckon the odds, abandoned their profit and fled. Falstaff alone stayed to make one or two valiant flourishes with his sword; but then, valuing his life above his livelihood, he too departed, whisking through the night like a runaway bull, bellowing with rage and terror.

The two young men gathered up the purses that had been left behind. They were almost helpless with laughter at the ease with which they had robbed the robbers.

Conspiring lords, no less than thieves, fall out; and there's betrayal and abandoning of friends in the higher world of politics no less than in the lower one of highway robbery. Hotspur had received a letter in his castle at Warkworth. It was from a gentleman on whom he'd counted for assistance, and who was now crying off.

"The purpose you undertake is dangerous," he read. He looked up. He scowled. "Why, that's certain," he muttered contemptuously. "'Tis dangerous to take a cold, to sleep, to drink; but I tell you, my lord fool, out of this nettle, danger, we pluck this flower, safety." He continued with the letter, becoming more and more exasperated with the writer's objections to the great enterprise. At length he flung the letter aside.

"By the Lord!" he exploded. "Our plot is a good plot, as ever was laid, our friends true and constant and full of expectation; an excellent plot, very good friends. Zounds, and I were now by this rascal," (he kicked angrily at the crumpled letter), "I could brain him with his lady's fan. Is there not my father, my uncle and myself?" he demanded, listing his fellow conspirators upon his fingers, "Lord Edmund Mortimer, my lord of York and Owen Glendower? Is there not, besides, the Douglas? Have I not all their letters to meet me in arms by the ninth of the next month?"

Then, after some further unflattering remarks about the letter writer, he decided he would set out that very night to meet with his dangerous friends. He told his pretty wife that he must go, but not why, or where.

"What is it carries you away?" she demanded.

"Why, my horse, my love, my horse," said he.

"Out, you mad-headed ape!" she cried. "I'll know your business, Harry, that I will."

But plead, threaten and cajole as she might, he would not tell her; and only in the moment of parting did he relent sufficiently to promise:

"Whither I go, thither shall you go too; today will I set forth, tomorrow you."

In the Boar's Head Tavern—a frowsy hostelry with as many nooks and cubbyholes as a nibbled cheese—the Harry of the south thought briefly of his glorious counterpart, that world's idol and pattern of honour. He shrugged his shoulders ruefully.

"I am not yet of Percy's mind," he confided to Poins, as the pair of them awaited the return of Falstaff from Gad's Hill, "the Hotspur of the north, he that kills me some six or seven dozen of Scots at a breakfast, washes his hands and says to his wife, 'Fie upon this quiet life, I want work . . .'"

Poins laughed; and so did Prince Hal, but with a touch of bitterness, as if he partly envied what he mocked. Then all thoughts of honour and glory were blown to the winds as, with a clatter of boots and a commotion of oaths, Falstaff and his men arrived. Torn, muddy and sweating from their adventure, they collapsed upon benches and chairs. Falstaff looked hard at Poins and the Prince.

"A plague of all cowards, I say," he remarked sombrely. "Give me a cup of sack, boy." A cup was fetched. He drank and made a sour face. He glared at the potboy. "You rogue, here's lime in this sack . . . yet a coward is worse than a cup of sack with lime in it."

To prove it, he turned his fat back on Poins and the Prince and drank again. Addressing his companions, and studiously ignoring the Prince, he continued to abuse cowards; until the Prince ventured to inquire the cause of his displeasure. Falstaff turned.

"Are you not a coward?" he demanded. "Answer me to that—and Poins there?"

"Zounds, ye fat paunch," cried Poins angrily, "and ye call me a coward, by the Lord, I'll stab thee!"

"I call thee coward?" wondered Falstaff, putting a table between himself and the indignant Poins. "I'll see thee damned 'ere I call thee coward, but I would give a thousand pound I could run as fast as thou canst."

At last the reason for the knight's black mood came out. The adventure upon Gad's Hill. In spite of monumental heroism, the like of which the world had never seen, it had been a defeat. He and his three fearless companions (who dimly nodded their battered heads) had boldly robbed some sixteen ferocious merchants; and then had had the cruel misfortune to be set upon and robbed themselves. (Again the companions nodded.) By how many? the Prince inquired, with a sly glance at Poins. By a hundred, at least, said Falstaff unblushingly; and even his companions gaped at the enormity of the lie.

"What, a hundred, man?" cried the Prince.

"I am a rogue if I were not at half-sword with a dozen of them two hours together," said Falstaff modestly, and went on to describe so desperate a battle that even a Hotspur would have paled at. Enemies, which seemed to multiply, as if they'd been put out at compound interest, came at him from every corner of the night; but still he duelled and still he fought, holding them all at bay—until, most treacherously, he was overcome.

"Three misbegotten knaves in Kendal green came at my back," he said bitterly, "and let drive at me, for it was so dark, Hal, that thou couldst not see thy hand."

The Prince nodded. Falstaff sighed and drank again, to drown the memory of that frightful time. Then the Prince called him a fat liar. Falstaff, much offended, demanded to know why. The Prince told him. How could he have known that the misbegotten knaves were in Kendal green when it was so dark he could not see his hand? Loftily, Falstaff declined to answer; so the Prince, with grim pleasure, went on to demolish the fat old man by telling him that the hundred he'd fought against had been no more than two; himself and Poins.

"What trick, what device, what starting-hole canst thou now find out," demanded the Prince, "to hide thee from this open and apparent shame?"

Falstaff was silent. His little eyes, like mice in a mansion, peeped from side to side. He frowned. He gnawed his lip. Then he beamed.

"By the Lord," he exclaimed, slapping his mighty knee with his plump hand, "I knew thee as well as he that made thee! Why, hear you, my masters," he asked of the company, "was it for me to kill the heir-apparent? Could I turn upon the true Prince?"

With huge innocence he turned from face to face, and outfaced them all. There was no demolishing Falstaff. The truth rebounded from his fat person as harmlessly as a spent arrow, and to accuse him of lying was like blaming the ocean for being wet. There was nothing for it but to laugh . . . at truth and lies and life itself.

In the midst of all the merriment, there came, like a spectre to the feast, a gentleman from the court with a message for the Prince from the King, his father. Falstaff went to inquire, and came back with uneasy news. Hotspur, Northumberland and Worcester, together with many powerful friends, were up in arms. The rebellion had begun.

"Thy father's beard," said the fat man, "is turned white with the news; you may buy land now as cheap as stinking mackerel."

The Prince was commanded to appear before his father in the morning; for, when all was said and done, Hal was the heir-apparent, and, when all was said and done, the King had need of him. Earnestly Falstaff exhorted his young friend to prepare himself and have some ready answer to the heavy reproaches that the King would undoubtedly heap upon his son's way of life. The Prince looked at the old man thoughtfully. Suddenly he laughed.

"Do thou stand for my father and examine me upon the particulars of my life."

Falstaff blinked. A look of startled fondness flickered across his wine-red face. "Shall I?" he wondered. He beamed. "Content!" he cried; and, settling himself royally in his chair, crowned his bald pate with a dirty tasselled cushion. Then, to the huge delight of the assembled thieves, potboys, and the blotchy hostess of the tavern, who was weeping and hiccuping with laughter, he addressed the Prince with all the dignity of a sorrowing father and a troubled king.

Meekly, and with bowed head, the Prince listened as his father, in the person of the raddled old knight, reproached him for his wild ways and low companions.

"And yet there is a virtuous man whom I have often noted in thy company," said Falstaff dreamily.

"What manner of man, and it like Your Majesty?" inquired the Prince, as if he did not know.

"A good portly man, i'faith," said Falstaff happily, "and a corpulent, of a cheerful look, a pleasing eye, and a most noble carriage; and now I remember me, his name is Falstaff . . ." He paused for the roars of laughter to die down, and then said most sincerely: "There is virtue in that Falstaff; him keep with, the rest banish . . ."

"Dost thou speak like a king?" interrupted the Prince, smiling, but with an edge to his voice; for Falstaff's open mockery of his father and himself had affected him more deeply than might have been supposed. "Do thou stand for me, and I'll play my father."

Cheerfully, and with a better grace than King Richard (whom Hal's father had deposed) the fat man resigned his throne and crown. He stood, humbly, before the new king, biting his thumbnail and tracing a pattern with his toe, the very image of an awkward prince. The Prince himself, seated in the chair of state, and wearing the cushion, regarded his mockery self with elaborate severity. The company laughed, expecting more comedy; and so indeed it began, with stern questions from the son-father and meek, apologetic answers from the father-son . . . for Falstaff had years enough to be Hal's father, and even his grandfather as well. Then the mood changed. The young man's voice grew harder, and his very youth seemed turned to stone.

"There is a devil haunts thee," he said, as if looking through Falstaff to himself, "in the likeness of an old fat man, a tun of man is thy companion. Why dost thou converse with that trunk of humours, that bolting-hutch of beastliness, that swollen parcel of dropsies . . . that reverend vice, that grey iniquity, that father ruffian . . ."

Mercilessly the Prince went on. Laughter died, smiles faded, and Falstaff himself grew uneasy, not because of the brutality of the young man's words, but because of what he dreaded might be in the young man's heart. This was the fat knight's only weakness: his deep love for Hal. It was the only point in his armour of lying, boastfulness and dishonesty through which he could be hurt.

"If to be old and merry," he protested, anxiously trying to defend himself, "be a sin, then many an old host that I know is damned . . . banish Peto, banish Bardolph, banish Poins—but for sweet Jack Falstaff . . . banish not him thy Harry's company . . . banish plump Jack, and banish all the world."

"I do, I will," said the Prince coldy; and at that moment he was indeed his father, the lean stern politician, Bolingbroke.

Urgently Falstaff attempted to plead more on his own behalf, when there came a loud knocking on the tavern door. The sheriff and the watch had come in search of the robbers from Gad's Hill. In particular, they were looking for a gross fat man . . .

Instantly Falstaff hid; and the Prince, forgetting everything but fondness, lied to save his friend.

"The man I do assure you," he promised the sheriff, "is not here."

Not satisfied, but forced to take the Prince's word, the sheriff departed. Falstaff was looked for and discovered fast asleep behind a curtain. He was quite worn out from all his labours and all his frights. Upon a sudden impulse, the Prince told Peto search the snorer's pockets. Nothing was found but a list of debts. The Prince sighed. All Falstaff's substance was in his flesh; he owned nothing but the listed recollections of food and drink. Hal shrugged his shoulders and departed to meet with his father, leaving behind the lying, boastful, laughing world of Falstaff for the grim world of honour, politics and war.

Of all the discontented barons who had gathered under the banner of Hotspur and Northumberland, none was more feared than Owen Glendower. Even Falstaff had quaked at the mention of him, for he was said to have power over the spirits and demons of the air. Deep in his Welsh stronghold, he strode back and forth, a short, fierce gentleman in a robe of silver stars and moons that billowed out behind him, and with a nose like the prow of a ship and deep-set eyes that burned like hot

cannons. In rolling Welsh tones, he informed his companions—Hotspur, Mortimer and Worcester—that he was so remarkable a personage that, at his birth, there had been strange portents in the sky and that the world itself had shaken.

Hotspur yawned. He had had more than his fill of wild Welsh magic. "Why so it would have done at the same season," he said, "if your mother's cat had but kitten'd, though yourself had never been born."

"I say the earth did shake when I was born," repeated Glendower, glaring at the impudent young man.

Hotspur said it did not; and the others, fearing for Glendower's rage, tried to keep Hotspur quiet. It was a hopeless task.

"I can call spirits from the vasty deep," said Glendower, darkly.

"Why, so can I," said Hotspur, not much impressed, "or so can any man, but will they come when you do call for them?"

It was an uncomfortable beginning to the enterprise; but then Hotspur was an uncomfortable young man. He lacked an easy temper. Unlike the other Harry, he could never have lived and laughed with a Falstaff. He loved honour too much, and he suspected all the world of trying to rob him of it. Presently, however, the differences between Hotspur and Glendower were resolved and the meeting ended with the coming in of wives, and Lady Mortimer singing a sweet song in Welsh and Lady Percy making amorous fun of her husband, so that, for a little while, honour, politics and war gave way to music, smiles and love.

Prince Hal stood before the King. He tried with all his might to look serious and contrite; but as his lean, stern father talked and frowned and sadly shook his head, and reproached him for his wild ways and low companions, the young man could not help thinking that his father was very like a thin imitation of Falstaff imitating the King. Then his father spoke, as he always did, of Hotspur, the too-glorious Hotspur. Even though Hotspur had rebelled against him, he was still admired; and, Hal knew, preferred above himself.

"What never-dying honour he hath got," went on the King, driving knives of envy into his son's heart, "against renowned Douglas . . ."

Silently the Prince stood as his father continued to heap praises upon the bright Harry of the north, at the expense of the dull Harry who stood before him. "Thou art degenerate," accused the King.

"Do not think so," cried Hal, "you shall not find it so!" and he poured out his bitterness against Hotspur and swore that he would prove himself to be the better man. "For the time will come," he promised, "that I shall make this northern youth exchange his glorious deeds for my indignities!"

So fiercely did he speak that the King's heart quickened and, for the first time, he saw in his son some glimmerings of the greatness he had hoped for; and when news came in that the rebels were gathering at Shrewsbury, he gladly gave the Prince command over an army to march against them.

"Let's away," he urged, laying a fond arm about his son's shoulders. "Advantage feeds him fat while men delay."

"Bardolph, am I not fallen away?" sighed Falstaff to his purple-nosed companion as the pair of them slopped into the Boar's Head Tavern. "Do I not bate? Do I not dwindle?" he wondered, patting his huge belly and finding it to be some inches from where he expected it. He sat down and regarded his countenance in the diminishing bowl of a spoon. "Why, my skin hangs about me like an old lady's loose-gown."

He was melancholy. It was not so much Falstaff as the world that was falling away. War was approaching, and his beloved Hal was now with his true father. The fat man felt himself neglected. He turned quarrelsome and accused the hostess of picking his pocket while he'd slept.

"I have lost," he complained bitterly, "a seal-ring of my grandfather's worth forty mark."

"O Jesu," cried the hostess indignantly, "I have heard the Prince tell him, I know not how oft, that that ring was copper!"

"The Prince is a Jack, a sneak-up!" snarled Falstaff, venting his spleen on the absent young man, "'sblood, and were he here I would cudgel him like a dog."

Even as he uttered the threat, the Prince came marching in. He was fresh and spruce and shining from his father's presence, and every inch the heir-apparent to the throne. At once the knight's melancholy left him; and he glowed as if his Hal had kindled him.

"Now, Hal, to the news at court," he demanded eagerly. "For the robbery, lad, how is that answered?"

All was well. The money had been paid back and Falstaff was no longer in danger from the sheriff. The Prince was good friends with his father; and, what was more, had procured Falstaff the command of a company of soldiers. The Prince was in high good spirits. The prospect of battle excited him, and the thought of meeting, at last, with his great rival, filled him with a fierce eagerness.

"The land is burning," he cried, "Percy stands on high, and either we or they must lower lie!"

"Rare words!" chuckled Falstaff, when the warlike Prince had gone. "Brave world!" And he settled down to eat his breakfast with an appetite restored.

Messengers crossed and re-crossed the land, galloping down narrow lanes and along broad highways on steaming horses, carrying rumour in their looks and news in their saddle-bags, from north to south, from south to north, to the King in London and to the rebel lords in Shrewsbury as the country plunged and staggered towards war. News came to Hotspur as he waited with Douglas and Worcester for his father and Glendower to join them, that his father was sick in bed and could not come. This was a great blow and Worcester cast doubts upon the sickness which he suspected to be caused more by caution than infection. Scarcely had this disaster been taken in than more messengers came, like doom-croaking ravens, to the rebel camp. Owen Glendower was delayed, and the King with all his people, was up in arms and marching north.

"What may the King's whole battle reach unto?" demanded Hotspur.

"To thirty thousand," answered the messenger.

"Forty let it be!" cried Hotspur, not in the least dismayed; for this was the cream of honour, to battle against impossible odds.

But the odds were not quite so great as Hotspur had been told. Already, and without a shot being fired or a sword being raised, the King's great

army had been reduced by a hundred and fifty. How so? Falstaff had sold them. By the authority entrusted to him, he had pressed into service only those who were rich enough to buy themselves out; in their place the knight was now the captain of some three hundred pounds and a band of ragged skeletons who had scarcely strength enough to march. Quilted, plumed and tasselled, like a pavilion filled with a gust of wind, the fat warrior rolled along the road to Coventry while his miserable little army picked their way painfully in his wake. Prince Hal, riding with the Lord of Westmoreland, came upon him and urged him to make haste, for the King's forces were already at Shrewsbury. He glanced back, and saw Falstaff's regiment.

"Tell me, Jack," he asked, "whose fellows are these that come after?"

"Mine, Hal, mine," responded Falstaff proudly.

"I did never see such pitiful rascals!"

"Tut, tut," exclaimed Falstaff, loftily waving aside all criticism, "good enough to toss, food for powder, food for powder . . ." he chuckled, "they'll fill a pit as well as better; tush, man, mortal men, mortal men."

The Prince frowned. Falstaff's harsh humour was not to his present taste.

"Sirrah, make haste!" he commanded. "Percy is already in the field!"

It was night-time in the rebel camp, and lanterns peered among the tents like creeping glow-worms. Hotspur was impatient for the coming battle. Time and again Douglas and Worcester urged him to wait until more men came in to swell his force. But Hotspur was a hero in the old style: caution, to him, was little better than cowardice.

A trumpet sounded, thin as a knife in the night. Voices murmured, lanterns gathered and threw up in their combined light, a herald emblazoned with the gaudy lions of the King. It was Sir Walter Blunt, a much-respected gentleman, come with an offer from the King. Swiftly he was conducted to Hotspur, who greeted him with affection and listened to him with courtesy. The message was that the King would know what were Hotspur's grievances so that they might be remedied without loss of blood. It was, all things considered, a fair and generous offer. But not to Hotspur, who admired the messenger but not the sender of the message.

"The King is kind," he said bitterly, "and well we know the King knows at what time to promise, when to pay," and then went on to deliver so damning an account of the King's misdeeds and the King's ingratitude, that no king could have endured it and remained a king.

"Shall I return this answer to the King?" asked Sir Walter, whose patience had been strained by the young man's furious recital of the wrongs done him.

Hotspur paused, and shook his head. The reproach in the herald's voice had moved him. "Not so, Sir Walter," he replied at length. "We'll withdraw awhile . . . go to the King . . . and in the morning early shall mine uncle bring him our purposes . . ."

"I would you would accept of grace and love," urged Sir Walter.

"And may be so we shall," returned Hotspur, but more out of kindness than belief.

The morning was pale and the sun bloody. It glinted on helmets and breast-plates like painted wounds. A herald's approach was sounded, and Worcester, that discontented, dangerous Earl, presented himself before the King. He had brought Hotspur's answer. It was violent and intemperate. Tight-lipped, he listened to the accusations of ingratitude, double-dealing and dishonourable theft of the crown. In part, he knew them to be true; but he was the King, and that high office absolved him from the crimes of private men. He was answerable only to God and his own heart. Government was all. Coldly he dismissed the accusations as being no more than the gilding of insurrection.

Prince Hal, stern in unaccustomed steel, stood beside his father. He surveyed the ranked soldiers whose pale faces looked anxiously at the day, as if wondering if they should see another.

"In both your armies," he said to the scowling Earl, "there is many a soul shall pay full dearly for this encounter if once they join in trial." He made no attempt to rebut Hotspur's charges or even to defend his father's name; instead, after paying due homage to Hotspur's courage and high honour, he offered himself in single combat against the other Harry, so that the blood of many might be saved.

It was a brave and chivalrous speech; it was a young man's speech; it was also, in the King's opinion, a foolish speech. It harked back to the old days of tournaments, that were long out of fashion.

"And, Prince of Wales, so dare we venture thee," he said, in public recognition of his son's valour; but then went on in a shrewder vein: "Albeit, considerations infinite do make against it."

This king was not so foolish as to risk all on one man's courage, particularly when he himself had the advantage in numbers. Besides, he suspected that his own Harry would be no match for the other. Accordingly he dismissed Worcester with no more than the offer of a pardon if the rebels would lay down their arms. Otherwise, they must take the dreadful consequences.

"We offer fair," he said. "Take it advisedly."

"It will not be accepted," said the Prince, when Worcester had departed. "The Douglas and the Hotspur both together are confident against the world in arms."

The King nodded. He knew that the battle must come.

"God befriend us," he said, as if to reassure his son, "as our cause is just."

He moved away, and with him went all the assembled earls, lords and captains, clanking grimly in their steel. The Prince, momentarily alone, frowned as he thought of the coming fight, of proud Hotspur who risked everything for honour, and of his father who risked nothing; of the justice of Hotspur's accusations, and the deviousness of his father's ways . . . and of good men dying for another's cause.

A loud clatter broke in on his thoughts, a mighty clashing, as of a kitchen in a gale. It was Falstaff in armour, and overflowing it, like too large a feast crammed into too few pots and pans. His breastplate lay upon his chest like a small tureen.

"Hal," he said uneasily, "if thou see me down in the battle and bestride me, so. 'Tis a point of friendship."

The Prince smiled ruefully at the fat and fearful old man. "Say thy prayers, and farewell."

"I would 'twere bed-time, Hal, and all well."

"Why, thou owest God a death," said the Prince.

"'Tis not due yet," cried Falstaff indignantly; but the Prince had gone to make ready for the battle. Falstaff shrugged his shoulders, and his armour chimed like church bells. He stared round at the little world of fluttering banners and painted shields, of kings and princes, and shivering wretches preparing to kill each other . . . for no better reason than for honour. He frowned, as if mightily puzzled.

"Can honour set to a leg?" he wondered. He pondered deeply; then shook his head. "No. Or an arm? No. Or take away the grief of a wound? No. Honour hath no skill in surgery then? No." He looked mournful, as if it was a real sorrow to him that honour could not undo the harm that honour had done. "What is honour?" he demanded. He thought again. "A word. Who hath it? Him that died a-Wednesday. Doth he feel it? No. Doth he hear it? No." With each repetition of the word honour, it seemed to become more meaningless. "I'll none of it!" grunted Falstaff at length; and, with a further shrug of his fat, plated shoulders, went off to lead his gnawed lambs to the slaughter.

Within this hellish cloud . . .

Worcester returned to the rebel camp. He said nothing of the offered pardon. He knew, full well, that it would never be extended to him. He would be made to bear the blame for all. His only hope lay in the chance of battle, and he was prepared to shed the blood of thousands to save his own. No matter; Hotspur's bright glory would cover all; for many misshapen creatures creep along under the richly embroidered cloak of honour.

The sky was melancholy; and the wind, blustering across the field outside Shrewsbury, seemed to cause the opposing forces to bend and tremble, like the shaking of wheat. Suddenly tiny voices shouted; trumpets shrieked as if in fright; and the ground began to shudder under the advancing thunder of horses' hooves. Slowly at first, and then with gathering speed, the armies rushed towards each other, so that, for a moment, they might have been intent upon a wild and joyous meeting. Then they met.

Shouts and screams of men and horses filled the air. Cannons roared; bright figures crashed and struggled; thick flowers of dust bloomed among them, and spreading, formed a huge rolling cloud that obscured all but the jagged edges of the conflict. Within this hellish cloud, men ran hither and thither, bleeding, screaming, cursing, looking for other men to kill. Among them, Hotspur searched for the other Harry, and the other Harry searched for him. Fat Falstaff searched for safety; and the wild Scot, Douglas, searched to kill the King. But the world, that day, seemed full of kings; that careful man, the true King, had dressed many in his armour. See! here was another! Douglas attacked, and in moments the royal armour fell and blood rushed out of it. Hotspur appeared, like the spirit of battle.

"All's done, all's won!" panted Douglas, "here breathless lies the King!"

But it was only another image he had killed; it was Sir Walter Blunt.

"Up and away!" cried Hotspur; and the two great soldiers vanished into the murky air.

There was quiet for a moment; and safety. The large shape of Falstaff appeared, very cautiously, as if he was squeezing sideways through a narrow gap in the air. He advanced, clutching a sword that had seen

much action, but had wisely taken no part in it. He stumbled over the dead man.

"Soft! Who are you? Sir Walter Blunt—there's honour for you!"

He shook his head; then looked about him as if for his followers. There were none. He shrugged his shoulders, and sighed:

"I have led my ragamuffins where they are peppered; there's not three of my hundred and fifty left alive, and they are for the town's end to beg during life."

Hal found him.

"What, standst thou idle here?" he demanded angrily. "Lend me thy sword."

But Falstaff would not part with it. Instead he offered his pistol.

"Give it me; what, is it in the case?"

"Ay, Hal," apologised Falstaff, "'tis hot, 'tis hot . . ."

The Prince took the case and drew out, not a pistol, but a bottle of sack. Furiously the Prince threw it at the fat man who mocked everything, and rushed away in search of Hotspur, his heart's enemy. Ruefully Falstaff stared after the enraged Prince; then he glanced down at the dead man. He shuddered.

"I like not such grinning honour as Sir Walter hath. Give me life," he grunted; and crept away, glinting and clanking, to find some safer place.

The smoky air seemed full of holes, like clearings in a noisy roaring forest, beyond which could be seen the shadowy shapes of struggling men. In one such clearing stood the King, the true King. His companions had left him to stiffen resistance where it faltered, so that briefly he was alone. An armoured figure came out of the dust. It was Douglas!

"Another king!" he shouted. "They grow like Hydra's heads . . . What art thou that counterfeit'st the person of a king?"

"The King himself."

"I fear thou art another counterfeit!" cried Douglas; but nevertheless, attacked.

The Scot was the younger man, and the stronger, and the true King staggered under his blows. In moments he would have fallen and joined all his images in death, so that true and false would have been one; but the Prince appeared. At once he drew off Douglas, and they fought. Douglas was fierce and powerful, but Hal had learned his fighting, not on the field of chivalry, but in the murky lanes and byways where cut-throats lurked. He was more than a match for Douglas who, cursing, fled.

Hal extended his hand to his fallen father and drew him upright. The two looked deeply at one another; and, for a moment, in the smoke, fury and shrieks of the battle, there was a moment of reconciliation and peace. Then the King left the Prince and, even as he did so, the terrible moment came towards which Prince Hal's life had always been moving. Hotspur found him.

The two Harrys stared at one another almost with curiosity: the one who had just saved his father, and the other whose father had abandoned him in his need.

"Two stars," said Hal grimly, "keep not their motion in one sphere, nor can one England brook a double reign of Harry Percy and the Prince of Wales."

"Nor shall it, Harry," returned Hotspur, "for the hour is come to end the one of us."

So at last they fought, as it was certain that they should from the very beginning; and it seemed that all the world hung upon the outcome of the single combat that Hal had first proposed, and that his cautious father had rejected. But the real cause for which they struck and stabbed and hacked at each other, for which they glared and bled and hopped like iron toads, was not for the fate of kingdoms; nor was it for honour, but for the jealousy of honour.

Unknowingly they had attracted an onlooker. It was as if the brightness of the conflict had drawn a bloated moth. Falstaff hovered, anxiously watching the progress of the fight.

"To it, Hal!" he urged his beloved Prince. "Nay, you shall find no boy's play here, I can tell you!"

So intent was he on watching the conflict, that, before he knew it, he himself was set upon by Douglas, still searching for kings. He was too heavy to run, and too fat to dodge, so he exchanged one or two valiant blows with the fierce Scot, and, as soon as he conveniently could, fell to earth with a dreadful clatter and a dying grunt. And then lay still. Douglas left him; and, at that very instant, Hal stabbed Hotspur to the heart.

"O Harry, thou hast robbed me of my youth!" sighed Hotspur, as he

lay, and bitterly whispered away the last of his life. "Percy," he breathed, "thou art dust, and food for—"

"For worms, brave Percy," completed the Prince; for Hotspur was dead. Sadly now the conquering Harry looked down on his rival; and grieved. He knew that he had killed not only Hotspur's youth but his own.

Suddenly he spied the huge form of Falstaff, lying like a fallen world; and his grief passed from the general to the sharply particular.

"What, old acquaintance," he wept, "could not all this flesh keep in a little life? Poor Jack, farewell! I could have better spared a better man."

He left the scene of the dead hero and the coward; and, so much for the dues of honour, his tears were for the coward.

An eye opened in Falstaff's head. It swivelled cautiously from side to side. Safety. Falstaff arose. "The better part of valour," said the knight, "is discretion, in the which better part I have saved my life."

His wandering gaze fell upon the dead Hotspur. Alarm seized him. What if he was not quite dead? "Why may not he rise as well as I?" wondered Falstaff fearfully. He looked carefully about him. Nervously

he raised his sword. "Nobody sees me," he muttered; and, with a quick movement, stabbed the dead man through the thigh.

Hotspur made no defence. "Come you along with me," grunted Falstaff; and began to heave the remains of the hero on to his broad back.

While he was thus engaged, the Prince and his younger brother returned to the scene. They stared at the resurrected Falstaff in amazement. The knight, quite unabashed at having been caught out in so gross a deception, regarded the two Princes with fat pride. He cast down Hotspur's misused body, declaring:

"There is Percy. If your father will do me any honour, so: if not, let him kill the next Percy himself. I look to be either earl or duke, I can assure you."

The Prince's wonderment turned to indignation.

"Why, Percy I killed myself, and saw thee dead."

"Didst thou?" said Falstaff pityingly. "Lord, Lord, how this world is given to lying! I grant you I was down, and out of breath, and so was he, but we rose both at an instant and fought a long hour by Shrewsbury clock."

Prince Hal, much divided between the claims of pride, honour, and old friendship, shook his head and smiled.

"If a lie may do thee grace," he murmured to the old rogue who, in many ways, had been a wiser and a better father to him than his own, "I'll gild it with the happiest terms I have."

A trumpet sounded, the rebels were in retreat. The King had won the day; and Hotspur, with all his honour, justice and high nobility, was in the dust. But Falstaff had survived.

"I'll follow," he said, preparing to roll on after the victors, "as they say, for reward. He that rewards me, God reward him."

So the fat man strode on, with his head high and his chest thrust out, but some little way behind his paunch.

More work was to be done. Battles were to be won against Mortimer, Glendower and the Duke of Northumberland. But the King was confident. The father had forgiven his son; all that now remained was for the son to forgive his father.

Hamlet

It happened in Denmark, long ago. High up on the battlements of the castle at Elsinore, two sentinels, their cloaks snapping in the whipping dark, met at the limit of their watch: the one ending, the other beginning. Their faces, seen faintly by the light of a thin seeding of stars, were white as bone. It was midnight. Presently they were joined by two companions, and the relieved sentinel took his departure, very gladly. The three remaining stared uneasily about them.

"What, has this thing appeared again tonight?" asked one of the newcomers, a young man by name of Horatio.

"I have seen nothing," answered the sentinel, but softly and with many a wary look about him.

For two nights now the sentinels had seen a strange, unnatural sight. Between midnight and one o'clock, a phantom figure had soundlessly stalked the battlements. It had been, so far as could be made out in the shaking dark, the spirit of the dead King.

"Tush, tush, 'twill not appear," murmured Horatio. He was a visitor to Elsinore from Wittenburg, where he had been at the University with Prince Hamlet, the dead King's son. Being a student of philosophy and not much given to dreaming, he had little faith in ghosts, phantoms and spectres of the night. He smiled at his pale companions, who had dragged him up to this cold, dark, windy place with their fantastic tale of—

"Look where it comes again!"

He looked; and his sensible eyes started from his sensible head. All reason fled for in weirdly gleaming armour and with weightless tread, the dead King stalked slowly by! The watchers, huddled in their cloaks, trembled with amazement and dread.

"Speak to it, Horatio!" breathed one, for the apparition seemed to linger. Horatio made the attempt, as boldly as he was able; and the night seemed to freeze as the dead King turned upon them a shadowy countenance that was grim with grief. Then it stalked away, and vanished into some invisible curtain of the night.

They watched after it till their eyes ached with staring; then they turned to one another in bewilderment. What could be the meaning of the apparition? Why had the dead King returned, and with looks so heavy with despair? Horatio, a little recovered in voice and colour, supposed the cause to lie in some danger to the state. Fortinbras, the Prince of Norway, was arming to seize back the lands that the dead King had boldly conquered. Surely it was this threat that had troubled the King's spirit and had dragged it from the grave?

But even as he proposed such a cause, which seemed likely enough, the ghost returned, as if to deny it.

"Stay!" cried Horatio, "if thou hast any sound or use of voice, speak to me!"

But it would not. It raised its arms as if in horror. From far off, a cock crew. The phantom wavered, became insubstantial, then faded, leaving on the dark air no more than an impress of measureless grief and despair.

"It was about to speak when the cock crew," whispered one.

"And then it started like a guilty thing upon a fearful summons," said Horatio; and straightway it was agreed that Prince Hamlet should be told of what had been seen. If to no one else, the dead father would surely speak to his living son.

The King, the great, good King, loved and honoured by all, had been dead for two months. He had been stung by a serpent while sleeping in his orchard, and all Denmark had wept. But now the time for grieving was past: sad eyes gave way to merry ones, long faces to round smiles; and the heavy black of mourning, that had bandaged up the court, was washed away by a sea of bright colour. Yellow silks and sky-blue satins, encrusted with silver, blazed in the ceremonial chamber, and the walls were hung with glory. There was a new King—even though there was still the same Queen. She had married again, and with her dead husband's brother.

This new King was a sturdy gentleman, broad-shouldered and broad-featured, and much given to smiling—as well he might, for he had gained a luxurious throne and a luxurious queen at a stroke. Affably he conducted the affairs of state, dispatching ambassadors to Norway to patch up grievances and giving gracious permission to Laertes, his faithful chamberlain's son, to return to France whence he'd come to attend the coronation. Next, still smiling, and with his strong hand guarding the jewelled hand of his Queen, he turned to her son, Prince Hamlet, a young man in black, like a plain thought in a gaudy world.

"But now, my cousin Hamlet, and my son—"

"A little more than kin, and less than kind," murmured the Prince, with a look of dislike and contempt.

Anxiously the Queen, his mother, begged him to forsake his dark looks and dark attire. He answered her with scarcely more courtesy than he had shown the King. The King, hiding his annoyance, added his own urgings; and the young man submitted—to the extent of agreeing to remain at court and not return to school at Wittenberg as he had wished. The King was satisfied and, with more smiles (which he dispensed like the small coin of royal charity), he left the chamber with the backward-glancing Queen upon his arm. As if on apron-strings, the crowding courtiers followed.

Hamlet was alone. Long and hard he stared after the departed court. The look upon his face, had it been seen by the royal pair who had inspired it, would have chilled their hearts, made stone of their smiles, and poison of the lust of their bed. Dull hatred oppressed the young man's mind: hatred for the corrupted world in which he was imprisoned, hatred for life itself, and loathing and disgust for the Queen, his mother, who, so soon after her noble husband's death, had married so wretched a creature as the dead King's brother.

"O most wicked speed!" he cried out in anguish, as, helplessly, his imagination both probed and shrank from the hateful circumstance. "To post with such dexterity to incestuous sheets!"

But someone was coming! Hastily he hid all evidence of his breaking heart under his customary mask of indifferent courtesy.

"Hail to your lordship," a gentleman said, coming into the chamber.

"I am glad to see you well," responded Hamlet, scarcely looking up, and with the distant cousin of a smile. Then he saw that the gentleman was no tedious courtier. It was Horatio, his old school friend Horatio, from Wittenberg!

At once, surprise and delight overspread his countenance. His gloom vanished and his sunk spirit revived. In a moment he was all quickness and liveliness and eager hospitality, as he greeted his good friend from Wittenberg, where life had been clear and honest, where the plain rooms had been enriched with noble ideas, not sullen tapestries, and the talk had flowed like wine. Warmly he included in his greeting Horatio's two companions, who were soldiers of the Royal Guard. Then, turning to his friend, he inquired:

"But what is your affair in Elsinore?"

"My lord, I came to see your father's funeral."

"I prithee, do not mock me, fellow student," said Hamlet, his smile, like the sun in winter, forgetting its warmth. "I think it was to see my mother's wedding."

"Indeed, my lord," admitted Horatio, gently, "it followed hard upon."

"Thrift, thrift, Horatio. The funeral baked·meats did coldly furnish forth the marriage tables," said Hamlet. Then his bitter mood lightened and his smile regained some warmth. "My father," he murmured softly, "methinks I see my father—"

Horatio and his companions started. "Where, my lord?"

"In my mind's eye, Horatio," said Hamlet; and his listeners grew easy again.

"I saw him once," said Horatio. "'A was a goodly king."

"'A was a man," said Hamlet, as if wanting to dispense with all worldly distinction of office. "Take him for all in all: I shall not look upon his like again."

Then Horatio told him. Eagerly, and yet careful to keep within the exact observation of a scholar, he told of the appearance of the dead King upon the battlements. "I knew your father," he assured the Prince. "These hands are not more like."

Hamlet listened, with fiercely beating heart; but old Wittenberg habits of argument, question and debate made him cautious.

"Armed, say you?"

"Armed, my lord."

"From top to toe?"

"My lord, from head to foot."

"Then saw you not his face?" demanded Hamlet, triumphantly.

"O yes, my lord, he wore his beaver up."

There was no doubt. The spirit had been, to all intents, the ghost of Hamlet's father. With huge and dreadful excitement, Hamlet promised that he would join Horatio and the soldiers on the battlements on the following night.

"My father's spirit—in arms," he breathed, when he was alone. "All is not well . . ."

Laertes was for France. Handsomely dressed in the newest fashion for his journey, he came to bid farewell to his sister Ophelia and give her such advice upon the perils and pitfalls of the world as he thought to be necessary. She was young and fair and modest as a bud. She was of so yielding a nature that she dared not call her soul her own, and had put it, trustingly, in the care of her brother and her wise old father, Polonius, the chamberlain. She had confided in Laertes that Prince Hamlet had, of late, caused her to believe that he loved her; and now, as she sat in a window seat, stitching some nursery proverb into a sampler, she listened as her brother solemnly warned her of the danger of passion and the unsteady nature of a young man's love. She nodded and nodded, and, when he had finished, she looked up and expressed the timid hope that he would practise as he had preached. Indignantly he protested his own virtue, and was about to depart when his father, Polonius, appeared.

"Yet here, Laertes? Aboard, aboard for shame!" cried the old gentleman; and then, taking advantage of the moment, saw fit to advise his son, even as his son had advised his sister. But yet there was a difference; for while Laertes had warned his sister of dangers that might threaten her from without, Polonius warned of those subtler dangers from within. Although they were, for the most part, threadbare maxims such as Ophelia might have embroidered on her samplers, they were not unfitting.

"Costly thy habit as thy purse can buy," said Polonius, severely eyeing his over-dressed son, "but not expressed in fancy: rich, not gaudy . . ."

At the mention of "purse", the young man's hand had gone helplessly to his side, which caused Polonius to warn, "Neither a borrower nor a lender be . . ." The young man grew red; but, nevertheless, listened patiently until his father had done. Then, turning to his sister and reminding her of his own advice, he took his departure in a blaze of mostly good intentions.

"What is't, Ophelia, he hath said to you?" asked her father suspiciously.

Timidly Ophelia confessed that it had to do with the Lord Hamlet. The old man nodded; he had suspected as much.

"What is between you?" he demanded. "Give me up the truth."

"He hath, my lord, of late," murmured the girl, dividing her looks between her proverb and her father, "made many tenders of his affection to me."

"Affection!" exclaimed Polonius contemptuously. "Pooh, you speak like a green girl!" And then and there he berated her soundly for her foolishness in believing in a prince's love. He warned her (as her brother had done) of the danger that might lie in Hamlet's fondness—a danger not only to herself, but, more importantly, to that wily politician who was her father. Sternly he forbade her to have any further talk with Prince Hamlet; and she, mild Ophelia, who had already given up the charge of her soul, now gave up the charge of her heart. "I shall obey, my lord," she said.

The night was bitter and the frozen stars peered secretly down upon the three cloaked figures who stood upon the castle's battlements.

"What hour now?" asked Hamlet for perhaps the hundredth time.

"I think it lacks of twelve," answered Horatio.

If the dead King was to appear, his time was almost come. Suddenly there came the sound of festive trumpets and the double thunder of a cannon.

"What does this mean, my lord?" wondered Horatio.

It was a custom, expounded Hamlet, with a sour smile, for such uproarious noise to accompany the revelry and drinking of the King. It brought the nation into disrepute, and made them seem to be no more than idle drunkards, so that, whatever of good there was, was lost in bad report. From this, Hamlet's unresting mind hovered over the curious circumstances of how a single defect in a man might, in the general view, taint and discolour his fairest virtues.

"Look, my lord, it comes!" Horatio's voice was sharp with fear; his hand shook as he pointed.

Hamlet turned. His face grew pale, his eyes huge, and his expelled breath made a thread of grey amazement in the air.

"Angels and ministers of grace defend us!" he cried out.

Upon the dark battlements stood his dead father! All in armour, as cold and lifeless as himself, the dead King gazed with tragic sorrow upon his shaking son. He beckoned, and Hamlet made to follow. Urgently his companions—Horatio and the sentinel—tried to prevent him, for they dreaded that the spirit might be malevolent and would tempt the young Prince to his death. Savagely Hamlet threw off the restraint and threatened to strike with his sword if he should be hindered any more.

"Go on," he cried to the beckoning ghost, "I'll follow thee!"

The dead King stalked on and the wild Prince went after, till both were lost from sight.

"Let's follow!" urged the sentinel, fearful for his Prince.

"To what issue will this come?" whispered Horatio.

The sentinel stared into the freezing darkness in which the dead King and his son had vanished. "Something is rotten in the state of Denmark," he said.

Father and son stood close together in a secret fold of the night. The young man shuddered as the unnatural chill of his dead father struck through to his heart.

"Mark me," whispered the ghost.

"I will," breathed his son.

"My hour is almost come," sighed the spirit; and, as it told of the grim and hateful regions to which it was soon condemned to return, Hamlet stared into his father's shadowy, unhappy eyes and longed, with all his heart, to kiss his freezing hand and pour out, into his hollow ear, all the love and devotion that death had stopped.

Upon the dark battlements stood his dead father!

"List, list, O list!" begged the ghost, with sudden urgency. "If thou didst ever thy dear father love—"

"O God!"

"Revenge his foul and most unnatural murder!"

"Murder!"

The stars glared, the battlements shuddered, and Hamlet's heart ceased as the terrible word was uttered. Murder! And revenge!

"Now, Hamlet, hear," whispered the ghost. "The serpent that did sting thy father's life now wears his crown!"

"O my prophetic soul! My uncle!"

Sombrely the dead man observed and approved the quickening of anger in his son, and went on to unfold the hideous circumstance of the crime, of how the King's loving wife, Hamlet's mother, had been seduced by the King's wretched brother, and then, how that brother had poured poison in the sleeping King's ear.

"Thus was I, sleeping, by a brother's hand, of life, of crown, of queen at once dispatch'd . . ."

Consumed with rage and horror, the son listened to his father's words, each one of which seemed a command for revenge upon the unwholesome pair whose faint rejoicings, from time to time, mocked the night.

"But howsomever thou pursuest this act," warned the ghost, with a sudden tenderness made horrible by its hopelessness, "taint not thy mind nor let thy soul contrive against thy mother aught. Leave her to heaven . . ."

Hamlet's heart ached with pity, for he saw that his father's spirit was tormented by love no less than by hate: both had outlived the grave. But now the night was wearing threadbare, and the phantom shivered as the dark grew thin and patched. "Fare thee well," it whispered. "Adieu, adieu, adieu. Remember me." Then it was gone and Hamlet stood alone.

Breathing harshly he leaned against the battlements and rested his head upon the cold stone, as if to support his staggering mind. Far, far below, a wild sea crashed and raged against the rocks at the base of the cliff upon which the castle stood; but darkness and disturbance reduced its fury to silent, tumbled lace. Yet had it been seen in all its huge madness, it would have seemed no more than distance had made it beside the raging in

Hamlet's soul. He raised his head and, with eyes blazing with tears, swore to heaven that he would be the instrument of the ghost's revenge. He would wipe from his mind all the calmness, wisdom and fine thoughts he had learned in happy Wittenberg, and leave behind only —revenge!

"O most pernicious woman!" he wept, as again he heard sounds of distant revelry. "O villain, villain, smiling damned villain!" With trembling hands he drew a book from his pocket—a student's book in which observations of life and nature were noted down. "Meet it is I set it down," he muttered, as if to calm his extreme agitation by such scholar's habit, "that one may smile, and smile, and be a villain." He wrote so fiercely that he scored the paper through. He put the book away. "It is 'Adieu, adieu, remember me'," he repeated. "I have sworn't!" He drew his sword as if meaning, then and there, to rush down into the black castle and kill its poisoned heart.

But he heard voices calling. His companions were searching for him. Desperately he searched for some secret place in his mind where he might hide the dreadful knowledge he possessed; he would not, he dared not, confide what the ghost had revealed. When his companions found him, and eagerly questioned him, he answered them with wild, fantastic humour which, to his great relief, bewildered them into asking no more. Nonetheless he made them swear, upon the cross of his sword, that they would never tell of what had happened that night. This they did, and more than once; for wherever they stood, Hamlet heard the ghost, deep in the earth, calling: "Swear!"

"This is wondrous strange," said Horatio, troubled by his friend's frantic manner.

"And therefore as a stranger give it welcome," returned Hamlet; and then, with a sad smile at his old school friend, said: "There are more things in heaven and earth, Horatio, than are dreamt of in your philosophy."

He made them swear again, this time that, if his mad humour should continue, they would never betray that they suspected what lay behind it. He trusted no one, least of all himself. His heart was so full that he dared not trust his tongue not to betray him. Madness would be his refuge and hiding place of truth, until the time was ripe for his revenge.

Revenge! He shrank within himself as the full horror of his circumstance came upon him. What was he, Horatio's fellow student, doing in this dark world of murder and revenge, of treacherous kings and faithless queens, of creeping courtiers and poison? Most bitterly he sighed:

"The time is out of joint. O cursed spite, that ever I was born to set it right."

Laertes was in France and out of his father's sight, but by no means out of that cautious old gentleman's mind. Polonius did not trust his son; and perhaps not without cause. He sent a servant to spy on him and on what company he kept.

Polonius, cunning old adviser to king after king, deemed it his duty to know everything. Consequently if walls had ears, they were Polonius's; if keyholes had eyes, they were likewise, Polonius's. Yet this abundance of knowledge did not make him wise; it made him merely knowing. Thus when his daughter Ophelia came to him, as she was in duty bound, and told him that the Lord Hamlet had appeared in her room while she was sewing, with the looks of a melancholy madman, he sought no further for a cause than in disappointed love. "Have you given him any hard words of late?" he asked.

"No, my good lord," she answered, with a downcast look, "but as you did command, I did repel his letters and denied his access to me."

"That hath made him mad," pronounced Polonius. "Come, go we to the King. This must be known . . ."

But Hamlet's strangeness had already troubled the smooth surface of the court, puzzled the smiling King and vaguely distressed the easy Queen. Knowing that nothing would be got from the loyal Horatio, two other school friends of Hamlet had been sent for, in the hope that they would discover the cause of the Prince's change. Rosencrantz and Guildenstern, two courtly scholars, so alike in bows and smiles and flattered pleasure at being Royally summoned, that the King was hard put to know which was Guildenstern and which was Rosencrantz. However, the two fledgling courtiers had no such difficulty in knowing the King, and divining, amid the oiled smiles that slipped from face to face, that they would be well paid for spying on their old friend and smelling out the secrets of his heart.

"Heavens make our presence and our practices pleasant and helpful to him," said Guildenstern to Hamlet's mother, judging that such tender interest would concern her more than it would the King.

But it would seem that the young men's skills were not to be needed. No sooner had the bowing pair departed, to search out Hamlet, than Polonius came bustling in, stuffed with good news. First, from Norway. Young Fortinbras asked for no more than the free passage of his army through Denmark to some distant spot. Next, and best of all, the cause of Hamlet's madness had been discovered. Polonius had found it out. What was it? The King and Queen waited while the old politician, who could never be plain, used up words like stuffing, to swell the importance of a small goose before serving it up.

"More matter with less art," said the Queen impatiently and Polonius, thus brought, unwillingly, to the point, produced a letter written by Hamlet to Ophelia. It was a love letter of the most sentimental kind.

"Came this from Hamlet to her?" wondered the Queen, as if surprised that her son could pen such poor stuff.

It had indeed.

"But how hath she received his love?" asked the King, curiously.

Polonius, uninterested in his daughter's heart, replied by explaining that he had thought it fitting to put a stop to the business. "Lord Hamlet," he had warned his daughter, "is a prince out of thy star. This must not be." Very properly he had forbidden her to speak with the Prince again. But since then he had learned of such matters from his daughter as had left him in no doubt as to what had staggered the young man's brain. Unrequited love.

"Do you think 'tis this?" asked the King of Hamlet's mother.

"It may be," sighed the Queen, over whose own heart love, passion and lust exercised a sovereign sway. "Very like."

But the King was not entirely convinced. He would like more evidence.

"How may we try it further?" he asked.

To Polonius, the ever-resourceful Polonius, this presented not the smallest difficulty. Hamlet, he recollected, was accustomed to walk in the lobby for hours at a time. "At such a time," he proposed, with the heartless eagerness of the seasoned conspirator, "I'll loose my daughter to him." What passed then between the girl and the Prince might easily be overheard from a suitable place of concealment. (Such places were, to Polonius, as familiar as his study; and, doubtless, furnished with comfortable chairs). Readily the King fell in with the scheme, but further talk was prevented by the appearance of Hamlet himself. He was reading a book; and so deeply was he sunk in it that he might have been walking upon some lonely heath, instead of through the richly peopled rooms of the royal palace of Denmark. In appearance, Hamlet was somewhat declined. His shoes were unfastened, his stockings wrinkled, and his shir. hanging loose, like a limp surrender. Polonius nodded knowingly. He urged the King and Queen to depart and leave all to him, which they did most gladly. Hamlet seemed not to see them go.

"How does my good Lord Hamlet?" inquired Polonius, with the patient kindness that might be offered to an idiot or a child.

"Well, God a-mercy," returned the Prince, not looking up.

"Do you know me, my lord?" pursued Polonius.

The Prince looked at him carefully. "Excellent well," he said. "You are a fishmonger."

Somewhat taken aback, Polonius denied the charge, and then found himself caught in a swirling net of nonsense, of daughters, maggots and graves, from which he was glad to escape, when Rosencrantz and Guildenstern, out of breath from searching, at last found their friend.

"My excellent good friends!" cried Hamlet, throwing off all his madness and most of his melancholy in a moment. "Good lads, how do you both?"

They laughed, and he laughed; and, for a little while, they were no more than three good friends delighting in each other's shrewd wit and wisdom; and, for a little while, the grim horror and despair of Hamlet's situation seemed to him to be no more than an evil dream . . . until, in all innocence and courtesy, he asked:

"But in the beaten way of friendship, what make you at Elsinore?"

"To visit you, my lord," they answered promptly, "no other occasion."

A little too prompt; and accompanied by looks that were a little too innocent. In moments, they who had been commissioned to worm out Hamlet's secret, had their own uncovered before they had so much as begun. They were forced to admit that they had been sent for by the Queen and King; and it needed no great skill on Hamlet's part to guess the reason. Bitterly he stared at them and reflected on how easily they had been corrupted by the poisoned world of the court. Anxiously they tried to make amends and lift the Prince's spirits. They told him that they had passed on their way to the castle a company of actors who were coming to perform before the court. It was, it seemed, a company from the city that the Prince knew well.

In spite of himself, the Prince smiled. He delighted in the play and the company of players, those excellent fellow creatures whose highest aim was to please, seemed to him the best in the world. He looked forward keenly to their arrival; but then, remembering the two pupil-spies who stood anxiously by him, he felt a pang of pity. "You are welcome," he said. "But my uncle-father and my aunt-mother are deceived."

"In what, my dear lord?" asked Guildenstern, hopefully.

"I am but mad north-north-west," said Hamlet seriously. "When the wind is southerly, I know a hawk from a handsaw."

Before they could unravel Hamlet's meaning—if, indeed, there was any—Polonius entered with the news that the players had arrived.

"The best actors in the world," read out Polonius, from the company's extensive advertisement, which reached down, like a paper apron, almost to his knees, "either for tragedy, comedy, history, pastoral, pastoral-comical, historical-pastoral, tragical-historical, tragical-comical-historical-pastoral . . ." he drew breath and read on, until the players themselves appeared.

They came into the grand ceremonial chamber where real kings and real queens and real princes held sway, and were not in the least abashed. They wore their paper crowns, clutched their wooden swords, and shrugged their patchwork gowns with a dusty dignity and a seasoning of pride.

"You are welcome, masters!" cried Hamlet, and shook them all warmly by the hand. He looked fondly into each well-remembered face, commented ruefully upon the damage done by years, then begged the chief actor to recite, then and there, a certain speech for which he had a particular affection.

The actor, a grand figure of a man, with the nose and eye of a battered eagle, recollected the speech and straightway launched it, as gloriously as a galleon, its sails full of wind. Either by chance, or design, the speech was from a tale of old Troy, and was full of murdered kings, revenge and mourning queens. Absorbed, Hamlet listened.

"Look," exclaimed Polonius admiringly, when the actor paused, "whe'er he has not turned his colour and has tears in's eyes. Prithee no more."

The players, pleased with the reception of this modest sample of their art, were preparing to be bustled away by Polonius to their quarters, when Hamlet detained their principal.

"Can you play 'The Murder of Gonzago'?" he asked quietly, for a curious idea was fermenting in his mind. The actor nodded. "We'll ha't tomorrow night," murmured Hamlet. "You could for a need study a speech of some dozen or sixteen lines, which I would set down and insert in't, could you not?"

The player, familiar with the vanity of poet-princes, agreed; then followed the busy chamberlain. Rosencrantz and Guildenstern likewise, bowed themselves away, doubtless to report to the King. Only Hamlet remained.

The Greek Prince, of whom the player had so roaringly told, had killed a king as bloodily quick as sword could strike; but the damned King of Denmark still lived. The Trojan Queen had rent her garments and shrieked aloud to heaven when she had seen her husband dead; but the Queen of Denmark still sighed and smiled in the bed of her husband's murderer. The player who had presented the scene had wept real tears over those long-dead griefs; the Prince of Denmark, with father murdered, mother lost to shame, and himself urged, by his father's ghost, to revenge, did nothing. "Bloody, bawdy villain!" he cried out, as his uncle's smiling face forced itself before his mind's eye. "Remorseless, treacherous, lecherous, kindless villain!" He stormed and waved his arms, even as the player had done; then shook his head. Ranting words were not to the purpose. Better think carefully of the speech he would write for tomorrow night's play. He nodded grimly. It was in his mind that the speech and the play together would represent, as nearly as was possible, the exact circumstance of his father's murder. His uncle, watching it, could not fail to be struck to the soul, and betray his guilt to the world. That is, if he *was* guilty. Hamlet frowned. Though the ghost's accusation had been, at the time, terrible in its certainty, now, in the light of a later day, it seemed remote, doubtful, and even fantastic. "I'll have grounds more relative than this," decided the undecided Prince. "The play's the thing, wherein I'll catch the conscience of the King!"

Ophelia, in her best and most delicate attire, sweetly perfumed and with sufficient red in her cheeks to sharpen her natural modesty, waited meekly while her father, closely huddled with the King and Queen, and Rosencrantz and Guildenstern, murmured about the Lord Hamlet. They were gathered in the lobby where, daily, Hamlet walked; and where she, as her father had expressed it, was to be loosed to the Prince. Presently the two young men took their bowing departures, and the Queen, after speaking kindly to Ophelia, also went away.

"Ophelia, walk you here," said her father, taking her firmly by the arm and examining her critically as if to see if anything further might be done by way of improvement. He was anxious to be proven right in his judgement that the Prince's madness had been brought on by love for his daughter. He pressed a book into her hands and bade her read it so that her solitary walking should seem plausible. Then he and the King secreted themselves in a curtained alcove that might have been expressly made to hide such a King and such an adviser. The girl looked unhappily towards the curtain. Angrily Polonius gestured her away. The Prince was approaching. Ophelia, divided between obedience to her father, and shame for the part she had been told to play, opened her book, and shrank into the furthest obscurity she could find.

The Prince also was reading; but there was a deeper likeness between Hamlet and Ophelia than such outward show. Each had been commanded by a father, one living, one dead, to play a part for which nature had not fashioned them: Ophelia for deceit, and Hamlet for murderous revenge. In order to overcome his nature and keep his anger hot, he had returned to the book in which he had so fiercely scored his fury while the ghost's words still sounded in his ears and tore at his heart. But no such tempest tossed him now.

"To be, or not to be, that is the question:" he mused; for he had, in turning the pages, come upon the notes he had made of a great debate at Wittenberg, in which the old question had been closely argued, of whether it was better to live or to die. The arguments were strong upon both sides. Indeed, for a time, it seemed that he who argued for death had the stronger case, as he piled up, in a grim edifice, all the agonies of living that might, by the single stroke of death, be utterly demolished. And yet, as his opponent shrewdly pointed out, the death-lover, in spite of all his excellent reasons, still lived. Why did he shrink from the one act that would, by his own admission end his sufferings? The answer, as Hamlet gave it murmured utterance, was as sombre as the question. "The dread of something after death, the undiscovered country, from whose bourn no traveller returns, puzzles the will, and makes us rather bear those ills we have than fly to others that we know not of."

He shut the book and helplessly considered how closely the swaying of the argument reflected the swaying of his mind. He longed for death, which would have absolved him from the hideous duty that had been laid upon him; but he dared not rush into it. Self-murder was as repugnant to him as the murder of another. "Thus consicence doth make cowards of us all," he sighed bitterly, "and thus the native hue of resolution is sicklied o'er with the pale cast of thought . . ."

A flicker of silk and the movement of a pale hand caught the corner of his eye. He looked round and saw Ophelia. Gently she greeted him. Gently he responded. Timidly she approached him and held out a little box of trinkets he had given her. She wanted to return them. He denied all knowledge of them. Bewildered, she protested; and then came out with such a sentiment as might well have been stitched on one of her samplers: "For to the noble mind rich gifts wax poor when givers prove unkind."

Hamlet laughed, somewhat harshly. He did indeed love Ophelia, but for her dear soul and not for her unformed mind. In her stiff words he smelt out the instruction of her pompous meddling father; and he became very angry. Even she, even the lovely, simple Ophelia, was being poisoned by the general poison of the court. Savagely he turned upon her and lacerated her with the insensate fury of his tongue—even though he knew full well that no fault attached to her. But he knew that whatever he said would pass directly to her father, who was an ever-open channel to the King.

"I did love you once," he said abruptly.

"Indeed, my lord, you made me believe so," faltered the girl.

"You should not have believed me," dismissed the Prince, hiding his pain under contempt. "I loved you not."

"I was the more deceived," whispered Ophelia, not knowing whether she was on her head or heels.

"Get thee to a nunnery!" shouted Hamlet wildly. Yet at the same time, he ached with pity and remorse for the frightened girl. But Ophelia could never walk the bloody path of revenge to which he was condemned. He wished only for her to escape from the foul corruption of Elsinore. "Where's your father?" he demanded suddenly.

"At home, my lord," lied Ophelia, horribly confused. And yet it was no lie she told, for Polonius's home was wherever he might hide and overhear. Nonetheless she grew pale, fearing that Hamlet had spied her father spying.

"I have heard of your paintings well enough," jeered Hamlet, seeing false colour, like treacherous flags, thrown up in her vacant cheeks. "God hath given you one face and you make yourselves another . . . Go to, I'll no more on't, it hath made me mad. I say we will have no more marriage. Those that are married already—all but one—shall live. The rest shall keep as they are. To a nunnery, go!"

With that, the mad Prince fled, leaving the girl he loved amazed and weeping on her knees. A moment later, the King and Polonius crept out of their concealment.

"Love?" said the King, his broad face bereft of smiles. "His affections do not that way tend, nor what he spake, though it lacked form a little, was not like madness. There's something in his soul . . ."

Polonius agreed, for he was not the man to disagree with his king; but he still maintained that neglected love had been the cause. "How, now, Ophelia?" he said impatiently, as his daughter's sobbing distracted him. "You need not tell us what Lord Hamlet said, we heard it all." Then, continuing to the King, proposed that the Queen might be better able to worm out her son's secret. If such a circumstance could be arranged, he, Polonius, (needless to say), would be concealed and hear all.

"It shall be so," nodded the King. "Madness in great ones must not unwatched go."

Hamlet, his face pale and his eyes glittering with excitement, waited in the great hall where the play was to be performed. Horatio was with him. Horatio knew all. Together they were to watch the King to see if he betrayed his guilt as the play unfolded the crime.

"They are coming to the play!" cried Hamlet, as the customary trumpets and drums sounded the approach of the King. "I must be idle. Get you a place!"

There was a buzzing and murmuring and laughing, and rustling and shuffling, as the King and Queen and courtly audience came in and flowed, like a silken sea, over the gilded chairs and stools and cushions that had been made ready.

"Come hither, my dear Hamlet," invited the Queen, a treasure store of pearls and diamonds and brilliant smiles, "sit by me."

Curtly the Prince declined. He took his place by Ophelia, whose brightest jewels were her eyes. But his preference seemed more spiteful than fond. He taunted her with lewd remarks that made her blush with misery, until the players' trumpet sounded the beginning of the play. The audience grew quiet, leaned forward, and misted over into a single monster of many mouths and eyes. All watched the stage—save Hamlet and Horatio, who watched the King.

At first, there was a dumb show. Gaudy painted figures stalked stiffly to and fro, and enacted, wordlessly, what might, or might not have been, the tale of a royal poisoning. The Player King grimaced, clutched air, and perished in dire agony. The King of Denmark's smile seemed nailed to his face. The dumb show ended to applause like a thin shower of hail. The dead king revived, bowed, and begged all to attend to what should follow.

"Is this a prologue, or the posy of a ring?" demanded Hamlet, consumed with impatience.

"'Tis brief, my lord," murmured Ophelia.

"As woman's love," said Hamlet, with a sharp, accusing look at the Queen.

Now the play began in earnest; and, though the king wore a tinsel crown, and the queen was no better than a padded boy, they spoke their love so eloquently that the Queen of Denmark sighed. But the King of Denmark's smile still seemed nailed to his face.

"Madam how like you this play?" asked Hamlet.

"Have you heard the argument?" demanded the King. "Is there no offence in't?"

"No, no, they do but jest—poison in jest. No offence i' the world."

"What do you call the play?"

"The Mousetrap."

The play continued. The Player King lay sleeping on the boards. A murderer entered. "Thoughts black, hands apt, drugs fit, and time agreeing," he hissed; and crept towards the sleeper with black cloak trailing, like some malignant bat. He drew out a phial, unstoppered it and, with horrid smile, poured its deadly contents into his victim's ear. The King of Denmark's smile was gone!

"A poisons him i' the garden for his estate!" cried Hamlet, unable to contain his fierce joy. "The story is extant and written in very choice Italian. You shall see anon how the murderer gets the love of Gonzago's wife—"

The King of Denmark stood up. His eyes were blazing with anger. His face was grey with guilt.

"Give o'er the play!" cried Polonius, urgently.

"Give me some light!" shouted the enraged King. "Away!"

The play was cut off, ended before its ending. The audience had gone. Tumbled stools and chairs bore testimony to the haste of the departure. The bewildered Player King crept back to recover his tinsel crown. Then he went away, sadly shaking his head. The performance had not gone well.

But to Hamlet and Horatio the play had succeeded beyond all expectation. The King was guilty; the ghost had been honest. A furious excitement filled the Prince. He had at last set events into motion. Action had begun! His mood found expression in wild laughter and wild words, as if he had drunk strong wine. Rosencrantz and Guildenstern, pale with uneasiness, came to tell him that the King's rage had worsened. Hamlet was not distressed. The Queen, also, was much agitated.

"She desires to speak with you in her closet before you go to bed," said Rosencrantz, reproachfully.

"We shall obey," announced Hamlet, "were she ten times our mother."

Now came Polonius, limp with concern, and with the self-same message from the Queen. She would speak with her son.

The King was with Rosencrantz and Guildenstern. Breathing heavily, for his anger had by no means subsided, he confided that he thought it dangerous for the Queen's mad son to remain in court. God knew what he might do next. He must be sent away. Rosencrantz and Guildenstern, being the Prince's trusted friends (the trusted friends bowed), must accompany him to England. And without delay. No sooner had the two pupil-spies left the King, than the master-spy joined him. Polonius. His news was that Hamlet, even now, was on his way to his mother. He, Polonius, would hide and overhear whatever passed between them. The old eavesdropper hastened away, and the King, from force of habit, smiled. But it was a smile that died almost as soon as it had been born.

"O my offence is rank," he cried out in wretchedness. "It smells to heaven."

The play, with its presentation of the murder, had opened up his soul and exposed the breeding poison in it. He had murdered his brother and stolen his brother's wife. He was in agony for what he had done; and a double agony, for, though he bitterly repented his deed, he could not repent the possession of the gains it had brought him. "Help, angels!" he groaned, and knelt to pray forgiveness from God.

So deeply was he lost in his despairing plea to heaven that he never heard the soft footfall behind him, nor the sharp indrawn breath. Hamlet stood behind him, with sword upraised. He had, in passing, glimpsed the kneeling King. At once the rich, broad back invited him to the hideous duty he knew he must perform. He hesitated.

"Now might I do it," he breathed. The sword remained unmoving. The man was praying. To kill him now would send his soul to heaven. Better wait for a worse time; then he would go to hell. Silently the Prince withdrew and went upon his way.

"My words fly up," sighed the King, rising to his feet, "my thoughts remain below. Words without thoughts never to heaven go."

Hamlet, in obedience to her wishes, came to the Queen, his mother. His mood was black with self-contempt. He had failed. Revenge had been within his grasp, and his sword had stuck in the air. It had not been because the King was at his prayers that the avenger had spared him, but because the avenger was not, by nature, an avenger. As always, thought had come between Hamlet and the deed. The consequences, like the long shadow of action, ever cooled him as he drew close. Action must needs be hot . . .

The Queen was in her bedchamber. Her hair was loose and streaked with silver, as if she had been too long in the moon. Beside her yawned the royal bed, gorged with kissing pillows and silken sheets.

"Now, mother, what's the matter?" demanded Hamlet harshly, as the rage against himself turned against the hateful scene before him.

Sharply, she reproached him. More sharply he reproached her.

"Come, come, you answer with an idle tongue," cried the Queen, with the authority of an outraged mother.

"Go, go, you question with a wicked tongue," returned Hamlet, with the authority of an outraged son. His words grew savage, violent; his look was wild, his sword was in his hand. Alarm seized the Queen. She tried to leave. Hamlet gripped her arm and forced her to sit upon the bed.

"What wilt thou do?" she shrieked in terror. "Thou wilt not murder me? Help, ho!"

"What ho! Help!" A voice, shrill with alarm, cried out from behind a curtain.

"A rat!" shouted Hamlet, whirling round in amazed fury. "Dead for a ducat, dead!"

He plunged his sword deep into the curtain. He felt it enter more than cloth and air. He heard the sighing cry of a life escaping!

"What hast thou done?" cried out the Queen in dread.

"Nay, I know not," whispered Hamlet, staring at his dripping blade. He trembled with excitement. "Is it the King?"

He drew back the curtain. Polonius glared up at him. He had killed the eavesdropping old man. Action, at last performed, had mocked him. His heart ached with horror and pity. "Thou wretched, rash, intruding fool," he mourned, "farewell. I took thee for thy better." He let fall the curtain and turned to his white-faced mother. "Peace, sit you down," he muttered, "and let me wring your heart."

She sank back upon the bed and tried, unavailingly, to shut her ears against such words as no son in all the world had ever stabbed a mother with. Tears made rivers in her cheeks and drowned her pearls as Hamlet

He plunged his sword deep into the curtain

pitilessly laid bare his mother's easy lust and the shameless corruption of her bed. Her husband-lover—

"A murderer and a villain!" accused Hamlet.

"No more," wept the Queen.

"A king of shreds and patches—"

Suddenly he fell silent. His looks altered and he seemed to stare into vacancy. He uttered words that made no sense.

"Alas, he's mad," breathed the Queen. She sat, not daring to move, till her son's fit should be over.

It was no madness that had suddenly stopped his tongue and engrossed his looks. The ghost had returned! The dead King's hopeless eyes dwelt forlornly on the bed, then fixed themselves upon the Prince.

"Do not forget," uttered the spirit. "This visitation is but to whet thy almost blunted purpose." Its bleak, unhappy gaze turned upon the trembling Queen. "Speak to her, Hamlet," pleaded the dead King, as an aching memory of fondness stirred the ashes of his heart. Hamlet obeyed.

"How is it with you, lady?"

"Alas, how is't with you?" asked the Queen, who saw no ghost but only her mad son transfixed. "Whereon do you look?"

"On him, on him," cried Hamlet, pointing to his father and striving, with all his might, with all precise detail and exact picture, to make his mother see the figure by the bed. But all she saw were the bed's hangings, and Hamlet, mad.

"Why, look you there," cried the Prince, "look how it steals away. My father in his habit as he lived! Look where he goes even now out at the portal!" But she saw neither the ghost's coming, nor the ghost's going. It had not appeared to remind her of forgotten love, but to remind Hamlet of neglected revenge.

The scene had been strange and terrible and the King, had he heard of it, would have been filled with dread. But the quiet spy behind the curtain had overheard with an unrecording ear.

"This counsellor is now most still, most secret, and most grave," said Hamlet, as he dragged the dead Polonius from the room, "who was in life a foolish prating knave . . . Goodnight, mother."

He had hidden the body and would not confess where. It seemed he mocked his own bloody act by hiding the spy who could no more hide himself. Concealment had brought about Polonius's death; now death brought about his concealment. To all urgent questioning the Prince replied in a vein that was tragical-comical.

"Now, Hamlet, where's Polonius?"

"At supper."

"At supper? Where?"

"Not where he eats, but where a's eaten."

But soon the body was found and taken to the chapel. And, that very night, the mad and dangerous Prince was dispatched to England, in the close care of his good friends, Rosencrantz and Guildenstern. Dearly would the King have liked to dispatch him to join Polonius, but he dared not. The Queen's love for her son and the people's love for their Prince stood in his way. But England would serve his darker purpose. He entrusted, to Rosencrantz and Guildenstern, a sealed letter for the English King. In it he required that Hamlet should directly be put to death.

Ophelia begged to see the Queen. But the Queen was reluctant. Her soul was too burdened with her own griefs to endure the sight of Ophelia's. Nonetheless she was prevailed upon to see the girl, so Ophelia entered.

She wore, as was proper for her visit, her best and most delicate attire; but had buttoned it all awry, as if she knew she ought to be modest but could not recollect how. She had painted her cheeks, but one less skilfully than the other. Her hair was down and still wild from sleep for, although she had remembered to dress everything else, she had forgotten her head. Which was not to be wondered at: the murder of her father by her one-time lover had quite blown out the candle of her mind. She smiled absurdly at the Queen, and then began to sing. But there was more madness in her music than music in her madness, for she kept neither tune nor time. The songs she sang were lewd fragments and snatches that came weirdly from her lips. God knew what they meant to her, or where she'd gathered them, or for how long her modesty had kept them folded, like bride-gowns, at the bottom of her mind.

The King came in and, together with the Queen, looked on dismayed. "O Gertrude, Gertrude," he sighed to his wife, when the girl, with a dozen or more "Goodnights", had drifted meaninglessly away, "when sorrows come, they come not single spies, but in battalions . . ."

Laertes, the mad girl's brother and son of the murdered man, had returned from France and, even now, was in the city where rumour and discontent were inflaming his already unsteady nature. Bitterly the Queen began to reproach the unthinking insolence of the common people, when the sound of a furious commotion was heard. Doors splintered, steel clashed, and voices shouted. A moment after, Laertes, with sword drawn and some half-dozen wild-looking fellows at his heels, burst in. He glared about, saw the King, and bade his followers leave him and guard the door.

"O thou vile King!" he accused. "Give me my father!"

The Queen tried to hold him back.

"Let him go, Gertrude," said the King calmly. "Do not fear our person. There's such divinity doth hedge a king, that treason can but peep to what it would . . ."

195

Laertes faltered. Royalty awed him, and so did the thought of the King's Swiss guards. He took his advantage where it lay, and grew peaceable. Then Ophelia came back. As if reminded of a childish duty neglected, she had returned with a gift of flowers. She had gathered them from somewhere wild, for her gown was stained and torn and her white arms scratched. She smiled at her brother as if he was a stranger.

"O heavens," wept the young man, seeing the ruins of his sister, "is't possible a young maid's wits should be as mortal as an old man's life?"

She began to sing, no lewd fragments now, but the mournful ditty of a burying. Then she gave away her flowers, telling the proper virtue of each as she gave them to her brother, to the King, and to the Queen . . .

"There's rue for you. And here's some for me. We may call it herb of grace a Sundays. You must wear your rue with a difference," she said to the Queen, with an eerie cunning smile. She returned to singing, and presently, with a quick, "God be wi' you!" fled from the room.

The King, with cautious sympathy and enclosing arm, led the distressed brother aside, and promised to tell him how the tragedies had come about, and who had been to blame: not him—not him . . .

Two sailors, rough and slanting, with cutlasses wide enough to divide a man, brought a letter to Horatio, who had remained in Elsinore, and waited while he read it. The letter was from Hamlet. He was in Denmark. The vessel on which he'd sailed had been pursued by pirates. The ships had briefly grappled. Hamlet had boarded the pirate and been taken prisoner. His own ship had escaped and continued on to England. Since then he had come to terms with his captors. They were good fellows and would bring Horatio to where Hamlet now waited. Also, they had letters for the King.

At once, Horatio went with one of the sailors to meet with Hamlet, while the other took his letters to the King.

The King was still with Laertes. He had told the young man how Hamlet had murdered Polonius and had become dangerous to the throne itself. Laertes listened, and wondered why the King had done nothing against the murderer.

"Break not your sleeps for that," murmured the King, smiling his old smile that slipped round his lips like oil. "You shortly shall hear more . . ."

It was then that he was given the sailor's letter. Hastily he read it. Rage and amazement filled him. Hamlet was returned. Hamlet who should, by all the King's shrewd scheming, have been dead in England, was once more in Denmark. Tomorrow he would be coming to the court.

"Let him come!" begged Laertes, wild with hatred for his father's killer and longing only to destroy him. The King, desiring Hamlet's death no less, paced to and fro, brooding upon some means whereby this might be brought about, a means by which no blame should be laid at any door and even the Queen should think it an accident. His Queen was always in the front of his thoughts. His love for her was almost a sickness, equal with his guilt. He paused in his pacing, and beckoned Laertes to his side.

"What would you undertake," he asked softly, "to show yourself in deed your father's son more than in words?"

"To cut his throat i' the church!" came the prompt reply.

The King shook his head. The scheme he had in mind was different. Hamlet, who delighted in swordplay, was to be tempted into a fencing match with Laertes. One of the weapons would be unbated and needle-sharp. With this, Laertes might, as if by unlucky chance, kill his man. As he confided the scheme, the King watched the young man shrewdly, to see if so mean and dishonourable a proposal repelled him. But Laertes was Polonius's son, and guile and concealment were in his blood. He entered into the scheme with all his heart, and gilded its cunning with some of his own. He had brought back from France a deadly poison, and with this he'd anoint his sword. It was a poison for which there was no remedy, and the merest scratch would procure Hamlet's certain death. The King smiled. Poison was the means whereby he had gained his Queen and crown; it was fitting that poison should be the means whereby he secured them. It must be by poison. Therefore, if Laertes failed to wound the Prince, a poisoned cup should be awaiting Hamlet when he paused to quench his thirst.

So Hamlet's death was encompassed; but even as it was nodded upon, there came news of another, lesser death. The weeping Queen came in to tell that Ophelia had been drowned. Frail mad Ophelia was dead. The news brought forth no wild excess of grief; but was received with quietness, as if this was calamity's fragile herald, sent in advance of its huge self.

A gravedigger was singing at his work. A jovial soul: the deeper he dug, the higher rose his spirits, and his song flew up in snatches, together with flying clods of earth. Hamlet and Horatio, on their way from the seashore to the castle, drew near; and the gravedigger, finding he had attracted a noble audience, paused, beamed, and wiped his brow. Amused by such good cheer among the bones, Hamlet fell into talk with the man; and Horatio could not but smile to see how his friend readily forgot his griefs and troubles in the pleasure of argument and debate, for the scholar-prince got as good as he gave. The gravedigger, by toiling so long among the grinners, had come by a shrewd and bony wit.
"What man dost thou dig it for?"
"For no man, sir."
"What woman, then?"
"For none neither."
"Who is to be buried in't?"
"One that was a woman, sir; but rest her soul, she's dead."
Presently he threw up a skull. Whose was it? Why, it was the old King's jester, Yorick . . .
"This?" murmured Hamlet, taking the skull in his hands and gazing at it, so that his sad smile was answered by its sightless grin.
"E'n that," said the gravedigger.
"Alas, poor Yorick," sighed the Prince. "I knew him, Horatio . . ." As Hamlet mused, the gravedigger continued with his work, for the grave's tenant was approaching to take possession of the premises. A sombre procession moved towards the grave, with a coffin borne on a swaying tide of black. The King and Queen were among the mourners: plainly the burial was for one of high estate. Hamlet and Horatio drew back, to observe the scene from a distance. The coffin was lowered into the earth, but the priest intoned no prayer; for the death had been doubtful. Suddenly, from among the mourners, Laertes stepped for-

ward; and Hamlet saw that the grave he had laughed over had been made for Ophelia. He cried out in anguish; but his cry was quite lost in the shouted grief of Laertes, whose words and feelings were as extravagant as his attire. His black was a whole night to Hamlet's little corner of dark; his grieving was a tempest to Hamlet's aching sighs. Frantically he leaped down into the grave to catch up his sister for one last embrace; and Hamlet, enraged that Ophelia, whom he had loved, should be used as a property for such gaudy grief, rushed forward to grapple with Laertes in the grave. Fiercely they fought until they were dragged apart. Then Hamlet, much ashamed, retired with Horatio; and the burial of Ophelia was concluded.

"Strengthen your patience," murmured the King to Laertes, and reminded him that revenge would soon be his.

"So Guildenstern and Rosencrantz go to't," murmured Horatio. He and Hamlet were alone in the great hall of the castle; and Hamlet had told him how, on the ship bound for England, he had found, in the cabin of his two good schoolfriends, a sealed letter to be given to the English king. He had opened it and read therein his own death warrant. So he had, most skilfully, exchanged for another in which he had put forward Rosencrantz and Guildenstern in place of himself. Thus those two gentlemen had sailed on to England bearing with them, not Hamlet's, but their own deaths.

"Why, man, they did make love to this employment! They are not near my conscience," cried Hamlet, as if to defend himself against the sad regret he sensed in Horatio's words. Regret there certainly had been, not for Rosencrantz and Guildenstern, but for Hamlet himself. His was the tragedy, not theirs. Sadly Horatio gazed at the brilliant, lively and noble young Prince who had been dragged back into an ancient, corrupt world of poison, murder and revenge.

As they talked, there was a gust of perfume, a rustle of satins, and a courtier came into the hall. He was a delicate gentleman with a feathered bonnet and butterfly hands. He talked very roundabout, and with so many bows that his listeners marvelled at his flexibility. His message, when at last it was unravelled, was from the King, and was amiable enough. Having heard that, of late, Laertes had won a great reputation for fencing, and knowing Hamlet's fondness for the sport, the King had laid a wager on the outcome of a match between them—that is, if the Lord Hamlet was agreeable to trying his skill against Laertes. Thus appealed to, Hamlet could not refuse. He was proud of his skill as a swordsman and always eager for a chance to show it off.

"Sir, I will walk here in the hall," he informed the courtier. "Let the foils be brought, the gentleman willing, and the King hold his purpose, I will win for him and I can; if not, I will gain nothing but my shame and the odd hits."

When the courtier had departed, Hamlet frowned and shook his head. He knew not why, but a strange uneasiness had seized him.

"If your mind dislike anything, obey it," said Horatio anxiously. "I will forestall their repair hither and say you are not fit."

Hamlet smiled and shook his head. "We defy augury," he said. "There is special providence in the fall of a sparrow. If it be now, 'tis not to come; if it be not to come, it will be now; if it be not now, yet it will come. The readiness is all . . ."

Trumpets announced the approach of the King. The courtier had delivered his message promptly. The King and Queen entered the hall attended by all the court. Two servants carried a table, and a lord bore a bouquet of swords, like a bridesman of Death.

All was smiles and good humour, as if Hamlet's madness had never been. "Come, Hamlet, come," urged the affable King; and he drew the Prince and Laertes together so that they might clasp hands and seal their friendship in forgiveness.

"Give me your pardon, sir," said Hamlet warmly, for there was no enmity in his heart for Laertes. "I have done you wrong."

Laertes responded with equal generosity, and the King's smile broadened. The swords were offered. Laertes, being the quicker, chose first. "This is too heavy," he said with a frown, flourishing the weapon he had drawn. "Let me see another." Plainly he was a most fastidious swordsman. At length he found a blade to his satisfaction. The swords were offered to Hamlet, who cheerfully took the first that came. The two young men saluted each other in steel, and awaited the King's word for the bout to begin.

The King called for wine so that he might drink Hamlet's health should he win. The cups were filled and set upon the table. The King, with a royal gesture, held out a splendid pearl. If Laertes should be defeated, the pearl would be cast into Hamlet's cup of wine. The court murmured, and applauded the magnificence of the prize.

"Come, begin!" exclaimed the King. "And you, the judges, bear a wary eye."

Swords touched, and the judges, two dancing, skipping, hopping courtiers, followed the weaving blades. The fencers, both in black, for

each mourned a murdered father, circled one another, made swift lunges, darted back, lunged again, parried, thrust, riposted—

"One!" cried Hamlet, triumphantly.

"No!" cried Laertes.

The judges were appealed to, and declared: "A hit, a very palpable hit."

"Well, again!" demanded Laertes.

"Stay," ordered the King. "Give me drink. Hamlet, this pearl is thine." He cast it into Hamlet's cup, and offered it to the Prince. But Hamlet would not drink. He would try another bout first. He and Laertes fenced again; and again Hamlet scored a hit.

"Our son shall win," said the King. The Queen smiled proudly, and offered her son her napkin to wipe his sweating brow.

"The Queen carouses to thy fortune, Hamlet," she said, and took a cup of wine.

"Gertrude, do not drink!" muttered the King, his face grey with horror.

"I will, my lord," said she. "I pray you pardon me."

The cup she held was Hamlet's cup. She drank the poison that had been laid for her son.

"My lord, I'll hit him now!" whispered Laertes to the King.

"I do not think it," said the King, whose eyes were upon his poisoned Queen, and whose whole world was beginning to crack and crumble about him.

"Have at you now!" shouted Laertes, seeing Hamlet unprepared. He thrust at him, and caught him on the wrist. Hamlet looked down amazed. He was bleeding. Laertes' sword had been unbated! He looked up at Laertes and saw guilt and hatred in his eyes. Bewilderment, then fury seized him. Though he never knew it, he had been fighting for his life. Savagely he flung himself upon Laertes, and beat the weapon from his hand. He picked it up, and contemptuously flung Laertes his own. They fought again: Laertes in terror, and Hamlet with all the skill at his command.

"Part them," cried out the King, "they are incensed!"

"Nay, come again!" shouted Hamlet, and, with a sudden thrust, pierced Laertes through.

Now the poison was spread, the poison that had, so long, rotted away the castle of Elsinore; and it was a poison, like the venom Laertes had brought back, for which there was no remedy. The Queen, the easy, lustful Queen, felt agony seize her. She cried out: "The drink, the drink! O my dear Hamlet! The drink, the drink! I am poisoned!" She fell back, and with lifeless eyes stared at her son.

"Let the door be locked!" shouted Hamlet. "Treachery! Seek it out!"

"It is here, Hamlet," sighed Laertes, bleeding from his wound, and dying from the venom of his own blade. "Hamlet, thou art slain. No medicine in the world can do thee good; in thee there is not half an hour's life . . ." So Laertes, while there was still breath in him, confessed his treachery, and pointed to the one whose crime, like Cain's, had brought about so many deaths. "The King—the King's to blame."

There was no delaying now, no breathing time for thought. With a terrible cry, Hamlet rushed upon the King and stabbed him with his sword. But, like a serpent, the King would not die.

"Here, thou incestuous, murderous, damned Dane, drink off this potion!" the avenger cried and forced the poisoned cup between the King's unresisting lips, and made him drink. "Follow my mother!"

"He is justly served," breathed Laertes; and with the last of his life, begged forgiveness of Hamlet for what he had done. Like Hamlet, he had avenged his father; and, like Hamlet, he died for it.

"I follow thee," murmured Hamlet, over the young man who now lay quiet and still. "I am dead, Horatio," he whispered to his friend who had come forward to support him. He trembled as a chill began to invade him. Then he smiled ruefully. "This fell sergeant, Death, is strict in his arrest . . ."

There came a sound of martial music and gunfire from outside the castle walls. A messenger entered, to tell that Fortinbras, the victorious Prince of Norway, was approaching. With a last effort, Hamlet roused himself. He was a Prince, and his concerns were now with the state, good order, and the well-being of his people. "The election lights on Fortinbras. He has my dying voice," decreed the Prince. Then, all strength spent, he fell back in Horatio's arms. "The rest is silence," he sighed.

Through veils and veils of tears, Horatio gazed down upon the quiet countenance that rested against his arm. "Good night, sweet Prince, and flights of angels sing thee to thy rest."

It was thus that Fortinbras found them, the dead and those who still lived, in the great hall of the castle of Elsinore.

"Let four captains bear Hamlet like a soldier to the stage," said Fortinbras, when he had heard Hamlet's story, "for he was likely, had he been put on, to have proved most royal . . ." The captains lifted up the dead Prince and carried him away. "Go, bid the soldiers shoot," commanded Fortinbras; and solemn gunfire roared in honour of the Prince of Denmark.

Romeo and Juliet

In old Verona, where the streets were hot and narrow and the walls were high, where men were as bright as wasps and carried quick swords for their stings, there lived two families—the Capulets and the Montagues—who hated each other worse than death. They had but to pass in the street and they were at each other's throats like dogs in the sun. Cursing and shouting and bawling, and crashing from civil pillar to post, they filled the good people of Verona with fear and anger to have their city's peace so senselessly disturbed.

They were at it again! In the buzzing heat of a July morning, two lazy no-good servants of the Capulets had spied two strolling men of the Montagues. Looks had been exchanged, then words, and in moments the peaceful market was in an uproar as the four idle ruffians set about defending their masters' honour by smashing up stalls, overturning baskets, wrecking shops and wounding passers-by, in their valiant endeavours to cut each other into pieces.

Benvolio, a sensible young Montague, came upon the scene and tried to put a stop to it; Tybalt, a young Capulet so full of fury that he sweated knives, promptly went for Benvolio; old Montague and old Capulet appeared and tried to draw their doddering swords—that surely would have shaken more like straws in the wind than lightning in the sky. Men

205

shouted, women screamed and rushed to drag wandering infants into safety . . . and bloody riot threatened to swallow up all the fair city, till the Prince of Verona, with soldiers, came furiously into the square.

"Rebellious subjects, enemies to peace!" he roared; and, by dint of stern anger and sterner threats, restored some semblance of peace. The vile destructive brawling between the Montagues and the Capulets incensed him beyond measure.

"If ever you disturb our streets again," he swore, "your lives shall pay the forfeit."

When the Prince had gone, taking old Capulet with him, (to remove one half of the quarrel and so leave the other without an object), Lady Montague spoke to Benvolio.

"O where is Romeo, saw you him today?" she asked. "Right glad I am he was not at this fray," she added, as if Romeo, her only son, was as hot-headed as any and would surely have come to grief among the flashing swords and blundering fists. But Romeo had been elsewhere, wrapped in a melancholy that was most mysterious to his parents.

"See where he comes!" exclaimed Benvolio, as the young man in question drifted dolefully into the square, as if he was a ghost under instruction to haunt it. "So please you step aside," he urged old Montague and his wife, "I'll know his grievance . . ."

The parents departed, leaving Benvolio to penetrate the inscrutable mystery of his cousin Romeo's gloom. It proved no great task, as Romeo was all too willing to talk. He was in love. Hopelessly. He doted to distraction upon a glorious creature by the name of Rosalyne; and she would have nothing to do with him. So far as she was concerned, he was dust. Consequently he had been mooning all morning, lovesick, in a grove of sycamores.

Patiently Benvolio listened to the extensive catalogue of Rosalyne's amazing charms. He shook his head, and ventured to suggest that, if only Romeo looked about him, he might find others as fair. Impossible! The world was not so rich as to hold another such as Rosalyne. Benvolio expressed doubts, but Romeo was adamant; and so they continued, strolling through the golden warm streets of Verona, Romeo all melancholy passion and Benvolio all cheerful good sense.

"Why, Romeo, art thou mad?" began Benvolio when a servingman, much bewildered and with a paper in his hand, accosted them.

"I pray, sir, can you read?"

It seemed the fellow's master had entrusted him with a list of guests to be invited to a banquet that night. But, being no scholar, he could make neither head nor tail of the writing. Obligingly Romeo read out the names. They were a distinguished company—and among them was Rosalyne!

Where was the feast to be? Alas! at the house of old Capulet. A dangerous place for a Montague. But, if he went masked and in fantastical costume, as was the custom for uninvited guests at such a feast . . .

"Go thither," urged Benvolio, anxious to cure his cousin of that sickness called Rosalyne. He had noticed that on the list had been the best beauties of Verona, beside whom Rosalyne might well not shine so bright. "Compare her face," he advised shrewdly, "with some that I shall show; and I will make thee think thy swan a crow."

They met that night in the street outside the Capulet's house: Romeo, Benvolio and Mercutio, who was a kinsman of the Prince and Romeo's dearest friend. He was a lively, mocking youth, as full of bubbling

laughter as a glass of good wine. They met by torchlight with some half dozen others, all in fantastical costume and gilded masks—as if King Midas had patted their heads and made fortunes of their faces.

Like gorgeous dragonflies, with partly folded wings, they leaned against the high wall that enclosed the Capulets' orchard, laughing and talking and trying, by all manner and means, to lift up Romeo's depressed spirits. But he, dressed as a rather splendid pilgrim, (in deference to the notion that any place that held Rosalyne must be a holy shrine), remained as dull as lead. Neither Benvolio's urging nor Mercutio's wit affected him. He stayed glum; and, furthermore, had had a strange premonition that the night's festivities would turn out to have been the beginning of a journey to the grave.

At length the maskers gave up their efforts and, with their gloomy companion, went into the feasting house. At once they were dazzled by a blaze of candles and a blaze of beauty . . . of silks and satins, soft white skin and dark, delighted eyes.

"You are welcome, gentlemen!" cried old Capulet, in holiday robes and cheerful to see so fine a company of maskers at his feast. "Come, musicians, play. A hall, a hall, give room! And foot it, girls!"

Music scraped and set a pulse, and the dancing began. Gowns rustled, filling the air with perfume; buckled shoes, like bright mice, twinkled in and out of richly swinging hems; fingers touched, hands entwined; masks and faces bobbed and turned, exchanging silver looks for golden smiles. All were dancing, but Romeo. He stood, marble pilgrim, stock-still and amazed! At last he spoke, to a servant standing by.

"What lady's that which doth enrich the hand of yonder knight?"

"I know not, sir," returned the servant.

"O she doth teach the torches to burn bright!" breathed Romeo, as he gazed at the girl whose beauty had, in an instant, overturned his heart. But though he had spoken softly, it had been too loud.

"This by his voice should be a Montague!"

Tybalt had recognized the masker! He was enraged that one of that hated name should dare to mock the Capulets' feast with his presence! He sent a page for his rapier.

His uncle, old Capulet, sharply bade him keep his temper. It was a

A light appeared in a window

night of feast and revelry, and not to be spoiled. He command Tybalt to leave Romeo in peace.

"I'll not endure him!" cried Tybalt furiously.

"He shall be endured!" ordered old Capulet, with mounting indignation. "I say he shall. Go to, am I the master here or you? Go to!"

Unable to contain his anger, Tybalt departed. There was vengeance in his heart. He vowed that he would call Romeo to account for the supposed insult to the Capulets.

Romeo, unaware of the sudden hatred directed against him, moved among the dancers towards his sudden love. At last he stood before her and his eyes, inside his golden eyes, shone with rapture. Her loveliness had increased a hundredfold with nearness. Startled, she looked at the pilgrim and, such was the warmth of his passion, that she took fire herself.

Their hands touched; they spoke, half-humorously, half-solemnly. He begged a kiss. She was too young to hide her heart, and too innocent to pretend an innocence. She granted the request. Then, like children for the first time having tasted strawberries, they wanted more. They kissed again . . .

"Madam, your mother craves a word with you."

The world outside broke in upon them, in the shape of a female with a billowing bosom and skirts that might have covered half a county. Reluctantly the girl parted from her passionate pilgrim, and went in answer to the summons.

"What is her mother?" asked Romeo, following her every movement till she was lost among the throng.

"Her mother is the lady of the house," answered the female complacently. "I nurs'd her daughter that you talked withal. I tell you," she confided, with a wink and a nudge and a knowing smile that creased up her face like a marriage bed, "he that can lay hold of her shall have the chinks."

She bustled away after her charge, leaving Romeo dismayed. He, the son of Montague, had fallen in love with the daughter of Capulet! Despairingly he cursed the night in which he had been so blessed, the night when Romeo first set eyes on Juliet.

The maskers left the house and met outside, by the orchard wall, meaning to make a night of it in Verona's hot dark streets. Romeo was not among them. They called him, searched for him, tried to conjure him up in the name of his fair Rosalyne and all her delicious parts. In vain. He did not appear; so they went away, laughing loudly at the foolish melancholy of love.

Romeo heard them go. "He jests at scars," he murmured, ruefully reflecting that, to him, love was falling among roses and being savaged by their thorns, "that never felt a wound."

He had climbed the high wall and was hiding in shadows within the Capulets' orchard. His situation was dangerous, but love lent a brightness to it, just as danger lent an edge to his love. He gazed up toward the dark side of the house. A light appeared in a window, before which there was a balcony, like a carved stone pocket some dozen feet from the ground. The window opened and on to the balcony stepped Juliet. She looked out on to the night, and sighed.

"O Romeo, Romeo, wherefore art thou Romeo?" she inquired most earnestly; and then, with gentle longing, urged: "Deny thy father and refuse thy name." She, like Romeo, had discovered that her greatest love was her father's greatest hate. She frowned and shook her head. "'Tis but thy name that is my enemy," she argued with ingenious philosophy. "What's in a name? That which we call a rose by any other name would smell as sweet; so Romeo would, were he not Romeo call'd . . ."

So she continued, putting her case before an audience of moon and stars, until Romeo came from among the shadows and stood beneath the balcony. At once she was alarmed; then, when she saw who it was, was fearful for his safety in her father's garden; then ashamed when she realised that he must have overheard her private confession of love.

Eagerly Romeo dismissed the danger and rejoiced in the confession which, by its frankness, had short cut all tedious custom of roundabout approach and, in the twinkling of an eye, had plunged them both fathoms deep into each other's hearts, as if they had lived there all their lives. Even so, she begged him to leave as she feared more and more for his safety.

"O wilt thou leave me so unsatisfied?" pleaded Romeo.

"What satisfaction canst thou have tonight?" she answered gently.

"Th' exchange of thy love's faithful vow for mine!" he cried.

A voice called from within the room. It was Juliet's Nurse. Hurriedly Juliet begged Romeo to wait and went inside. A moment later she was back on the balcony.

"Three words, dear Romeo," she whispered down; and then, scorning arithmetic, went on with many, many more. If Romeo was honourable, and his purpose marriage, she would send to him tomorrow so that he might tell her the time and place where the ceremony might be performed.

Again the Nurse called and again Juliet seemed plucked inside, as by an apron string; and again came back at once. More arrangements were made for the following day, and more love exchanged until, at last, there was no avoiding the parting.

"Good night, good night," sighed Juliet. "Parting is such sweet sorrow that I shall say good night till it be morrow."

She went back into her room. Romeo waited a little longer and then climbed back over the orchard wall. Rosalyne and all her charms had been swept from his mind and heart; and Juliet, too, had quite forgotten that she had been betrothed that very morning to a rich young man of her father's choice.

As soon as it was light, Romeo sought out his confessor, Friar Laurence, in a monastery some little way out of the town, and begged the worthy priest to marry him to Juliet that very day. At first the good Friar was too taken aback by the sudden setting of Rosalyne to comprehend the glorious sunrise of Juliet; but then, seeing the strength of Romeo's love, and knowing the honesty of his heart, and thinking that by such a union the hatred between the Montagues and the Capulets might be buried forever, he agreed to perform the ceremony. It was to take place in the holy Friar's cell on that afternoon. In high delight Romeo returned to the sunshine town to await Juliet's messenger.

While Romeo had been away from his house on his mission of love, Tybalt had called on a mission of hate. Not finding Romeo, he had left a letter, challenging the son of Montague to a duel to the death. This challenge had been found by Benvolio and Mercutio, who were still seeking their companion who had given them the slip on the previous night.

"Romeo will answer it," said Benvolio.

"Any man that can write may answer a letter," chuckled Mercutio; and the pair went their way through the bright streets, making fun of Tybalt and his fury.

Presently they met Romeo; but before they could tell him of the challenge, Juliet's Nurse, with skirts rolling and bosom billowing, came majestically down the street.

At once the three friends, overcome by the female's size and dignity, set about her like mad butterflies mocking an old cabbage. They twisted

her, turned her, upended her words and her wits till she shook with indignation in all her bulging parts. At last she managed to say that it was Romeo she looked for, and Romeo alone; so Mercutio and Benvolio went away, laughing their heads off—and clean forgot about Tybalt and his murderous letter.

As soon as they were alone, the Nurse begged Romeo to deal honestly with Juliet, who was very young. Romeo swore he would.

"Bid her devise," he pleaded with the Nurse, "some means to come to shrift this afternoon. And there she shall at Friar Laurence' cell be shriv'd and married!"

Gleefully the Nurse received the news. Although she knew that Juliet was already betrothed to another, the prospect of a marriage and a wedding night acted upon her like strong wine. After all, so long as there was a husband, it mattered little whether it was one man or another. Full of thoughts of the bounding joys of the marriage bed, she rushed away to tell her young mistress and to prepare her.

That very afternoon, in Friar Laurence's cell, Juliet and Romeo were married. Juliet became a Montague; and Romeo, in the same instant, became kin to all the Capulets. From the harsh soil of the two families' enmity, had sprung a single flower of love.

The day was hot and men's blood boiled in their veins. Tybalt, seeking a violent answer to his violent letter, came upon Romeo's two friends.

"Mercutio," he cried, with contempt in his voice and manner, "thou consortest with Romeo."

"Consort?" answered Mercutio angrily. "What, dost thou make us minstrels?"

Anxiously Benvolio tried to keep the peace that was so suddenly threatened. Romeo appeared. Tybalt turned aside from Mercutio.

"Well, peace be with you, sir," he said, "here comes my man." Coldly he insulted Romeo. Passers-by began to gather, but at a respectable distance; for surely there was going to be a fight. Tybalt challenged Romeo to draw his sword. Romeo refused. He had, within that hour, been married to Juliet and so was united with the house of Capulet. He would not, he could not shed any of their blood. But as the marriage was still secret, he was forced to hold his tongue.

"O calm, dishonourable, vile submission!" cried Mercutio, unable to understand Romeo's reluctance to fight. "Tybalt, you rat-catcher, will you walk?"

He drew his sword and, in a moment, he and mad Tybalt were thrusting and parrying and darting at each other with their shining deadly stings.

"Draw, Benvolio," cried Romeo, aghast. "Beat down their weapons. Gentlemen, for shame, forbear this outrage. Tybalt, Mercutio!"

He seized his friend, meaning to hold him back. Murderous Tybalt lunged; and his sword, like a thin snake, struck under Romeo's arm and pierced Mercutio's breast. Then he fled.

"I am hurt," muttered Mercutio, finding himself to be a sudden victim of the hatred between Capulet and Montague. "A plague o' both your houses."

"What, art thou hurt?" asked Benvolio, supporting Mercutio, who was sinking to the ground.

"Ay, ay, a scratch, a scratch . . ."

"Courage, man," urged Romeo, "the hurt cannot be much."

"No, 'tis not so deep as a well," agreed Mercutio, "nor so wide as a church door, but 'tis enough, 'twill serve. Ask for me tomorrow, and you shall find me a grave man. I am peppered, I warrant, for this world. A plague o' both your houses . . ."

He was carried into the nearest house and soon after, the news came out that Mercutio, brave, witty, laughing Mercutio, was dead. Even as Romeo stood, amazed and overcome with grief, and blaming himself for his friend's death, Tybalt returned.

This time Romeo did not refuse the challenge. He drew his sword, and, mad for revenge, beat down Tybalt's furious blade—which was

still red with Mercutio's blood—and killed him before he knew what he had done.

"Romeo!" cried Benvolio, terrified by the sudden disaster. "Away, be gone . . .! The Prince will doom thee death if thou art taken. Hence, be gone, away!"

Only then did Romeo understand. On the very day he had married, he had killed his new wife's kinsman and so condemned himself to death.

"O I am fortune's fool!" he wept, and rushed away; leaving Tybalt spidered on the ground and slowly reddening Verona's street.

He fled for sanctuary to Friar Laurence's cell and there, shaking and trembling, he learned that the Prince had been merciful. As the quarrel had been forced upon Romeo, the Prince had sentenced him to banishment instead of to death. He was to leave Verona and never set foot inside its walls again. Such was the Prince's mercy, but to Romeo it was worse than death. Not to see Juliet again was to condemn him to a living grave. The good Friar tried to reason with him, to teach him to make the best of the life that had been granted.

"Thou canst not speak of that thou dost not feel!" cried Romeo in despair. "Wert thou as young as I, Juliet thy love, an hour but married, Tybalt murdered, doting like me, and like me banished, then mightst thou speak . . ."

To this there was no answer; for who could know what Romeo felt but Romeo, and who could know that Juliet was his world? Had he been older, he might have been wiser . . . if indeed it's wisdom to be calculating in affection and circumspect in love.

There was a knock upon the door. It was the Nurse, come in haste from her mistress, who was in despair over the death of her dear cousin and the banishment of her husband. Romeo's remorse knew no bounds. He threatened to kill himself; but the holy Friar stayed his hand.

"Go," he advised the wildly grieving youth, "get thee to thy love as was decreed. Ascend her chamber—hence, and comfort her."

Hope revived as Romeo listened to the Friar's words. He would spend that night—his wedding night—in Juliet's arms; and early on the following day, he would go to Mantua where he would wait until his marriage might be made known and the Prince's pardon obtained. The Friar would send to him . . .

The orchard was dark, but the stars were pale. Presently a bird began to sing. The new husband and the new wife, sleepy from love, came out on to the balcony, which held them like another bed, a bed of stone.

"It is not yet near day," lied Juliet. "It was the nightingale and not the lark . . ."

Romeo shook his head. "It was the lark, the herald of the morn . . . Look, love . . . night's candles are burnt out."

"Yond light is not daylight," denied Juliet. "I know it . . ."

But it was to no avail. The night was over and the time for parting come.

"Farewell, farewell, one kiss and I'll descend," murmured Romeo. They embraced, and he slipped unwillingly from Juliet's despairing arms, and climbed down to the dark ground. He looked up and she, overhanging the balcony, with her willow hair weeping, stared down; and each, in that last moment, was chilled with a sudden foreboding and seemed to see the other pale and dead. Then Romeo was gone.

The Capulet's house was in sad confusion. Tybalt had been laid to rest and Juliet, supposedly grieving for her murdered cousin, was a ghost of sobs and tears. Old Capulet, ever impatient with the sorrows of the young—which, to him, were as trifling as the peevish mewing of a baby, to be quietened by a sweet or a new toy—spoke with his wife and the County Paris, the excellent and well-connected youth to whom he had betrothed his daughter.

"What day is this?" he demanded.

"Monday, my lord," said Paris.

"Monday! Ha ha! Well, Wednesday is too soon. A Thursday let it be, a Thursday, tell her," he instructed his wife, "she shall be married to this noble earl." He nodded with high satisfaction. A husband was the very thing to quieten his wailing child. "We'll have some half a dozen friends," he decided, "and there an end. But what say you to Thursday?"

The youth was in agreement and old Capulet was satisfied that the joyful tidings of such an occasion would put a stop to his daughter's grief.

The joyful tidings were received; but far from joyfully. Juliet was filled with dread and horror. Too frightened to confess that she was already married, and to a Montague, she sought frantically to avoid, to delay this impossible second marriage.

"Here comes your father," said Lady Capulet, shocked by her daughter's reluctance to obey her parents' command. "Tell him so yourself and see how he will take it at your hands."

The father was no better pleased. Turning in fury on his disobedient child, he shouted: "But fettle your fine joints 'gainst Thursday next to go with Paris to Saint Peter's Church, or I will drag thee on a hurdle thither. Out, you green-sickness carrion! Out, you baggage! You tallow-face!"

"Good father!" pleaded Juliet, weeping and on her knees.

"Hang thee young baggage!" raged her father. "Get thee to church a Thursday or never after look me in the face!"

Then, when the father and mother had gone, the Nurse took up their cause, but more gently.

"I think it best you married with the County," she urged; for a second marriage meant no more to her than another joyful, bounding wedding night. "O he's a lovely gentleman," she sighed. "Romeo's a dishclout to him . . ."

"Well, thou hast comforted me marvellous much," said Juliet, her last prop gone and with nothing left in all the world to cling to but Romeo's love. "Go in and tell my lady I am gone, having displeas'd my father, to Laurence' cell, to make confession and to be absolv'd."

To the monastery she went, and there, in the holy Friar's cell, poured out all her misery and despair. The old man listened and, moved by Juliet's all-consuming love for Romeo, and also concerned for the sin he would be bringing upon himself by performing a second marriage, devised a strange, fantastic plan. If this plan succeeded, then great happiness would be the result. If it failed, then Verona, Juliet and Romeo, Capulet and Montague, would stand for ever in the world's memory for love's tragedy.

This was the Friar's plan. He knew of a liquor that, if drunk, would produce so exact a counterfeit of death that none could tell the difference. This state would continue for two and forty hours, after which there would be a harmless awakening. On the Wednesday night, when she was alone, Juliet was to drink this liquor so that, when her people came to wake her in the morning for her wedding, they would find her seeming dead. Then, as was the custom, she would be laid in her best attire in the family monument. There, after a proper time, she would awaken and Romeo would be beside her. Letters would have been sent to Mantua telling him of the plan, so that he and Juliet might escape together to safety and happiness.

"I'll send a friar with speed," promised the old priest.

"Love give me strength," prayed Juliet, taking the vial of liquor from Friar Laurence. "Farewell, dear father."

In darkly winding Mantua, news came to Romeo from Verona. But not from Friar Laurence. It was news brought by Romeo's servant; and it was as black as hell. Juliet was dead.

"Leave me," muttered Romeo, sick with amazement and grief. "Hast thou no letters to me from the Friar?"

There was none; for what more could be told than that Romeo's world was lost and his life was a vain pretence? He went to buy strong poison from an apothecary; and set off for Verona and Juliet's tomb.

"Well, Juliet," he whispered, "I will lie with thee tonight."

The letter telling Romeo the truth of what had happened had never left Verona. The wretched brother who had been entrusted with it had been shut up in a house suspected of the plague, and it was night before he was freed.

He went at once to Friar Laurence and told him of the misadventure. The Friar was filled with deep concern. Juliet would soon awaken and she would be alone in a dead man's tomb. He himself must go to the monument and be on hand for the awakening.

The churchyard was dark and the yew trees stood black among the pale monuments, as if the day's mourners had left their shadows behind. Paris, the unlucky bridegroom who, on his wedding morning had come to claim his bride and found her dead, now came with tears and flowers to her midnight tomb. He sent his page a little way off, to warn him of any intruder, for he wanted to mourn and weep in solitude.

Presently the page whistled. Someone was approaching. Paris hid from sight. The intruder appeared. It was that Montague who had been banished for murdering poor Juliet's cousin. What further act of violence was he about to commit? Dear God! he was opening sweet Juliet's tomb!

"Stop thy unhallowed toil, vile Montague!" he cried. "Can vengeance be pursued further than death?"

Romeo turned. His face was pale, as if death had already touched it. He begged Paris leave him and be gone. Enraged, Paris tried to seize him for a felon.

"Wilt thou provoke me?" shouted Romeo. "Then have at thee, boy!"

They drew their swords, and there, among the solemn dead, they fought like madmen; until one, young Paris, fell dying to the ground.

"If thou be merciful," he begged his unwilling murderer, "open the tomb, lay me with Juliet."

"In faith I will," promised Romeo, but to a man already dead.

He dragged him into the monument and laid him down within the low, vaulted chamber where, among stored-up Capulets, long-since ransacked by worms, lay Juliet upon a bed of stone. Death had not yet begun to spoil her; she might be living still. He knelt beside her and made his sad farewell.

"Eyes, look your last. Arms, take your last embrace! And lips, O you the doors of breath, seal with a righteous kiss a dateless bargain to engrossing Death." Then, with a sudden joyfulness he cried, "Here's to my love!" and drank the apothecary's poison; and so, in an instant, ended for ever the parting from his love.

When Friar Laurence, old, hobbling, infirm and fearful, at last entered the tomb, Romeo was dead; and Juliet just awakening.

"O comfortable Friar, where is my lord?" she asked gently. "Where is my Romeo?"

Wretchedly he told her; and wretchedly begged her to come away.

"Go, get thee hence," she answered, with a dignity that would have humbled a king, "for I will not away."

The old priest, who had meant so well and done so ill, crept away from the consequence of his endeavours; and left Juliet alone with her dead.

Longingly she kissed Romeo's lips in the hope that some poison still remained on them. There was none; so she took his dagger and pressed it lovingly into her heart.

So, in old Verona, died Juliet and Romeo, who loved at last sight no less than at their first. The fathers—old Capulet and Montague—were grief-stricken by the tragic deaths of their children, and ashamed that their old hate had brought it about. They vowed eternal friendship to one another; and now the Capulets and Montagues, and old Verona, live only in the great love of Juliet and Romeo.

Othello

Night in Venice. A narrow street, dark as sin, with but a single lamp, like a false moon shakily doubling itself in the water. Two men stood together. One, Roderigo, a slender young gentleman with a disappointed face, a disappointed voice, and disappointed feathers in his bonnet, said:

"I take it much unkindly that thou, Iago, who hast had my purse as if the strings were thine, shouldst know of this."

"If ever I did dream of such a matter," returned Iago, angrily, "abhor me!" He was shorter than his companion, but very sturdy and compact, with every inch of him expressing energy. He was a soldier . . .

"Thou told'st me thou didst hold him in thy hate," persisted Roderigo, his lip quivering.

Iago scorned to deny it. His hatred for the man Roderigo had referred to was an honest hatred. Indeed, both he and Roderigo had cause enough to dislike that proud, boastful, vain personage, that "thicklips", as Roderigo contemptuously called him. He was a Moor and as black as a stove; and he had done both of them a bad turn. He was high general of the Venetian forces and had promoted, to be his second-in-command, one Michael Cassio, a fellow, in Iago's words, "that never set a squadron in the field, nor the division of a battle knows more than a spinster." By

223

all the rights of service and seniority, the place should have been Iago's; but he had been overlooked.

"'Tis the curse of service," sighed the soldier bitterly, "preferment goes by letter and affection, not by the old gradation . . ."

The Moor's offence against Roderigo struck no less deep. Even as he had denied to Iago a coveted place, so he had to Roderigo, a place in the bed of Desdemona, Senator Brabantio's wondrously beautiful daughter, a female of whom the young man had entertained the fondest hopes. That very night, the thicklips had married her. It was the shock of this that had caused Roderigo to reproach Iago, whom he had paid to assist him.

"Call up her father," urged Iago, anxious to make amends. "Rouse him, make after him, poison his delight . . ."

"Here is her father's house!" cried Roderigo, readily following wherever Iago led. "What ho, Brabantio! Signior Brabantio, ho?" he shouted; and banged, with moth-like fists, upon the door outside which he had so long sighed in vain.

"Awake! What ho, Brabantio!" bellowed Iago, in parade ground tones, for he judged that Roderigo's efforts would not have roused a mouse. "Thieves, thieves, thieves! Look to your house, your daughter, and your bags!"

The house shook. Invisible feet stumbled upon invisible stairs. Voices called, and sudden yellow light sketched round the shuttered windows. A casement opened, and, like an ancient cannon, Brabantio's venerable head poked forth and thundered loud annoyance. He looked down and saw two shadowy ruffians lurking below. One was known to him: he was the fool who had been pestering his door in pursuit of his daughter; the other he knew not. What the devil were they doing, shouting and banging and turning the night into bedlam? More casements opened and the tall dark mansion broke out all over with night-capped heads, like a plague of angry boils.

"Zounds, sir," shouted the unknown villain, loud enough for all Venice to hear, "you are robbed! Even now, very now, an old black ram is tupping your white ewe!"

"What profane wretch art thou?" roared the senator.

224

Othello, the Moor of Venice

"I am one, sir," returned the wretch, retiring a little, "that come to tell you, your daughter, and the Moor, are now making the beast with two backs."

The Moor and his daughter? The foul suggestion, so foully uttered, chilled the father's blood. Grey-faced with anger, he rushed away to assure himself that his daughter was still secure.

"Farewell, for I must leave you," muttered Iago rapidly to Roderigo. Much as he hated the Moor, it would be foolishness to stay and be produced against him; "for necessity of present life," he admitted with a rueful smile that went straight to Roderigo's understanding heart, "I must show out a flag, and sign of love . . ." Nonetheless, before he made off, he told Roderigo where the Moor might be found, so that he and Brabantio might have their revenge.

Moments after there was a howl of anguish from the house. The discovery had been made. Brabantio's daughter had betrayed her father's trust, and was gone! There was a violent commotion and Brabantio, sword in hand and with a robe flung hastily over his nightgown, rushed out like a madman. Servants, wrenched from sleep, half-dressed, bearing torches and weapons, crowded after.

"Who would be a father!" Brabantio cried aloud to the stars in the sky; and then to the despised Roderigo who, for a son-in-law, would have been an angel beside "the old black ram", "O that you had had her! Do you know where we may apprehend her and the Moor?"

Roderigo knew, and eagerly led the way; and was much encouraged by the betrayed father's heartfelt thanks.

Othello, the Moor of Venice, stepped out of the inn where he and his new wife had retired for the night. The thicklips, the old black ram, was tall and dignified, as became the great general in whom Venice had placed her trust. Splendidly robed, he enriched the night. Soldierly attendants waited respectfully upon him; and at his side stood his sturdy, faithful ensign, Iago.

Anxiously the ensign warned his general of Brabantio's wrath, which had been so foully abusive of the Moor that Iago admitted that his hand had gone to his sword. "Nine or ten times," he said gruffly, "I had thought to have yerked him here, under the ribs."

Othello smiled. The fierce loyalty of the plain-spoken, rough soldier warmed his heart; but an old gentleman's intemperate words should not be answered with blows. "Let him do his spite," said the Moor gently; and his voice was as dark and rich as his complexion. "My services, which I have done the signiory, shall out-tongue his complaints . . ."

Even as he spoke, torches and dark figures, bulky with shadows, came hastening towards them. Iago, fearing it was Brabantio with armed assistance, drew his sword. He begged Othello to go within; but it was not in the Moor's nature to hide. However, it was not the outraged father, but Michael Cassio, Othello's lieutenant, with officers, who had come in search of the general.

"The duke does greet you, general," said Cassio, saluting courteously, "and he requires your haste post-haste appearance, even on the instant."

The senate was in urgent session on account of warlike news from Cyprus, and Othello's presence was anxiously awaited. Othello nodded and bade Cassio wait while he returned briefly to the inn.

"What makes he here?" asked Cassio, when Othello had gone.

"Faith," chuckled Iago, "he tonight hath boarded a land carrack . . ."

"I do not understand."

"He's married," explained Iago; but before he could reveal to whom, the Moor had returned, wearing the chain and seal and buckling on the sword that denoted his high office. It was then that Brabantio, with Roderigo by his side, and a troop of armed friends and servants at his heels, rushed, like a crowd of angry fireflies, out of the night. Cassio and his men drew their weapons. Othello raised his hand. "Keep up your bright swords, for the dew will rust 'em!" he said; and such was his bearing and manner that he was instantly obeyed. "Good signior," he continued, turning to Brabantio, "you should more command with years than with your weapons."

"O thou foul thief!" shouted Brabantio, raging helplessly before the calm dignity of the Moor. "Where has thou stowed my daughter? Damned as thou art, thou hast enchanted her . . ."

He demanded that the Moor should be dragged off to prison; but this could not be. The Duke had sent for Othello, so the outraged father could do no more than to go with the black thief of his fair daughter, to lay his grievance before the senate.

In the sombre council chamber of the Duke's palace, the rich robed senators sat in gravely troubled state. White beards grew whiter as conflicting rumour blew a hostile Turkish fleet hither and thither, swelling its size and its threat to Cyprus with every gust that came. Then Othello entered. Every face turned towards the great general with such

eager welcome that those who accompanied him were quite overlooked.

"I did not see you," said the Duke to Brabantio, whose temper had not been improved by having been ignored; "welcome gentle signior, we lacked your counsel and your help tonight."

"So did I yours," returned Brabantio, who had not come to prevent the loss of Cyprus to the Turk, but the loss of his daughter to the Moor. Witchcraft must have been practised upon her, for by no other means could she have been persuaded to leave her father's house for the black embraces of Othello. Accordingly, the father demanded the full rigour of the law.

"What in your own part can you say to this?" asked the Duke, turning to the general. Although the state had need of Othello, neither the Duke nor the senate could dismiss Brabantio's complaint without a hearing; for he, too, was a senator.

"Most potent, grave, and reverend signiors," answered the Moor quietly, "that I have ta'en away this old man's daughter, it is most true: true, I have married her . . ." He spread out his hands. His wrongdoing amounted to no more than that. He sighed. He was a soldier and not practised in courtly speech. He knew that his rough tongue was unlikely to recommend him to the present assembly. "Yet," he went on, "by your gracious patience, I will a round, unvarnish'd tale deliver, of my whole course of love, what drugs, what charms, what conjuration," he smiled, "and what mighty magic, for such proceedings I am charged withal, I won his daughter."

The Moor's answer had been gentle; but its very gentleness only served to aggravate Brabantio the more. Loudly he insisted that witchcraft had been used—until the Duke somewhat impatiently suggested that witchcraft and magic were not very sensible charges to bring. The senators also were anxious to have done with this domestic dispute and to return to the more important matters of state.

"Send for the lady," offered the Moor, "and let her speak of me before her father." There was a general murmur of approval, for this seemed the wisest course. Othello despatched his ensign, Iago, to fetch Desdemona; and while all awaited her appearance, Othello begged leave to tell how he had won her love.

"Say it, Othello," said the Duke; and the grave senators settled back in their seats to listen and to judge.

"Her father loved me, oft invited me," began Othello, with a courteous bow towards the stony-faced Brabantio, "still questioned me the story of my life, from year to year: the battles, sieges, fortunes, that I have passed . . ."

As the Moor told of how he had related the strange and wonderful adventures of his life, and how Desdemona had listened breathless, been called away, and hastened back and begged to hear all again, and how she'd sighed, "'twas strange, 'twas passing strange; 'twas pitiful, 'twas wondrous pitiful . . ." the deep music of Othello's voice filled the chamber and drew the old senators forward in their seats. Some stroked their white beards, some rested their chins upon their fists, and here and there, hastily fastened robes parted to betray nightgowns—as if they were returning to the dreams from which they had been summoned. "This is the only witchcraft I have used," said the Moor softly, as Desdemona entered the chamber. "Here comes the lady, let her witness it."

"I think," said the Duke with a smile, "this tale would win my daughter too."

Desdemona, radiant in her bride joy, stood before the solemn assembly; but she had eyes only for her husband, and the brightness of her love seemed to dim the torches in their sconces. Even before her father demanded of her where her chief duty lay, he knew the answer, for it was written in her looks. Her duty, and her heart with it, now belonged to the Moor. So Brabantio, with a bitter sigh, accepted what he could not change. And the senate, with much relief that all had ended in love, turned their attention back to matters of war. Othello was to sail at once for Cyprus and command the garrison there. It was agreed that Desdemona should join him; she should sail attended by the general's faithful ensign, Iago, and be waited upon by Iago's wife. So the business of the night was concluded. The Duke and senators left the chamber; but not before Brabantio had turned and stared sombrely at his daughter's husband. "Look to her, Moor," he said, "have a quick eye to see: she has deceived her father, and may thee."

Two remained behind. They were the two whom the Moor had, all unknowingly, injured: Roderigo, the disappointed lover, and Iago, the disappointed ensign. Roderigo was all for drowning himself.

"Drown thyself?" jeered Iago. "Drown cats and blind puppies!" The silly young gentleman should put such thoughts right out of his mind. Instead, he should put money in his purse and follow his love to Cyprus. Did he not know that a Venetian lady like Desdemona would soon tire of her barbaric Moor, and look elsewhere for her entertainment? And where else should she look than to Roderigo? "Therefore put money in thy purse," urged Iago; and swore he would use all his skill for Roderigo to gain his heart's desire.

The forlorn young gentleman revived, and, like a weed after rain, put forth tiny flowers of hope. Iago was a shrewd fellow, and Roderigo was fortunate to have him for a friend. True, he was something of a rogue, but he was an honest rogue and he always took Roderigo into his confidence. You could trust a man like that.

"No more of drowning, do you hear?" cried Iago, clapping him on the back.

"I am changed," said Roderigo, bravely.

"Go to; farewell! Put money enough in your purse."

As Roderigo hastened away, Iago stared thoughtfully after him. He grinned amiably, and murmured: "Thus do I ever make my fool my purse." Then his brow darkened, and all pleasantry slipped from his face. Only hatred remained, hatred for the Moor. He had confided in Roderigo that he hated the Moor because he had promoted Cassio over him; but there was another reason that was far stronger. He suspected that Othello had slept with his wife. He had no proof of this; he had only suspicion based upon rumour. But it was enough. He told no one, because he was not a man who could endure being laughed at. He kept it within himself where it grew and grew like an ulcer on his soul. His very veins ran with poison. He began to pace to and fro, muttering to himself as thoughts of how he might obtain his revenge flickered through his mind. The Moor was an open man and trusted him; so much the worse for the Moor. Cassio was a handsome fellow, and spendthrift of his charm; so much the worse for Cassio. "Let me see . . . after some time, to abuse Othello's ear, that he is too familiar with his wife . . ." Suddenly he ceased his pacings. He laughed aloud and slapped his knee in triumphant delight.

"I ha't, it is engendered," he cried; "Hell and night must bring this monstrous birth to the world's light!"

A villainous sky and a villainous sea that rushed up to meet it, and villainous winds that blew where they chose, had smashed and bewildered the Turkish fleet, and blown the three vessels from Venice many miles apart. Cassio's ship was the first to arrive at Cyprus; then came the vessel bearing Desdemona with Iago and Emilia, his wife. Most courteously, and fondly, too, Cassio greeted his general's lady; and Iago observed with shrewd interest how the handsome young lieutenant could no more help striving to charm the beautiful Desdemona than he could help breathing. Then Othello's ship was sighted, and presently he came ashore to the loud rejoicing of the garrison and the people of the town.

In flying saffron cloak, bright armour and plumed helmet cradled in his arm, the great general strode forward to greet his wife.

"O my fair warrior!" he cried.

"My dear Othello!" she answered; and their embrace, she fair, he black, was like the engulfing of day by all-conquering night.

"O you are well tuned now," murmured Iago, the eternal observer, "but I'll set down the pegs that make this music, as honest as I am."

When the rapt lovers had departed and the onlookers had drifted away, Iago drew near his Venetian friend. Roderigo had followed Iago's advice. He had sold his property, filled his purse, and come to Cyprus, brave as a lily, though still somewhat green from the rigour of the sea. Had Roderigo noticed, Iago asked quietly, how fondly Desdemona and Cassio had met? Roderigo had, and had taken it for mere courtesy. Iago shook his head. "Lechery," he murmured, "by this hand; an index and prologue to the history of lust . . ." Roderigo was amazed, but then Iago was a shrewd fellow and knew more about such matters than he did. You could trust a fellow like Iago to know what was what. In short, Iago had no difficulty in persuading his friend into believing what he wanted to believe: that Desdemona had already tired of the ageing black Moor and was casting about for some younger, fairer object for her desires. If Roderigo still hoped to succeed, Cassio must be got rid of. Roderigo nodded as vigorously as he could, and listened while Iago, whose thoughts had not been idle, proposed his scheme. That night, Cassio was to be the officer of the watch. Now Cassio was a hot-tempered fellow and, if Roderigo provoked him into a fight, he would be discredited and the way to Desdemona would be clear. Roderigo beamed happily, and went away thanking his stars that a clever fellow like Iago was his friend and not his enemy.

"Welcome, Iago," said Cassio, coming briskly into the hall of the garrison castle; "we must to the watch." Being newly appointed, the young man was most prompt and careful in his duty. Iago, however, the seasoned soldier and good-humoured friend, pointed out that it was far too early, and suggested that they should drink Othello's health with some gentlemen of Cyprus who were waiting outside. Regretfully

Cassio shook his head. "Not tonight, good Iago," he protested; "I have very poor and unhappy brains for drinking . . ."

He had, he said, drunk one cup that night, and already it was affecting him. Iago laughed sympathetically and, good friend that he was, promised that, if Cassio would bring the gentlemen in, he, Iago, would drink up Cassio's wine for him. "I'll do it," said Cassio reluctantly, "but it dislikes me."

"If I can fasten but one cup upon him . . ." murmured Iago, when Cassio had gone. Cassio's having a poor head for drinking was an unlooked-for advantage, of which Iago meant to take the fullest opportunity. But, as it turned out, there was no need for him to exert himself. The gentlemen of Cyprus had already forestalled him. In they came, some half dozen merry gentleman, among whom was the governor, and all bearing bottles of wine.

"'Fore God," hiccuped Cassio, "they have given me a rouse already."

"Good faith, a little one," protested the governor, "not past a pint, as I am a soldier."

They all sat down, and Cassio missed his chair, but no one remarked on it. Iago, the soul of good fellowship, called for more wine, and began to sing. "'Fore God, an excellent song!" sobbed Cassio, for he loved a good tune and was moved by it. Iago sang again, and Cassio drank again. "'Fore God this is a more exquisite song than the other!" he wept; and had more wine. At length, having been briefly religious and talked of his soul, he stood upright, or nearly so. "Do not think, gentlemen, I am drunk," he announced solemnly. He pointed to Iago. "This is my ancient." He held up a hand and looked at it carefully. "This is my right hand," he decided at length; and then had no difficulty in identifying the other as his left. "I am not drunk now," he concluded, having displayed such clear-mindedness, "I can stand well enough, and speak well enough." Everyone agreed and Cassio, after some trifling disagreement with his sword, left the hall. When he had gone, Iago sighed and confessed it saddened him to see so fine an officer as Cassio brought low by drink.

"Is he often thus?" asked the governor. Iago nodded. Every night . . . The governor wondered that the general should trust such a man. Should not the ensign tell Othello of the lieutenant's infirmity? Iago shook his head. He was not the man to betray a friend's weakness. Suddenly there was a commotion outside. A moment later the door burst open and Roderigo rushed in, fiercely pursued by the drunken Cassio. "A knave teach me my duty!" roared Cassio, belabouring Roderigo with sword and fist. "But I'll beat the knave into a wicker bottle!"

"Good lieutenant," cried the governor, seeking to intervene, "hold your hand!" "Let me go sir," shouted Cassio, "or I'll knock you o'er the mazzard!"

"Away I say," whispered Iago to Roderigo, for his enraged pursuer had now turned upon the governor, "go out and cry a mutiny." Gladly Roderigo fled, and left the hall to wild confusion. Chairs and tables were overturned, bottles smashed and candles sent to blazing ruin. The governor cried out as Cassio's sword pierced him. An alarm bell began to ring and its brazen clamour filled the air.

"Hold, for your lives!"

Robed for the night, and gigantic in his anger, Othello stood in the hall.

"Hold, the general speaks to you," echoed Iago; "hold, hold, for shame!" and he took up his proper place by his general's side.

The fighting ceased and furiously the Moor demanded to know how it had begun. He asked Iago, from whom he knew he would get a plain, blunt answer. But Iago could not say. One moment all had been friends, and, in the next, they had been at each other's throats. He asked Cassio. But Cassio was too drunk to speak. Last of all he asked the wounded governor.

"Worthy Othello," said he. "I am hurt to danger. Your officer Iago can inform you . . ." The general turned again to his faithful ensign, and commanded him to speak.

"I had rather ha' this tongue cut from my mouth," muttered Iago, with such reluctance that all present admired him for the honesty of his feelings, "than it should do offence to Michael Cassio." Then he went on to tell what had happened, but in such a way that he seemed to be defending Cassio rather than damning him. When he had done, Othello laid a hand upon his shoulder. "I know, Iago," he said kindly, "thy

honesty and love doth mince this matter, making it light to Cassio."
Then, sternly, he turned to his lieutenant, whose countenance was red
with wine and shame. "Cassio," he said, "I love thee, but never more be
officer of mine."

So Cassio was ruined; and it seemed to that unhappy young man, as
everyone left the hall, that all the world now shunned him. Except for
Iago. That sturdy fellow had been the only one who had taken his part
and spoken up for him . . . even though it had done no good. It was Iago
who stayed behind, came up to him, patted him on the back and bade
him be of good cheer. Ah! he was a real man, a real friend! Thank God for
fellows like honest Iago! But it was no use. He was done for. He had lost
his good name. He began to weep, for he was still fuddled with drink.

Then Iago, shrewd fellow that he was, persuaded him that all was not lost. There was still a way by which he might regain the general's trust. "Our general's wife is now the general," said Iago; and suggested that Cassio should beg Desdemona to intercede with her husband on his behalf.

"You advise me well," said Cassio, upon such reflection as he was capable.

"I protest," said his good friend Iago, "in the sincerity of love and honest kindness."

In the morning, Cassio, through the good offices of Iago's wife, Emilia, who was Desdemona's attendant, approached his general's wife. They met in the gardens outside the castle, and the bright sunshine mingled their shadows as they talked. Iago had advised him well. Desdemona readily embraced his cause, and proved herself to be the "fair warrior" of Othello's greeting. She vowed she would not rest till she had gained a victory and restored Cassio to her husband's favour. "Madam, here comes my lord," warned Emilia, as Othello and his ensign approached. Hastily Cassio departed, for he did not feel equal, at that moment, to facing his general.

"Ha, I like not that," muttered Iago, observing the quick leave-taking.

Othello frowned, as if a pin had pricked him. "Was not that Cassio parted from my wife?"

"Cassio, my lord?" said Iago doubtfully, "no, sure, I cannot think it, that he would sneak away so guilty-like, seeing you coming."

But it had been Cassio. Desdemona admitted it as soon as Othello asked; and straightway began to beg and wheedle her husband into restoring the fallen lieutenant to his place. Othello tried to put her off but she so persisted, using her charms for weapons, that the great general was forced to acknowledge defeat. "Prithee no more," he laughed, "let him come when he will. I will deny thee nothing."

Desdemona, with Emilia attending her, departed in triumph. "Excellent wretch," sighed Othello, gazing after her, "perdition catch my soul, but I do love thee, and when I love thee not, Chaos is come again."

"My noble lord—" began Iago hesitantly; and then fell silent. Othello frowned again. (Again the pinprick). What was it his ensign found so hard to say? Something concerning Cassio. Little by little Othello dragged it out of him. Iago had not liked the familiarity with which Cassio had treated Desdemona. Had Cassio known the lady for long? Why yes, for almost as long as had Othello himself. Iago looked troubled, but would say no more. Othello pressed him, for something of Iago's uneasiness had communicated itself to him. He knew his ensign to be a plain blunt soldier who always spoke his mind. Why did he not do so now? He knew him to be a fellow not given to fancies; so what was it he knew about Cassio and Desdemona? Fear clutched at Othello's heart. His love for Desdemona was so great that the dread of losing her always lay in ambush. Fiercely he demanded that Iago should tell him what was in his mind. Stoutly Iago refused. His thoughts were his own and they might easily be unfounded. To let Othello know them might well be destructive of Othello's peace and his own honour as a man.

"Good name in man and woman, dear my lord," said the worthy soldier, shaking his head, "is the immediate jewel of their souls." He paused, and smiled ruefully. "Who steals my purse, steals trash," he said, thinking not a little of Roderigo, that "trash of Venice" as he had once called him, who had been his purse but who had now served his turn; "'tis something, nothing; 'twas mine, 'tis his, and has been slave to thousands: but he that filches from me my good name . . ." Thus Iago did indeed speak his thoughts, though none but he guessed how. He glanced at the great general by his side, a giant of a man who might, with one blow of his arm, have sent Iago headless to hell. He smiled inwardly. The Moor was unsettled. His confidence was shaken and his trust in his wife was already being nibbled at. "She did deceive her father, marrying you," he said softly, shrewdly feathering his poisoned darts with enough of truth to give them a surer aim, "and when she seemed to shake and fear your looks, she loved them most." When at length he departed, he begged Othello not to give way to unreasoning jealousy. After all, his own suspicions might be groundless. The general should satisfy himself. Perhaps it would be wiser for him to hold off giving Cassio back his place, and see if Desdemona's pleadings became more urgent.

Though the air was still and warm, the Moor shivered and swayed slightly, as a tall tree might be swayed by a small breeze, once it is rotted within. Desdemona returned with Emilia to remind him that the islanders were awaiting him for dinner. He answered faintly. She expressed concern. He pleaded a headache as the reason. She offered to bind the place with her handkerchief. "Let it alone," he said, brushing her hand aside, "come, I'll go in with you." She took his arm and together they went into the castle. The handkerchief fell unnoticed to the ground.

Emilia picked it up. She recognized it. It had been the Moor's first gift to Desdemona, and she had always set great store by it. Iago, Emilia's husband, had often asked about it. She smiled to herself. She would have it copied for him. She was sure he would be pleased. Even as the idea came to her, Iago appeared. She teased him with the handkerchief but he was too quick for her. He snatched it and would not give it up. She told him her mistress would be distressed to lose it. He shook his head. He had a use for it—and such was his cheerful smile that she could not suppose he meant any harm. She left him with the handkerchief in his hand. He was laughing . . .

"I will in Cassio's lodging lose this napkin, and let him find it," he murmured. He let it flutter from his fingers. "Trifles light as air are to the jealous, confirmations strong as proofs of holy writ."

Othello, having left the table, came out once more into the castle gardens: the soft golden sunshine was turned as hard and yellow as brass. He frowned and gnawed his lip and shook his head as if he was caught in an invisible net of flies.

"Look where he comes," breathed Iago; "not poppy nor mandragora, nor all the drowsy syrups of the world, shall ever medicine thee to that sweet sleep which thou owed'st yesterday."

"Avaunt, be gone!" cried Othello, seeing his ensign watching him with concern, "thou hast set me on the rack . . ."

Silently Iago exulted. Skilful soldier that he was, he had brought down an enemy a thousand times greater than himself. "Is't possible, my lord?" he exclaimed, in honest amazement when he perceived the huge extent of the Moor's anguish. The deadly seeds he had planted had lodged in a richer soil than ever he'd dared hope. Othello was great in all things: great in nature, great in war, great in love, and great in his despair. Like a coin turned, the noble head had become the unnatural beast.

"Villain, be sure thou prove my love a whore," raged the Moor, "be sure of't, give me the ocular proof. . ." He seized his ensign by the throat and threatened to kill him if the accusation prove false.

"Take note, take note, O world," cried Iago, struggling to free himself, "to be direct and honest is not safe . . ."

At once, Othello repented of his violence towards the honest soldier who had, after all, done no more than speak his mind. But, nonetheless, he demanded proof that Desdemona had been false with Cassio. Iago demurred. To observe them in the act would not be easy; even, as he put it, "were they as prime as goats, as hot as monkeys, as salt as wolves, in pride . . ." However, there had been an occasion when he had overheard Cassio murmuring in his sleep of his love for Desdemona, and cursing the Moor for having her. In addition, he spoke of a certain handkerchief, spotted with strawberries, that he believed to be Desdemona's, that he had seen in Cassio's hand.

This last, this trifle light as air, did indeed prove strong as holy writ. The handkerchief that, to Othello, had been the symbol of his love, now

became the symbol of love betrayed, and of vengeance. Savagely he demanded blood. "Within these three days let me hear thee say that Cassio's not alive."

"My friend is dead," said Iago quietly. Although he had planned only for anguish, ruin and despair, now that murder entered into the design, he accepted it. Just as other men were led by Iago, so was Iago led by his own devices––and willingly, too, for he knew that his own life stood in danger if Cassio should live to prove him a liar.

In another part of the gardens, Desdemona and Emilia strolled together. Desdemona was well-pleased with her victory over her husband and sent for Cassio, for surely now was the time when he would get back his place. Then she fell to wondering where she could have lost her handkerchief. "I know not, madam," muttered Emilia, looking the other way. Then Othello came and stood before his wife with countenance of frowning ebony. She smiled at him and reminded him of his promise. "What promise, chuck?" he asked, and the endearment came out harshly. "I have sent to bid Cassio come speak with you," she answered; and was troubled to see her husband suddenly rub his eyes as if they pained him. "I have a salt and sullen rheum offends me," he said, "lend me thy handkerchief." "Here, my lord," she offered. Othello stared at it. He shook his head. "That which I gave you," he said. She grew uneasy. The deep music that she loved so well in her husband's voice was changed. It sounded hard and menacing. "I have it not about me," she said, but Othello was not satisfied. The handkerchief had been more than a love token. It had belonged to his mother. It had been given to her by a magician who had warned her that if ever she lost it or parted with it, so she would lose her husband's love. In vain Desdemona protested it was not lost; and, hoping to turn his thoughts from the handkerchief, she reminded him of Cassio. "I pray let Cassio be received again." "Fetch me that handkerchief!" demanded the Moor. "Come, come, you'll never meet a more sufficient man," urged Desdemona. "The handkerchief!" "I pray talk me of Cassio," begged Desdemona. "The handkerchief!" shouted Othello, his fury mounting as Desdemona unknowingly damned herself with every word. At last he could bear it no longer and

She awoke and smiled up at him

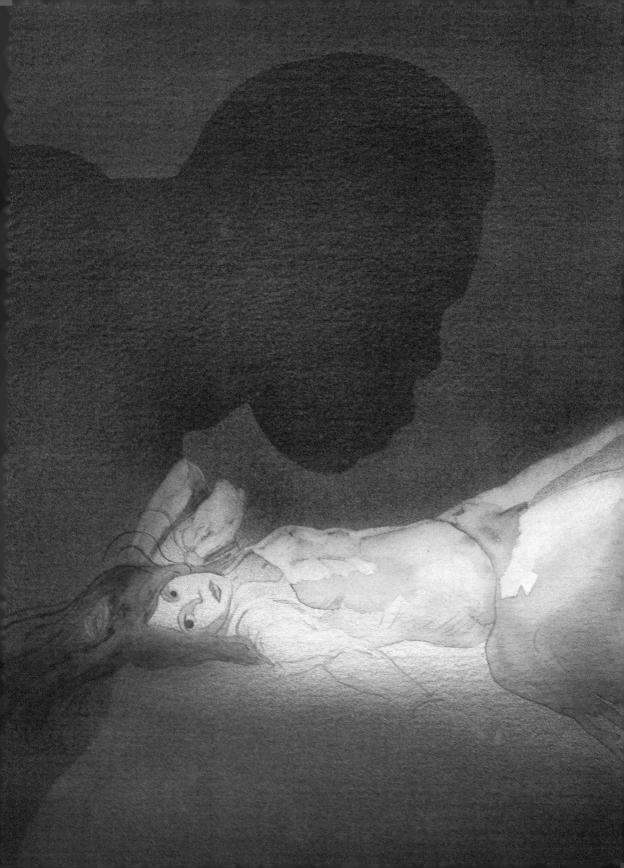

hastened away, leaving his wife fearful and amazed. "Sure there's some wonder in this handkerchief," she said to Emilia. "I am most unhappy in the loss of it." Emilia bit her lip. She knew she should have spoken before; now it was too late.

Cassio came, and sadly Desdemona told him that Othello's mood was such that now was not the time to speak with him. Then, seeing Cassio crestfallen, she promised she would go after her husband and beg him again on Cassio's behalf. Cassio looked hopeful, and Desdemona bade him walk about the gardens till he was sent for. This he did; and, in his strollings among the groves and lawns, met his mistress, Bianca, and gave her a handkerchief he had found in his lodgings. He asked her to have it copied, for it was a pretty trifle and it pleased him . . .

Presently he turned back towards the castle, for the reddened sun was sinking and making long graves for all the trees. Suddenly he saw Iago standing, and Othello lying senseless at his feet. "What's the matter?" he cried out, hastening towards them. Iago turned. His face was filled with concern. "My lord is fall'n into an epilepsy," he said in great agitation, "this is his second fit, he had one yesterday." "Rub him about the temples," urged Cassio; but Iago motioned him away. "Do you withdraw yourself a little while," he advised, "he will recover straight." With many a backward glance, Cassio went away, for already the general had begun to groan and stir and stare about him wildly.

"How is it, general?" inquired Iago with rough tenderness, "have you not hurt your head?"

"Dost thou mock me?" whispered Othello, for his fit had come upon him when Iago had told him that Cassio had confessed that he had lain with Desdemona. All his strength had left him and the world had rushed up about him as if to swallow him. He stood up, but was still unsteady and confused. He leaned upon Iago's shoulder, and was grateful to the sturdy ensign who stood by him in all things. Iago begged him to go stand among the trees, for Cassio was returning. If the general concealed himself, he would hear, with his own ears, the truth of his suspicions and so be removed from the torment of doubt.

As Cassio drew near, Othello, the great general, the noble Moor of Venice, hid among the trees like a furtive savage.

"How do you now, lieutenant?" greeted Iago, affectionately putting his arm about Cassio's shoulders, the better to guide him nearer to, or further from, the listening Othello, as the occasion demanded. Cassio sadly shook his head. "Ply Desdemona well," said Iago loudly, "and you are sure on't." Then, drawing him away, said softly, and with a knowing dig in the ribs, "Now if this suit lay in Bianca's power, how quickly should you speed!" Cassio laughed, and his laughter was yet another poisoned arrow in Othello's heart, for the Moor, having heard only Desdemona mentioned, thought that Cassio laughed contemptuously at his wife.

"I never knew a woman love man so," said Iago. "Alas, poor rogue, I think i'faith she loves me," said Cassio, with a boastful smile. And so it went on, with Iago most skilfully encouraging Cassio to talk freely of Bianca, while the hidden listener supposed the talk to be about his wife.

Presently Bianca herself appeared and, far from destroying Iago's device, she supported it, for she had brought with her the handkerchief

242

which she now displayed angrily to Cassio. "This is some minx's token," she said, tossing it contemptuously to him.

"After her, after her!" urged Iago, as the lady swept indignantly away. "Faith, I must," laughed Cassio, hastening after, "she'll rail i' the street else!"

"How shall I murder him, Iago?" pleaded the Moor, creeping out of the concealment in which he had endured the torments of hell. And yet, in all his darkness, there still flickered a fragile light as he thought of his beloved Desdemona and how she once had been. "But yet the pity of it, Iago!" he wept, "O Iago, the pity of it, Iago!"

"If you be so fond over her iniquity . . ." murmured Iago, anxiously; but there was no need, for, in the very next moment, Othello was plunged back into his night of madness and hate. "I will chop her into messes!" he raged and then, more calmly, though more terribly: "get me some poison, Iago, this night . . ."

"Do it not with poison," said Iago quickly. Like many a man whose soul is black as pitch, he was careful to keep his hands clean, as if, at the last judgement, he would be able to stand, like a Sunday schoolboy, presenting spotless palms. "Strangle her in her bed, even the bed she hath contaminated."

"Good, good, the justice of it pleases," agreed the Moor; and Iago, confident now that he had harnessed Othello's very nobility to his own ends, undertook to murder Cassio by midnight. No sooner had the murders been determined upon, than a trumpet sounded from within the castle, as if to seal the double deaths.

Lodovico, a great man in Venice and ambassador from the Duke, had arrived with a letter for Othello from the senate. He stepped out into the darkened gardens attended by torch-bearing servants and with the Lady Desdemona by his side. Othello received the letter with elaborate courtesy; and, while he read it, Lodovico inquired about Cassio, and was surprised to learn that he and the general were estranged. "But you shall make all well," said Desdemona.

"Are you sure of that?" Othello's voice was harsh and sudden, but as he was still reading the letter it was supposed his words concerned what he read. The letter had commanded him to return to Venice and to leave

Cassio in his place. This news, conjectured Lodovico, might well account for the general's frowns. The talk returned to Cassio, and Desdemona again spoke up on his behalf. "Devil!" shouted Othello; and struck her in the face! Lodovico exclaimed in amazement; he could scarcely believe what he had seen.

"I have not deserved this," whispered Desdemona, her white cheek stained with the Moor's furious hand. "I will not stay to offend you," she said, and turned to go.

"I do beseech your lordship," protested Lodovico, outraged by this treatment of Brabantio's daughter, "call her back!"

Othello shrugged his shoulders and called, "Mistress!" contemptuously. Desdemona turned. "What would you with her, sir?" asked the Moor. "Who, I, my lord?" said Lodovico. "Ay, you did wish that I would make her turn," answered the Moor wildly. "Sir, she can turn, and turn, and yet go on, and turn again . . ." He talked in fits and jerks, sometimes to Lodovico, sometimes to his wife and sometimes, it seemed, to his distracted self. Savagely he dismissed Desdemona, who went, with eyes brimming with uncomprehending tears; then, with a great effort at calmness, he bade Lodovico sup with him. "You are welcome, sir, to Cyprus," he said. His wandering gaze fell upon Iago. "Goats and monkeys!" he shouted frantically, and rushed into the castle.

"Is this the noble Moor whom our full senate call all in all sufficient?" wondered Lodovico. "This the noble nature, whom passion could not shake?"

"He is much changed," admitted Iago sadly, and went on to confide to the ambassador that it was only loyalty that prevented him telling what he knew concerning his general. "I am sorry that I am deceived in him," said Lodovico grimly; and, together with Iago left the garden that, like Eden, had witnessed a temptation and a fall.

His wife was a whore. The Moor was sure of it. Whenever she spoke, it was of Cassio. Whenever she pleaded, it was for Cassio. Whenever she praised, it was Cassio. Closely he questioned her assistant, Emilia. Nothing. He accused the whore herself. Nothing—nothing but denial. "What, not a whore?" he demanded incredulously. "No, as I shall be saved!" cried Desdemona. "I cry you mercy then," apologised the Moor with a mocking bow, "I took you for that cunning whore of Venice that married with Othello . . ." He would listen to her no more. Iago had told the truth. Iago was a soldier and had no cause to lie. The women lied to protect themselves. He flung some money at Emilia, as was due to her as keeper of a whorehouse, and left the room.

Desdemona wept in bewildered despair. She no longer knew her husband. Surely the savage, foul-tongued Moor who had just departed could not be the great and gentle Othello she had married? She begged Emilia bring in Iago, Iago, good Iago, would know what was amiss. But Iago could supply no reason for his gen ral's distraction other than troubled affairs of state. Emilia wondered if the cause of the Moor's change had been because some damnable villain had poisoned his mind . . . even as Iago's mind had once been poisoned against his wife with a slander about her and the Moor. "You are a fool, go to!" said Iago sharply; and then, in answer to Desdemona's plea that he should speak with Othello on her behalf, he said gruffly: "I pray you, be content: 'tis but his humour; the business of the state does him offence." "If 'twere no other—" faltered Desdemona, with sudden hope. "'Tis but so, I warrant you," said Iago quickly. "Go in," he urged, when trumpets announced the serving of supper, "and weep not; all things shall be well." So the two women departed, and neither of them knew their husbands: the one no longer saw the man in the monster, and the other had never seen the monster in the man.

A forlorn figure crept into the room; a miserable, neglected, ill-used figure, an emptied purse: Roderigo. He had come to complain bitterly of his treatment. He had given Iago enough jewels, as he put it, that would have "half corrupted a votarist", for Desdemona; and had got nothing in return. Now he was ruined. Patiently Iago listened; and effortlessly persuaded the wretched Roderigo into hoping again. If he would do but one thing, then success was assured. What thing? Why, kill Cassio! Though Roderigo had sunk as low in spirits as in money, so that he had nothing left to lose, he still shrank from undertaking murder. But the ruinous road on which he'd embarked was too steep and slippery for him to stop; and it needed little persuasion on Iago's part for him to take the final step. He was to lie in wait for Cassio outside Bianca's house, between twelve and one o'clock. Iago himself would be on hand, so that, if Roderigo failed in his first attempt, Iago would complete the deed. "It is now high suppertime, and the night grows to waste," murmured Iago, pushing Roderigo from the room: "about it!"

With the ending of supper, Othello seemed calmer, as if some inner conflict had been resolved. He left the table in company with Lodovico and bade Desdemona go to bed and dismiss Emilia for the night. He himself would join her presently. When he had gone, Emilia expressed some uneasiness, but Desdemona shook her head. "We must not now displease him," she said. Emilia sighed and began to unpin her mistress's hair. As she did so, Desdemona began to hum an air. She stopped and smiled sadly. "My mother had a maid called Barbary," she said, "she was in love, and he she loved proved mad, and did forsake her; she had a song of 'willow', an old thing 'twas, but it expressed her fortune, and she died singing it; that song tonight will not go from my mind." She sang the song in a quiet, lost voice, and when she finished, bade Emilia leave her. "Good night," she murmured; "mine eyes do itch; does that bode weeping?"

The night was black and airless, as if a thick blanket lay over the town, blindfolding the stars. In an obscure street, voices whispered. "Here stand behind this bulk, straight will he come, wear thy good rapier bare, and put it home, quick, quick, fear nothing . . ." "Be near at hand," pleaded the other, "I may miscarry in't." There was a mutter of impatience, then: "Here at thy hand, be bold, and take thy sword!" Faint fingers were pressed by firm ones round the weapon's hilt, and faint conscience was smothered by firm resolve. Soundlessly the whisperers parted, each to his station.

"Whether he kill Cassio," weighed up Iago, who had no great confidence in the ferocity of Roderigo, "or Cassio him, or each do kill the other, every way makes my game . . ." But it would be better, he reflected, for both to die: Roderigo because, if he lived, he would demand the return of the jewels he had given Iago for Desdemona; and Cassio —"if Cassio do remain," he breathed, in a sudden rage of envy, "he has a daily beauty in his life that makes me ugly: and besides, the Moor may unfold me to him . . .''

There was a sound of footsteps descending stairs. A door opened and Cassio, buttoning up his coat, came yawning out of Bianca's house. He had had a pleasant evening. He stepped into the street; and at once the night was full of thrusts and stabs and murder! Roderigo's blade, fierce as grass, pricked Cassio's coat. Cassio shouted, turned and pierced his attacker through. Roderigo shrieked and fell. Then came Iago, quick as thought, stabbed Cassio from behind, and fled.

Lodovico and his companions, who had been walking back to their vessel, heard the violent commotion. They were seized with alarm. Othello, who had accompanied them, heard Cassio's voice, crying out for a surgeon. So! Iago had kept his word! Faithful Iago had killed for his friend's sake. "Thou teachest me!'' he whispered, and crept back to the castle and his faithless wife.

The groans and cries had fetched out someone with a light. Thankfully Lodovico recognized Iago, the Moor's sturdy ensign. He was in his shirt as if the commotion had roused him from sleep. He searched the dark and

found Cassio lying in agony from a savage wound in his leg. Who had attacked him? "O help me!" came a faint voice. "That's one of them," groaned Cassio. "O murderous slave!" shouted Iago, "O villain!" and, like the loyal soldier he was, rushed upon Cassio's attacker with an avenging blade.

"O damned Iago!" screamed Roderigo, as he saw, in one frightful instant, the truth of Iago. "O inhuman dog!" Then Iago's dagger entered his heart. He died, and Iago was secure.

People came forward from the dark. Bianca rushed from her house, saw Cassio and cried aloud over his wound. The ground was searched; the dead attacker found. "Lend me a light!" cried Iago, who, in great concern, seemed everywhere at once. "Know we this face or no? Alas, my friend and my dear countryman Roderigo? No—yes, sure—O heaven, Roderigo!"

How had it come about? None could say. The only one who could have told, was dead. Sternly Iago turned upon Bianca: "This is the fruit of whoring," he said, and charged her with complicity in the crime. A chair was fetched and Iago helped the wounded Cassio into it. Honest Iago, good friend and faithful assistant to all.

The Moor, tall in his white and silver robe, stood beside his sleeping wife. By the light of a candle he gazed down upon her and marvelled at her pale beauty. "Yet she must die," he whispered, "else she'll betray more men." He knelt and, with great tenderness, kissed her lips. He was calm and gentle once more, and might indeed have been the noble Othello Desdemona had married. He kissed her again. She awoke and smiled up at him. "Will you come to bed, my lord?" Slowly he shook his head. "Have you prayed tonight, Desdemona?" "Ay, my lord." Sombrely he urged her to think of any sin she might have omitted and for which she might beg heaven's forgiveness. "I would not kill thy soul," he said. "Talk you of killing?" cried Desdemona, in sudden fear. He nodded; and Desdemona began to plead for her life. But Iago had done his work too well, and all Othello's nobility and strength of purpose was directed to one terrible end. Desdemona's pleadings and frantic denials of guilt served only to change him to iron. "O banish me, my lord, but kill me not!'' she wept, reaching up to embrace her murderer. He thrust her away. She clutched at his hand. "Kill me tomorrow, let me live tonight!" He flung her back upon the bed. "But half an hour," she pleaded, "but while I say one prayer!" "'Tis too late!" panted the Moor, his breast heaving and his eyes wild at the horror of what he was about to do. He seized a pillow and, with his black hands like huge spiders, forced it down upon Desdemona's terrified face. She struggled, cried out to God, but the Moor was implacable and her cries and struggles grew fainter and fainter until, at last, both were stilled.

"My lord, my lord!" Distracted, he thought the cry was his wife's, and he forced the pillow down harder; then he understood it was Emilia, outside the door. He became frightened and did not know what to do. "If

she come in," he muttered, "she'll sure speak to my wife . . ." Then bleak misery seized him as the full knowledge of what he had done flooded his soul. "My wife! My wife! What wife? A ha' no wife . . ." Emilia called again. Quickly he drew the bed curtains and let the woman in. She came with tumbled news of murders in the street. Roderigo killed and Cassio wounded. ("Not Cassio killed?")

"O Lord, what cry is that?" Emilia had heard a voice, as frail as air. She rushed to the bed, drew back the curtain and discovered the dying Desdemona. She looked in terror, shouted for help, then stared in accusation at the distracted Moor. "O who has done this deed?" she cried.

"Nobody, I myself," sighed Desdemona from her deathbed, "farewell." For the first and only time, Desdemona had betrayed her husband: to innocence. Othello had killed her life, but not her love.

"She's like a liar gone to burning hell!" shrieked Othello, turning away from Desdemona's sightless eyes. "'Twas I that killed her!" He could not endure the pain of forgiveness, which made his just vengeance small. "She was false as water!" he shouted, in answer to Emilia's bitter denunciations. "Thou as rash as fire!" cried Emilia. "Cassio did top her!" insisted Othello, striving, with all his might, to make the woman comprehend that he had killed for guilt. "Ask thy husband else . . ." "My husband?" "Thy husband!" But she would not understand, and it was as if she did not know such a man. "I say thy husband," repeated Othello furiously: "dost understand the word? My friend, thy husband, honest, honest Iago."

Emilia faltered. "If he say so," she whispered, "may his pernicious soul rot half a grain a day! He lies to the heart." She shook her head. It was not possible. She knew her husband. She loved him. He could never have kept hidden such monstrous wickedness. The Moor was mad. She shouted out for help. People came running. They burst into the bedchamber, stared in amazement and horror at the murdered Desdemona, and her murderer standing over her, stiff as wood. Iago was among them. Frantically Emilia demanded of him whether he had told Othello that Desdemona had been false. "I told him what I thought," said Iago, looking hard at the Moor. "But did you ever tell him she was false?" "I did," said Iago, not taking his eyes from Othello's, as if to keep his soul in chains. "You told a lie!" screamed Emilia, as she, like Roderigo, saw for the first time, the truth of Iago, "an odious, damned lie!" He bade her hold her tongue. She would not. She cursed him, she raged at him . . . "What, are you mad?" muttered Iago, his composure shaken as his wife so turned upon him. "I charge you, get you home!"

Suddenly Othello uttered a howl of despair and sank down upon the bed beside his murdered wife! Despairingly he sought to justify what he had done. He still believed in Iago. It was the very necessity of his soul. The handkerchief—he had seen it in Cassio's hand.

"Oh God, O heavenly God!" cried out Emilia and before Iago could stop her, she told all, that she had found the handkerchief and had given it to her husband. "Filth, thou liest!" snarled Iago; but, seeing that she was believed, moved at her, quick as a viper, and thrust his dagger into her side. As she fell dying, he fled, leaving behind consternation and intolerable dismay.

Othello rose. His sword was in his hand. The onlookers fell back, fearing that he was mad. But Othello's madness was passed. "Be not afraid," he said, "though you do see me weaponed: here is my journey's end." His voice had recovered its marvellous deep music, even as his mind had recovered the nobility of his soul. But it was too late. "O ill-starred wench," he sighed, gazing down upon the quiet Desdemona, "pale as they smock . . ." Then measureless grief overcame him, and he wept for Desdemona dead.

Iago had been seized, and now was brought back. Lodovico and officers accompanied him, and the wounded Cassio was carried in. Othello stared at the man who had ruined him. Iago stood before him, secured on either side by guards. "If that thou be'est a devil," cried Othello suddenly, "I cannot kill thee!" He struck at Iago with his sword. Iago staggered in the arms that held him. "I bleed, sir, but not killed," he muttered contemptuously. "I am not sorry neither," said Othello wearily, giving up his sword. "I'd have thee live, for in my sense 'tis happiness to die."

"O thou Othello, that wert once so good," said Lodovico sadly, "what should be said of thee?"

"Why anything," returned Othello, "an honourable murderer, if you will: for nought I did in hate, but all in honour." He turned to Cassio. "Will you, I pray, demand that demi-devil, why he hath thus ensnared my soul and body?"

"Demand me nothing," said Iago, grim with hatred for the world, "what you know, you know. From this time forth I never will speak word." The foulness of his soul had been exposed, and he knew it; but envious pride prevented his making confession.

"You must forsake this room, and go with us," said Lodovico, gently, to the Moor, "your power and your command is taken off." Othello listened and nodded. The officers moved forward to take him. The Moor held up his hand, and such was the dignity of his bearing that they fell back. "Soft you, a word or two before you go," he begged. "I have done the state some service, and they know't; no more of that; I pray you in your letters, when you shall these unlucky deeds relate, speak of them as they are; nothing extenuate, nor set down aught in malice; then must you speak of one that loved not wisely, but too well . . ." He spoke gently, and with a sad smile as he recalled his past valour and set it beside his present distress. He seemed so much at peace with himself that none noticed that he had drawn a dagger from his robe. Yet even if they'd seen it, none would have had the heart to stay his hand as he stabbed himself to the heart.

"I kissed thee ere I killed thee," he whispered, sinking on the bed beside his dead wife, "no way but this, killing myself, to die upon a kiss."

Iago looked on, seemingly unmoved. "To you, Lord Governor," said Lodovico to Cassio, "remains the censure of this hellish villain: the time, the place, the torture—O enforce it!"

A Midsummer Night's Dream

Hermia, who was small, dark and perfect, loved Lysander; and Lysander loved Hermia. What could have been better than that? At the same time, Helena, who was tall, fair and tearful, loved Demetrius.

But Demetrius did not love Helena. Instead he, too, loved Hermia . . . who did not love him. What could have been worse than that?

Now although Lysander and Demetrius were both young, handsome and rich, so that, to the untouched heart and the uncomplicated eye, there was nothing to choose between them, Hermia's father had made a choice. He had chosen Demetrius; and such was the harsh law of Athens, where they all lived, that Hermia had to obey her father and marry Demetrius, or be shut up in a nunnery for the rest of her life.

So Hermia was in despair, Lysander was in torment, Demetrius was triumphant, and Helena, loving and unloved, wept like a willow over a stream of her own making. It was a pitiable state of affairs, and it could not have been better put than by Lysander, who declared that:

"The course of true love never did run smooth."

But nonetheless, run it did, on eager, fearful feet, to a certain wood not far from the town. There, in the moon washed time of night, Lysander and Hermia planned to meet and fly to some distant place where they would be safe from the cruel Athenian law.

All would have been well had not Hermia, warm-hearted, confiding Hermia, told Helena, who was her longest, dearest friend. Helena, more doleful than ever, and hoping for no more than a glance of gratitude and a rag of his company, played the tell-tale and told Demetrius of the flight. Demetrius was outraged. He rushed off to the wood, meaning to win Hermia's heart by plunging his sword into Lysander's. And after him went Helena, in despairing pursuit.

Nor were these love-tangled four the only ones who went to the wood upon that Midsummer's night; for no man, not even a lover, can have the world to himself. Six good men and true, six solid workmen of Athens, engaged to meet there in secret. They were to rehearse a play for the festivities of Duke Theseus's marriage to Hippolyta, once his enemy but soon to be his love.

Very serious was their business, for if their play was chosen, they would all be given pensions and stand high in the esteem of their fellow workmen in the town. The play, as was right for a wedding, was of lovers; so the six good men and true, with their heads full of passions and pensions, went to the wood, where already, in thicket and clearing, there was love in earnest and love in despair.

It was a strange wood, as huge, dark and mysterious as a man's mind. It was haunted—and by more than spinning spiders, beetles, hedgehogs and softly gliding, spotted snakes. There were other personages who flickered among the shadows, darted across moonbeams, hung in the beating air and pursued mysterious affairs of their own.

"Ill met by moonlight, proud Titania!"

Oberon, dread King of the night! Shadowy, formidable, with train of goblins, sprites and elves; and with Puck, his grinning, mocking henchman by his side; stepped suddenly into the moonshine and stood, a dark threat in a silver world.

Over and against him, caught in brightness with delicate foot unplaced, Titania, his queen, drew back with hands upraised in anger.

"What, jealous Oberon? Fairies, skip hence! I have forsworn his bed and company!"

Strange quarrel between these powerful rulers of the night time world! Titania had as her attendant a changeling Indian boy that Oberon desired

for himself. But Oberon's request had been denied, and his command scorned. So there was discord in the world of spirits no less than in the world of men. In consequence, the very seasons had been disturbed: killing frosts and drowning floods had spoiled the spring and bewildered the summer, for a quarrel between so dangerous a King and so wild a Queen, made a sickness in Nature herself.

"Do you amend it then; it lies in you," accused Oberon. "I do but beg a little changeling boy . . ."

"Not for thy fairy kingdom!" vowed Titania. And, with her gossamer train attending, swept from the glade, leaving her shadowy lord to brood angrily on his disappointment.

"Well, go thy way," he murmured at length. "Thou shalt not from this grove till I torment thee for this injury."

Presently the notion of a strange revenge came into his ranging thoughts. There was, he knew, a certain purple flower that grew, far, far away in the west, that was possessed of an uncanny power. If the juice of this flower was dropped upon sleeping eyelids, then the sleeper, on awakening, would fall wildly, madly in love with the very next living creature—be it lion, bear, wolf or monkey, no matter how vile—that the magically anointed eyes beheld.

"Fetch me this herb," commanded Oberon to Puck, his lurking henchman, "and be thou here again ere the leviathan can swim a league."

"I'll put a girdle round about the earth," promised Puck, a prick-eared child with a crooked grin, whose chief delight was fright and confusion, "in forty minutes!" And off he sped, like a wicked arrow, from his dread master's side.

Lost in thought, the King awaited his servant's return until suddenly, the murmuring quiet of the wood was disturbed. There came a violent crashing, and rending, and gasping, and panting, as of wild beasts lost and confused. At once the brooding King drew the night about him, like a cloak, and became no more than the shadow of a shadow . . .

The commotion burst out into the pooled moonlight and made it shake.

"I love thee not, therefore pursue me not!" It was the furious Demetrius with Helena wailing hopelessly in his wake. "Hence, get thee gone and follow me no more!"

Her tale-bearing had done her no good. Instead of her lover's company, she'd gained only the sight of his avoiding back; and instead of his gratitude, she'd had only his shoulder-flung abuse. But still she pursued him, weeping and sobbing her love.

"I am your spaniel," she wailed; "and, Demetrius, the more you beat me, I will fawn on you. Use me but as your spaniel," she pleaded. "Only give me leave, unworthy as I am, to follow you!"

"I am sick when I do look on thee!" shouted Demetrius, feeling unwanted love at his heels like a stone in his shoe.

"And I am sick when I look not on you!" sobbed Helena.

"Let me go!" cried Demetrius, wild only to find Hermia and kill Lysander. "Or if thou follow me do not believe but I shall do thee mischief in the wood!"

He bore himself like a monarch . . .

But Helena was past caring. So far gone was she in love that custom, modesty, and maidenly restraint were but as specks on the horizon, and remembered only with a pang.

"We should be woo'd," she wept, "and were not made to woo!"

Demetrius escaped, and Helena, with a doleful cry, plunged after. The glade stood empty of all save moonlight and the memory of distress. Then Oberon became visible, as if in the thinning of a mist.

"Fare thee well, nymph," he murmured, gazing after the broken-hearted lady. "Ere he do leave this grove, thou shalt fly him, and he shall seek thy love."

As he stood meditating on how this reversal might be brought about, Puck returned breathlessly to his side, holding out the little purple flower. Oberon's eyes glittered mysteriously as he took it.

"I know a bank where the wild thyme blows," he whispered, as his fancy brought it before his mind's eye. "There sleeps Titania some time of the night." Dreamily he crushed the flower between his pale fingers so that its liquor ran into a cup, held out by the eager Puck. "And with the juice of this I'll streak her eyes, and make her full of hateful fantasies . . ."

He smiled vengefully; and then, remembering the distress that had passed so recently before his invisible eyes, he bade Puck take a little of the juice and anoint the eyes of the scornful youth so that, when he waked, he should dote to distraction on the tall, fair, tearful lady who had so unavailingly pursued him.

"Thou shalt know the man," he instructed, "by the Athenian garments he hath on."

"Fear not, my lord," assured Puck; "your servant shall do so."

Now the wood was quiet, and folded in night; and the moon's dream self drifted, among mirrored branches, in stream and pool. The two wanderers, dark master and quick servant, crept among the shadowy trees, each with his portion of the charmed liquor: the one to make love run mad, the other to make love run smooth and prosperous to life's end.

First Oberon found what he sought, and while Titania slumbered, and her drowsy sentinels nodded at their posts, he streaked her sleeping eyes with the purple flower's juice.

"What thou seest when thou dost wake," he breathed; "do it for thy true love take . . . Wake when some vile thing is near."

He left her sleeping and so cloaked and canopied in the garments of nature that the youth and the girl who came into the glade soon after saw nothing but leaves and flowers. But then they never looked to see a sleeping queen, for they had eyes only for each other.

Hermia and Lysander, those dear lovers in perfect accord, were weary from walking, and were lost.

"We'll rest us, Hermia," proposed Lysander, "if you think it good."

"Be it so, Lysander," agreed small, dark Hermia, with a downward cast of her eyes; "find you out a bed, for I upon this bank will rest my head."

"One turf shall serve as pillow for us both," said Lysander, with a tenderness that filled sweet Hermia with grave misgivings.

"Nay, good Lysander; for my sake, my dear, lie further off yet; do not lie so near."

Fervently Lysander protested that his intentions were most honourable and urged his lovely Hermia to reconsider her unkind decision. But Hermia shook her head.

"Lie further off, in human modesty," she insisted with gentle reproach. "Such separation as may well be said becomes a virtuous bachelor and a maid. So far be distant; and good night, sweet friend."

Lysander sighed but, deferring to his lady, found himself a bed some little way removed; and presently the lovers, united in spirit though divided in flesh, closed their eyes in sleep.

So they lay when Puck found them and, surprised and vexed to see so much distance between them, instantly took them for the youth and girl he had been told to find.

"This is he my master said despised the Athenian maid . . . and here the maiden sleeping sound, on the dank and dirty ground!" the goblin cried indignantly. "Pretty soul! she durst not lie near this lack-love, this kill-courtesy!"

Straightway and without another thought, he anointed Lysander's closed eyes with the charmed juice, and returned to Oberon, well pleased with his success.

No sooner had he departed than calamity came into the glade. It came with a rush and a cry and a moan and a wail. It came in the shape of doleful Helena. Chivvied by bush and fingered by briar, with her gown in as many tatters and shreds as her heart, she paused, panting for breath. She had lost Demetrius and knew not where to turn.

"But who is here?" she cried. "Lysander on the ground?"

She rushed and knelt beside him, hanging her anxious face above his, like a sad moon with lips, eyes and streaming silken hair. "Lysander, if you live, good sir, awake!"

He awoke, opened his bewitched eyes, saw Helena (for there was little else within his scope!) and loved her madly, as he had never loved before!

Shocked beyond measure, Helena drew back, reminded Lysander that it was Hermia he loved—

"Not Hermia but Helena I love!" cried Lysander. "Who will not change a raven for a dove?" And he poured out so wild a torrent of passion that Helena quailed before it and thought herself to be most unkindly mocked.

"O that a lady of one man refused," she sobbed, "should of another therefore be abused!" And she fled from the clearing, dismayed.

Lysander, seeing the sleeping Hermia, wondered how he could ever have loved her.

"Hermia," he cried—but softly for he did not want to awaken her, "sleep thou there, and never mayest thou come Lysander near!"

Then off he rushed in pursuit of Helena, who pursued Demetrius, who, in his turn, pursued Hermia, who laying sleeping and abandoned, with nothing for company but troubled dreams.

She awoke and called out for Lysander. There was no answer. She looked: the glade was empty. She called again:

"Lysander! lord! What, out of hearing? Gone? No sound, no word?"

She trembled, she shook, she cried out in terror; and then, like Helena before her, fled from the clearing, dismayed!

The glade was still and the troubled moonlight calm again; so that the disturbed bushes and shaken leaves were restored to skilful silverware. Oberon's queen still slept upon her secret couch; her magically anointed eyes had yet to open . . .

"Are we all met?" came a plain, sturdy voice.

"Pat, pat," came another; "and here's a marvellous convenient place for our rehearsal."

The six good men and true, the six worthy workmen of Athens, clumped into the moonlight glade, paused and peered thoughtfully about them.

"This green plot shall be our stage," decided Peter Quince, a carpenter by trade. He was the most scholarly of the company and was to produce the play.

The parts had been given out and all was now to go forward, exactly as it would be before the Duke. That is, if their play was chosen.

"Peter Quince!"

Nick Bottom, the weaver, spoke up, and everybody paid attention. Among every company of men there is always one to be reckoned with, one that it is good to have on your side, one whose abilities mark him out as a mine of intellect and a tower of strength.

Such a man was Bottom the weaver: large, big-faced and with little eyes ringed round with red, as if to emphasize their importance. He was down for Pyramus in the play, which was the lover's part and the most important; for none but Bottom could have undertaken it. He might have played Thisbe, the lady, with equal success; he might have played the Lion, who frightened poor Thisbe away; he might have played any or all of the other parts—for he had a genius for each of them, as everyone agreed—but he had to play Pyramus, for none but Bottom could have undertaken it. Without Bottom there could be no Pyramus; and without Pyramus there could be no play. The whole enterprise was founded on Bottom; and without a Bottom it would· have fallen through.

"Peter Quince!"

"What sayest thou, bully Bottom?"

Bottom had a great deal to say, and all of it good sturdy sense. He had discovered that Pyramus, in the play, was to kill himself, which would distress the ladies in their audience to such an extent that the hoped-for pensions might well be in peril. Everyone nodded wisely and looked to Bottom for a solution. They were not disappointed.

"Write me a prologue," said Bottom, "to say we will do no harm with our swords, and that Pyramus is not killed indeed. Tell them that I, Pyramus, am not Pyramus, but Bottom the weaver. This will put them out of fear."

He smiled, and everyone looked relieved. Truly was Bottom a man of infinite resource, and a very presant help in time of need.

So the rehearsal went forward, with tireless assistance from Bottom, who was never at a loss to improve the play. With all solemnity the six good men and true transformed themselves into ardent lovers, a ravening lion and a patient wall (for a wall was required and there was none nearby); and Peter Quince, with book in hand, sometimes admiring, sometimes critical, guided the progress of the play.

But Peter Quince was not the only auditor; or, for that matter, the only critic of the proceedings.

"What hempen homespuns have we swaggering here, so near the cradle of the Fairy Queen?"

Puck, lurking among leaves, peered out at the worthy workmen's solemn antics. He grinned crookedly, and his eyes glittered like spots of dew.

"I'll meet thee, Pyramus, at Ninny's tomb," announced Francis Flute, the bellows-mender, who, though he had a beard coming, and was bashful about it, played the lady Thisbe.

"Ninus' tomb, man!" cried Peter Quince, crossly. "Why you must not speak that yet; that you answer to Pyramus." Then, losing patience with Flute, who, though earnest, was slow of learning, accused him bitterly: "You speak all your part at once, cues and all." He shook his head and sighed. Come what would to try him, the play must go on. "Pyramus, enter!" he called. "Your cue is past . . ."

Bottom, who had retired within a hawthorn brake, stepped forth with that mixture of modesty and expectation that marks the well-graced actor who knows that all eyes will be upon him, and the rest of the company ignored. His expectations were answered. All eyes were most certainly upon him—and to a bulging extent.

His companions stared, glared, shook, trembled, turned white, turned grey . . . and most precipitantly fled! Bottom, surprised, could make

261

nothing of it. He shook his head. Peter Quince returned, briefly and timorously. He stared at Bottom, appalled.

"Bless thee, Bottom, bless thee! Thou art translated."

Then he retired again in melancholy terror. Bottom frowned and looked down upon himself to see what cause there was for dismay. None. There were his own stout arms, his own good stomach, his own sturdy legs that ended up, as might have been expected, in his own large, familiar boots. All that he could see was as it should have been, and proper to Bottom. It was only what he saw with that was not. From the neck down he was Bottom the weaver; from the neck up he was—a monster!

While he had waited in the hawthorn brake, listening for his cue, Puck had touched his broad brow and made it harsh and hairy, had touched his nose and made it a muzzle, and had touched his ears and made them grow. In short, he had clapped upon the shoulders of the unsuspecting Bottom, the sickening head of an ass!

"I see their knavery," said Bottom, by way of a dignified reproof to his departed companions; "this is to make an ass of me . . ." He walked up and down and began to sing in a loud voice to keep up his spirits. He was divided between mystification and anger over the behaviour of his friends; for he, no more than any man, could see that he had a donkey's head.

Puck watched with rare delight, and guided the weaver's steps nearer and nearer to the bed of the Fairy Queen. Suddenly she awoke, and opened her anointed eyes.

"What angel wakes me from my flowery bed?" she cried, hearing Bottom's braying voice and then seeing him in all his hairy, long-eared glory.

Bottom acknowledged the greeting of the Fairy Queen, and then continued with his song, for he was not a man easily amazed.

"I pray thee, gentle mortal, sing again!" begged Titania; and, helpless with admiration, confessed to the donkey-headed Bottom that she loved him at first sight.

"Methinks, mistress, you should have little reason for that," said Bottom in all honesty; and went on to express a wish to find his way out of the wood. But that was not to be.

"Thou shalt remain here," commanded Titania, "whether thou wilt or no. I am a spirit of no common rate," she declared, rising from her couch in all her strange beauty and majesty. "And I do love thee; therefore go with me."

Bottom bowed his long-eared head in courteous assent, and bright Titania awarded him four gossamer sprites to tend upon him and supply his every want. So Bottom, whom nothing could surprise—for, though he had an ass's head, he had a rare soul—went affably with the Fairy Queen, while the four sprites waited on his smallest command. He bore himself like a monarch . . .

These matters Puck reported to his master, who nodded, well-pleased by the grotesque punishment that had been visited on his disobedient Queen.

"But hast thou," he asked, "yet latch'd the Athenian's eyes with the love-juice, as I did bid thee do?"

"I took him sleeping," promised Puck, "that is finish'd, too." Even as he said it, Demetrius and Hermia came into the glade.

"Stand close;" murmured Oberon, dissolving into a kind of mist, "this is the same Athenian."

"This is the woman," agreed Puck, thinning by his master's side; "but not this the man."

Puck had blundered. Demetrius still loved Hermia, who still loved Lysander, who now, by reason of Puck's mistake, loved Helena who, therefore, must still love where she was despised.

"See me no more!" cried small dark Hermia, wearied and distressed by the unwanted Demetrius. And she plunged away in pursuit of her lost Lysander. Demetrius gazed after her in despair.

"There's no following her in this fierce vein," he sighed regretfully; and, overcome with weariness from the chase, lay down to rest.

"What hast thou done?" demanded Oberon, vexed by his servant's error. "About the wood go swifter than the wind, and Helena of Athens look thou find!"

The goblin vanished and Oberon softly approached the sleeping Demetrius.

"When his love he doth espy, let her shine," he whispered, anointing the sleeper's eyes with the liquor of the purple flower. "When thou wak'st, if she be by, beg of her for remedy."

Even as this was done Puck returned, leading in his invisible wake the melancholy Helena who, in her turn, was followed by the eye-bewitched Lysander. Demetrius awoke, opened his charmed eyes, saw Helena and straightway fell madly, wildly in love with her! No sooner had he declared himself, than Hermia returned and there followed a scene of such frantic confusion, such anger, such reproach, such accusation and denial, such brandishing of fists and flashing of eyes, such wounding with words and breaking of hearts, that, had there been mortal eyes to watch, they would have made a waterfall of tears, instead of glinting with merriment at love's calamity.

"Lord what fools these mortals be!" chuckled Puck, as the four lovers raved and ranted and wept in the moonlit glade.

"You juggler! You canker-blossom!" shouted Hermia, maddened by the very sight of Helena, once without a lover and now the undeserving possessor of two. "You thief of love!"

"Have you no modesty, no maiden shame?" wondered Helena, tottering like a stricken willow before the injustice of Hermia's reproach. "You puppet, you!"

"Puppet?" shrieked Hermia, mortified by so unkind a reference to her brevity of inches. "Thou painted maypole!"

"Let her not hurt me!" screeched Helena, skipping, like a timid doe, behind Demetrius and Lysander, as Hermia flew at her with upraised nails. "She was a vixen when she went to school!"

The quarrel leaped and blazed. Spiders, beetles, serpents and distracted birds fled from the heated scene; and the passions of the four lovers could no longer be confined within the pressing limits of the glade. Demetrius and Lysander, unable to endure each other's existence for an instant more, reached for their swords and rushed away in search of plainer ground where they might make fountains with each other's blood.

The two ladies thus abandoned in the moonlight, and panting from their recent exertions, eyed each other with strong dislike and deep distrust. Then first one, and then the other, retreated and vanished into darkness, to seek kindness and security among the less wild beasts that might inhabit the wood.

"This is thy negligence," accused Oberon, coming out from leaves and regarding his henchman with disfavour. "Still thou mistak'st, or else committ'st thy knaveries wilfully."

"Believe me, king of shadows, I mistook," protested Puck, whose goblin heart had, nonetheless, been gladdened by the sight of the crossed and crossing lovers. The four-fold enmity that had sprung from a single misplaced love had furnished him with much salty delight.

But now it was to be ended. Oberon commanded Puck to prevent the coming battle between Lysander and Demetrius, and then to undo the harm that magic had done with magic again. While Puck was so employed he would find the donkey-doting Titania and gain his chief object which was to take her Indian boy.

"Up and down, up and down," cried Puck, who foresaw as much confusion in undoing confusion as in making it, "I will lead them up and down!"

Away he sped into the wood where first he found Lysander, baffled by thicket, ditch and moonshine, shouting for his enemy and waving his sword wherever there was space to do so.

"Where art thou, proud Demetrius?"

"Here, villain, drawn and ready!" answered Puck, in Demetrius's voice.

"I'll be with thee straight!" swore Lysander and went off as round-about as Puck could lead him, fighting with bushes, branches and shadows every step of the way.

Next he taunted Demetrius with Lysander's voice; then back to Lysander, then Demetrius again, then with goblin speed, to furious Lysander. He was here, he was there, he was in front, he was behind, he was everywhere, he was nowhere!

"Follow my voice!" he called; and follow it the maddened lovers did, until the wood was filled with shouts and cries and grunts and gasps, and the glitter of swords as they slashed at moonbeams and pierced the dark. Then, little by little, the passionate enemies grew slower in their motions. Their limbs ached and their bright swords, no longer flashing, helped them, like sticks or crutches, on their weary way. At length first one and then the other tottered into the very glade from which they'd set out; and, unaware of each other, thankfully lay down and went to sleep.

"O weary night, O long and tedious night!" wailed Helena, straying upon the scene and seeing nothing but her own sadness. Her heart was broken. She sighed and sank down upon the grass and prayed for sleep.

"Yet but three?" cried Puck, examining with interest the unconscious contents of the glade. "Come one more, two of both kinds makes up four!"

"I can no further crawl, no further go;" sobbed Hermia, shredded alike by misery and briar. "Here will I rest me till the break of day!"

And she joined the three sleepers to make up the goblin's four.

"Sleep sound!" whispered Puck and, darting forward, squeezed the fateful juice into Lysander's dreaming eyes. "When thou wak'st," he promised, "thou tak'st true delight in the sight of thy former lady's eye!"

He vanished, leaving the four strewn upon the grass, like fallen warriors on love's battlefield.

"Come sit thee down upon this flowery bed," begged the Fairy Queen, marvellous in the moonlight, "while I thy amiable cheeks do coy . . . and kiss thy fair large ears . . ."

Bottom, sturdy, donkey-headed Bottom, brayed with pleasure and with dignity, submitted himself to Titania's embrace.

Crowned and wreathed and stuck all over with admiring roses, Bottom laid himself down upon Titania's couch, while his attendant

sprites scratched him and tickled him and supplied his every want. Presently, the weariness of endlessly fulfilled desires overcame him.

"I have," he declared with a yawn, "an exposition of sleep come upon me."

"Sleep thou," murmured the Fairy Queen. "O how I love thee! How I dote on thee!"

So Bottom slumbered, and his loud snores made a thunderous lullaby that soon lulled Titania and her court into sleep. Sleep! The glade was filled with it, and the very moonlight seemed to dream. Bushes nodded and flowers turned and dozed, as Oberon and his henchman came softly among them. The king of shadows, having obtained the Indian boy, looked down with pity on his bewitched queen.

"I will undo this hateful imperfection of her eyes," he whispered; and doing so, with the juice of another herb, bade Titania wake.

"My Oberon!" she cried, "What visions have I seen! Methought I was enamoured of an ass!"

"There lies your love," said Oberon; and Titania gazed appalled upon the vision of flowery, snoring, donkey-headed Bottom.

"How came these things to pass?" she demanded; but Oberon smiled and shook his head. Then, bidding Puck restore Bottom to his human state, he took Titania by the hand and led her, dancing, from the sleeping scene.

The sounds of hounds and horn came winding through the wood. Duke Theseus and his future queen were out upon the morning's hunt.

Presently the Royal riders entered the glade and gazed down in wonderment upon the sleepers.

"My lord, this is my daughter here asleep!" cried Hermia's father, who was of the company. Seeing how things were, he demanded that the full rigour of the law should be visited directly on his truant child.

But when the lovers were awakened, all could see that, either by magic, witchcraft, or merely by true love finding out true heart (which must be magical enough!), each now loved where he should, and each was beloved by whom she would. So the angry father was overruled. It was a day of forgiveness; it was Duke Theseus's wedding day.

"In the temple, by and by with us," he decreed, "these couples shall eternally be knit."

So Hermia and Lysander, Demetrius and happy Helena, winding arms and linking looks and smiles, followed the Duke and his company out of the glade, all spite and anger, all tears and heartbreak having faded into the semblance of a dream.

"When my cue comes, call me and I will answer."

Bottom awoke. He was alone. He scratched his head and, to his great relief, found that it was the proper head for Bottom. He shook it. It was indeed the self-same head he'd had for as long as he could remember. And yet there was a difference. There was a dream inside it, a dream of such brightness that Bottom, when he thought about it, shone like a star in boots. He smiled, and it was a rare smile, for Bottom, of all mortals, had walked, waking, in the kingdom of dreams.

"I will get Peter Quince to write a ballad of this dream," he decided. "It shall be called, 'Bottom's Dream', because it hath no bottom."

With that he went back to the town where his companions greeted him with relief and joy. Now the play could go forward, for Bottom was come among them again; and none but Bottom could ever have played Pyramus. Their pensions were certain and, for bully Bottom, as Flute the bellows-mender put it, "sixpence a day in Pyramus, or nothing."

That very day the Duke and his queen, and the two pairs of lovers, were married with due solemnity; and that night the tragedy of Pyramus and Thisbe was enacted before them with all the delicacy, wit and grace that Peter Quince and his company could command. Snug the joiner played the Lion to perfection, and Snout the tinker rose to great heights as the Wall. Starveling the tailor shone in the necessary part of the man in the moon; and Flute was a Thisbe to wring all hearts. But bully Bottom the weaver was best of all. He lived Pyramus, he died Pyramus, and lived again to take his bow, so powerfully that there was not, as they say, a dry eye in the house . . . although whether the tears shed were of grief or laughter, none could say.

The play done, the married lovers went their ways to bed. For a little while the hall was empty; then Puck and Oberon and Titania, with all their gossamer train, came with glow-worm lamps to bless the house and bid goodnight.

Macbeth

Three old women out in a storm. But what old women, and what a storm! It banged and roared and crashed and rattled. The sky was quick with sudden glares, and the earth with sudden darknesses, darknesses in which wild images of rocks and frightened trees, like scanty beggars in the wind, leaped out upon the inner eye! And the old women! Ancient hags with backs hooped like question marks and their shabby heads nesting together, like brooding vultures . . .

"When shall we three meet again?" howled one, above the shrieking of the wind. "In thunder, lightning or in rain?"

"When the hurly-burly's done!" came an answer, lank hair whipping and half muffling the words. "When the battle's lost and won!"

"Where the place?"

"Upon the heath."

"And there to meet with Macbeth!"

The sky stared, then shut its eye . . . and when it looked again, the old women had gone. Had they been real or had they only been fantastic imaginings made up out of strange configurations of the rocks? Yet their words had been real enough. There was a battle being fought, and there was a man called Macbeth.

Macbeth! A giant of fury and courage, his sword arm whirling and beating like a windmill as he fought for his king against the treacherous enemies who sought to overturn the state. So tremendously did he fight that he made killing almost holy, and they say his blade smoked with traitors' blood.

A soldier from the battlefield, a gaudy, staggering patchwork of blood and gashes, came stumbling into the royal camp to tell the King of Macbeth's mighty deeds, of how he had come face to face with the worst of the King's enemies and, with one blow had "unseamed him from the nave to the chops, and fixed his head upon our battlements".

Amazed, good King Duncan listened to the eager account of his general's almost supernatural bravery and success; and, while he stood wondering how he might justly reward such service, news came of yet another victory. The treacherous Thane of Cawdor had been captured. The King sighed. The price of victory was high. He had once loved and trusted Cawdor.

"Go pronounce his present death," he commanded sombrely; "and with his former title greet Macbeth . . . What he hath lost, noble Macbeth hath won."

He sent two messengers post-haste to greet the great general with his new title and with the heartfelt gratitude of his King.

The King's messengers travelled swiftly, but even before they had set out, other messengers were on their way to meet Macbeth, messengers who travelled as fast as thinking, messengers whose purpose was as dark as the King's was bright: the three old women of the storm.

It was towards evening. There was thunder in the air and little lightnings, like bright adders, wriggled across the sky. Here and there on the open heath naked trees seemed to hold up their hands in fear and dismay; and the three old women crouched and waited, still as stones. Presently there came a rolling and a rattling, as if a small thunder had lost its way and was wandering in the dark. The three old women nodded.

"A drum, a drum! Macbeth doth come!"

The drummer was Banquo, friend and companion-in-arms of Macbeth. The drum he carried had been salvaged from the battlefield, taken, perhaps, out of the cradling arms of some dead drummer-boy. Cheer-

"A drum, a drum! Macbeth doth come!"

fully he thumped it as he and mighty Macbeth strode on through the gathering night, their kilts swinging and their heads held high.

Suddenly they halted and the drum ceased like a stopped heart. Their way was barred. Three old women had appeared before them, three hideous old women who crouched and stared. For an instant, an uncanny fear seized the two warriors; then Banquo recovered himself. Imperiously he thumped on his drum and demanded:

"What are these, so withered and so wild in their attire?"

Silence. He thumped again.

"Live you?"

Their silence remained unbroken.

"Or are you aught that man may question?"

At this, the old women's eyes glinted, and slowly each raised a finger to her lips. Thus they crouched, like crooked answers awaiting only the right question, and the right questioner. They turned to the great, battle-stained figure of Macbeth. For the smallest moment, he hesitated; then commanded:

"Speak if you can! What are you?"

The right questioner. One by one they rose and greeted him.

"All hail Macbeth, hail to thee, Thane of Glamis!"

His rightful title, and Banquo thumped approval on his drum.

"All hail Macbeth, hail to thee, Thane of Cawdor!"

The drum faltered . . .

"All hail Macbeth, that shalt be King hereafter!"

King! The drum stopped. King! It seemed that another drum was beating. Macbeth could hear it, thudding and thundering in his ears. It was his furious heart! He trembled and grew pale, fearing that Banquo would hear the tell-tale sound. But Banquo was no more proof than he against the golden promise in the weird old women's words.

"If you can look into the seeds of time," he begged them eagerly, "and say which grain will grow and which will not, speak then to me . . ."

As before they answered, one by one.

"Lesser than Macbeth and greater," promised the first.

"Not so happy, yet much happier," promised the second.

"Thou shalt get kings though thou be none," promised the third.

"Stay, you imperfect speakers!" shouted Macbeth. "Tell me more!"

But even as he spoke, the weird sisters vanished, as abruptly as if, whispered Banquo, "The earth hath bubbles as the water has, and these are of them . . ."

It was then, as the two men stood, staring at one another and wondering if what they had seen and heard had been real, that the King's two messengers appeared, and the first of the weird sisters' prophecies came true. The King had made him Thane of Cawdor!

"What! Can the Devil speak true?" cried Banquo, involuntarily; and Macbeth's thoughts turned helplessly to the second prophecy: he would be King! If one had come true, why not the other? Dark thoughts filled his head, thoughts of how that prophecy might be made to come true. He tried to put them from him. He shook his head violently. "If Chance will have me King," he reasoned to himself, "why Chance may crown me without my stir."

But Chance proved as wayward as a woman, first offering, now denying. When he returned to the royal camp with the messengers, he heard King Duncan pronounce Malcolm, his son, as heir to the throne of Scotland. Chance had mocked him; all was lost. Then Chance offered again. The kindly King declared that he would travel to Inverness, and stay one night as the guest of his loyal and well-loved subject, Macbeth.

"Stars, hide your fires!" whispered Macbeth, as he set off ahead of the King to warn his wife to prepare for the royal night. "Let not light see my black and deep desires!"

The lady of the castle had a letter in her hand. Over and over again she read it as she paced back and forth across her tall chamber where the light came through a narrow window like a knife. Each time she crossed the beam, her red hair blazed, as if there was a furnace in her head. The letter was from her husband, Macbeth. It told of his meeting with the weird sisters, of their strange prophecies, and of how the first had already been fulfilled. She put the letter aside.

"Glamis thou art," she breathed, "and Cawdor, and shalt be what thou art promised . . ."

King! He must be King! But how was it to be brought about? Even as she wondered, a servant entered the room.

"What is your tidings?" she demanded.

"The King comes here tonight."

She caught her breath; she started violently.

"Thou'rt mad to say it!" she cried out, before she could prevent herself; for in that instant she knew that the messenger had announced the death of the King. She and her husband together would murder him.

When her husband came, wild and breathless from his furious ride, she embraced him passionately; and, as they talked in low, rapid tones of the approaching King, she saw in his face that his thoughts were the same as hers. Yet perhaps they showed too plainly . . .

"Your face, my Thane," she warned him, "is as a book where men may read strange matters."

He nodded; then he faltered a little. Between the thinking and the doing of a deed, there was a line to be crossed. Though he was mighty in the trade of public blood, he shrank from private murder in the dark.

"We will speak further," he muttered.

But she would have none of it. Fate had promised him the crown, and the crown he would have.

"Only look up clear," she commanded. "Leave all the rest to me."

It was late afternoon when King Duncan, his two sons and his nobles, reached Inverness; and the lady of the castle, all smiles and bending like a flower, came out to greet them.

"Give me your hand," said the gentle King, and the lady, with welcome in her face and murder in her heart, gave the King her hand and drew him into her house.

That night, sounds of cheerful feasting filled the air; torches flamed in the stony passages and courtyards, making fantastic shadows of the hurrying servants, and the castle ran red with wine. But Macbeth, the host, was not at the feast. He had left the table in a mood of sudden horror at the thought of what he was to do. He stood alone in a courtyard, close against the wall.

"He's here in double trust," he whispered wretchedly: "first as I am his kinsman and his subject, strong both against the deed; then as his host who should against his murderer shut the door, not bear the knife myself."

"Why have you left the chamber?"

It was his wife. She had come in search of him. Her looks were fierce. He tried to avoid them.

"We will proceed no further in this business."

Furiously she turned on him for his cowardice.

"I dare do all that may become a man," he protested; "who dares do more is none."

Her eyes blazed, her scorn increased and stung him unbearably. He weakened. "If we should fail?"

"We fail!" she cried triumphantly. "But screw your courage to the sticking-place and we'll not fail!"

He stared at her, and she at him. He bowed his head. The matter was settled.

Past midnight. The feast was ended and the feasters all in bed. The torches were out and the castle was dark and quiet. Yet there was an uneasiness in the air, and sleep was restless. Two men crossed a court that was open to the black sky. One was Banquo, the other was Fleance, his son. A light approached.

"Who's there?"

It was the master of the house with a servant carrying a torch. His face was a rapid mingling of firelight and shadows, now seeming to scowl, now to grin, now plunged into utter gloom.

"I dreamt last night of the three weird sisters," murmured Banquo to his friend. "To you they have showed some truth."

"I think not of them," said Macbeth, and looked away. The friends parted. For a moment, Macbeth stared after Banquo and his son. Then he turned to his servant. "Go bid thy mistress," he ordered, "when my drink is ready she strike upon the bell."

The servant departed, and Macbeth waited, listening. Once again, horrible thoughts filled his head, and strange fancies . . .

"Is this a dagger which I see before me?" he breathed; for he did indeed

seem to see such a weapon, eerily in the air, and it was thick with blood. Then, faintly, he heard the sound of a bell. Although he expected it, had been waiting for it, he started violently when it came.

"Hear it not, Duncan," he whispered, "for it is a knell that summons thee to heaven or to hell." Then, drawing his own dagger, he crept from the court like a ghost.

There was silence. Nothing stirred, nothing breathed. Then Lady Macbeth appeared. Her face was white; her eyes blazed with inward fire. She waited. Suddenly an owl screamed, and the night sighed. She stared towards the chamber where the King slept.

"He is about it."

A shadow moved. It was Macbeth.

"My husband!" she cried, and tried to embrace him. He pushed her aside.

"I have done the deed," he said, and stared down at his hands. He was holding two daggers: their blades and his hands were dripping with blood.

"This is a sorry sight," he said.

"A foolish thought, to say a sorry sight," cried she. But for once her words had no force for him. What he had done had put him out of her reach. To her, he had done no more than to kill an old man to get a crown; to himself, he had murdered sleeping innocence, he had murdered his own honour, he had killed his own soul. Already, he was a man apart.

"Why did you bring these daggers from the place?" she demanded. "They must lie there. Go . . ."

He shook his head. "I'll go no more. I am afraid to think what I have done; look on't again I dare not."

"Give me the daggers!" she exclaimed contemptuously. "The sleeping and the dead are but as pictures . . ."

She seized the daggers and left him. No sooner had she gone than there came a knocking on the outer gate. He shook and trembled and stared down at his murderer's hands. Lady Macbeth returned. Her hands were now as guilty as his.

"My hands are of your colour," she said, holding them up before him; "but I shame to wear a heart so white." She rubbed her hands together, and, as if comforting a child, said: "A little water clears us of this deed."

Then the knocking was heard again. It was loud and urgent. Husband and wife stared at one another—and fled.

It was Macduff who knocked at the gate, Macduff, the great Thane of Fife. He had come to rouse the King. His knocking had been so loud that all the castle had been awakened—all, that is, except for the King.

"I'll bring you to him," offered the master of the house. "This is the door," he said, gesturing with a white hand and a whiter smile. He stood aside and Macduff went in to the King.

He waited, at ease, it seemed, with the world. He waited for Macduff to cross the outer chamber; to reach the inner chamber; to open the door. He waited, still easy, until he heard the shout, the cry, the shriek of discovery, as Macduff saw what lay on the bed within. Then Macduff ran out. His looks were wild and frantic. The King was dead! He had been slaughtered as he slept!

"Murder and treason!" he shouted. "Banquo and Donalbain! Malcolm, awake!"

Murder and treason! The castle rocked. The very stones seemed to shake and glare. Murder and treason! Torches, like maddened fireflies, rushed hither and thither, throwing up faces, like sudden paintings of amazement and horror, as nobles and servants came tumbling upon the scene. Murder and treason! The King had been killed in the night! Who had done it? Why, his guards, of course, who else? Question them! Impossible! Macbeth had already stopped their tongues. Rage had overcome him and he had slaughtered them for the crime!

"Wherefore did you so?" demanded Macduff, a terrible suspicion awakening in his heart.

"Who can be wise, amazed, temperate and furious, loyal and neutral in a moment?" cried Macbeth. "No man."

The King's two sons looked fearfully to one another. Their father had been murdered. Would they be next?

"Where we are, there's daggers in men's smiles," muttered one.

"Therefore to horse," answered the other, "and let us not be dainty of leave-taking but shift away!"

They fled from the hall and from the castle, and from Scotland itself, leaving behind the dead King, the crown—and Macbeth.

The old women's prophecy was fulfilled. The grain they had spied in Macbeth's heart had grown and flourished in that dark place. He seized the crown and mounted the throne. He was King, and none dared oppose him: not murdered Duncan's sons, not great Macduff, nor even Banquo, who, of all men, knew enough to bring him down.

"Thou hast it now," murmured Banquo thoughtfully: "King, Cawdor, Glamis, all as the weird women promised; yet I fear thou playedst most foully for it . . ."

He was at Forres in the royal palace, soon after Macbeth and his Lady had been crowned. There was to be a banquet that night. All the Scottish nobles, himself included, had been summoned to do homage to the new King. Banquo watched, but kept his thoughts to himself. This was partly caution, and partly because he also had been given a promise by the weird sisters. Though he would not be King himself, he would be father to kings.

"Ride you this afternoon?" inquired Macbeth, coming upon his old companion-in-arms, and fondly greeting him.

"Aye, my good Lord," answered Banquo, and confided that he would not be back till an hour or two after nightfall.

"Goes Fleance with you?"

"Aye, my good Lord . . ."

Macbeth nodded, and wished Banquo and his son Godspeed.

"Fail not our feast," he said and stared after Banquo long and deep. He had not forgotten the old women's prophecy to his friend; and the recollection of it festered in his heart.

A servant approached, bringing in two strange, muffled-looking men. They were grim fellows that the world had treated badly; and, in return, they were prepared to take their revenge upon the world—and upon Banquo, in particular.

They talked together and soon the matter was settled between them. The men departed, and Macbeth breathed harshly. "It is concluded!" he whispered. "Banquo, thy soul's flight, if it find heaven, must find it out tonight!" His friend and his friend's son were to be murdered that night.

"How now, my Lord? Why do you keep alone?"

Lady Macbeth approached the brooding King. Her face was worn, her eyes had lost their fire. She scarcely knew her husband any more. The deed he had done had set him apart, and now they seemed to face different ways: she without, and he, within.

"What's done is done," she urged; for to her it was, but not so for him.

"We have scorched the snake, not killed it," he warned. Banquo and his son still lived.

"What's to be done?" she asked. He shook his head.

"Be innocent of the knowledge," he bade her, "dearest chuck, till thou applaud the deed . . ."

Banquo was not at the feast. All the world was there, laughing, smiling, jesting, drinking—but not Banquo. Macbeth, the royal host, walked among his guests in high good humour, found a place at table, sat down . . .

"We'll drink a measure," he proposed; when he saw a man appear in the doorway, a grim, muffled-looking man whose eye caught his, and who beckoned. Macbeth left the table and went to the man. He stood close, stared at him.

"There's blood upon thy face," he murmured.

" 'Tis Banquo's then."

"Is he dispatched?"

"His throat is cut."

Macbeth nodded. And Fleance? What of the son? The man shook his head. The son had escaped. Dismay filled Macbeth's heart. Then he recovered himself. The worst, at least, was done. Banquo was dead. He dismissed the man and returned to the feast. He hesitated. The guests looked up at him.

"May it please your Highness sit?"

Macbeth frowned in puzzlement. "The table's full," he said.

"Here is a place reserved, Sir."

"Where?"

"Here, my good Lord."

He looked. He grew deathly white. He shook and trembled till he could scarcely stand. He tried to speak. His voice was thick with dread.

"Which of you have done this?"

The place offered to him was filled. Banquo was sitting in it! Banquo, his head half off, and all painted with his life's blood! Grimly the ghost of the murdered man glared at his murderer.

"Thou canst not say I did it," groaned Macbeth; "never shake thy gory locks at me!"

Amazement seized the table as the guests saw the whitened King shake and stare and mutter at an empty stool. Urgently the Queen tried to calm the company, and still more urgently to calm her frantic husband.

"Why do you make such faces?" she whispered to him. "When all's done, you look but on a stool!"

Neither she nor anyone else could see what he could see. The ghost had come for him alone. Then it departed and briefly Macbeth recovered himself. But not for long. The gashed and bleeding spectre returned, and its dreadful looks drove the King into a frenzy.

The feast broke up in dismay, and the guests rose in confusion. The King was ill. What was wrong?

"I pray you speak not," cried the distressed Queen; "he grows worse and worse. Question enrages him. At once, good night. Stand not upon the order of your going; but go at once!"

Once alone, the Queen and King stared at one another across the ruins of the feast.

"It will have blood, they say," muttered Macbeth; "blood will have blood."

The Queen was silent.

"How sayest thou, that Macduff denies his person at our bidding?" he murmured, his thoughts turning to another enemy as he recollected that Macduff had failed to attend the feast.

"Did you send to him, Sir?"

"I heard it by the way," he said; "but I will send." Another crime, another murder . . . but did it matter any more? "I am in blood stepped in so far," he sighed, "that, should I wade no more, returning were as tedious as go o'er."

He shook his head. On the next day he would seek out those who had first set him on the dark and bloody path along which he had already travelled so far. The weird sisters.

"More shall they speak," he said; "for now I am bent to know by the worst means the worst."

They were waiting for him, even as once they'd waited before. They knew he would come. They waited in a dark room in a dark house in

Forres, not very far from the royal palace; and, while they waited, they made ready.

"Double, double toil and trouble," they chanted, as they moved about a cauldron that smoked and reeked in the middle of the room; "fire burn and cauldron bubble." And into it they cast weird, unholy things.

Then they stopped.

"By the pricking of my thumbs," cried one, "something wicked this way comes!"

It was Macbeth. They stared at him, but did not speak. As before, they were answers awaiting a question.

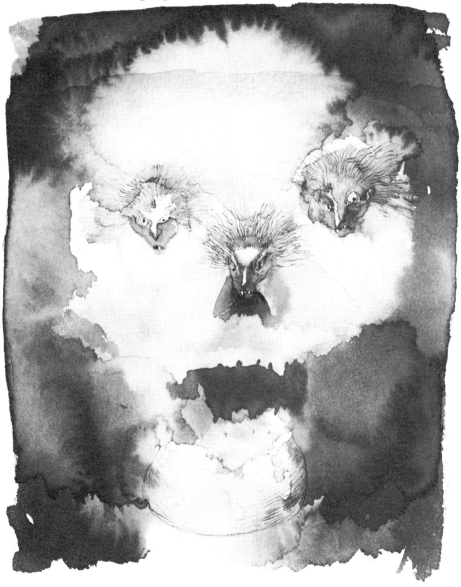

"What is't you do?" he demanded, gazing at the cauldron.

"A deed without a name."

"Answer me to what I ask you."

"Speak," said one. "Demand," said another. "We'll answer," said the third. Then the first said: "Say if thou'dst rather hear it from our mouths or from our masters."

"Call 'em," commanded Macbeth; "let me see 'em."

The weird sisters obeyed. They poured blood into the cauldron, and presently there arose from it, wreathed in smoke and wearing a warlike helmet, a severed head. It hovered in the air and stared at Macbeth.

"Tell me, thou unknown power . . ." he began; but one of the sisters bade him only listen, as the apparition already knew what he had come to ask.

"Macbeth, Macbeth, Macbeth," it chanted; "beware Macduff! Beware the Thane of Fife!"

Then the head dissolved and its place was taken by another, even stranger sight. There floated in the air before him an infant, a little child all streaked with blood.

"Macbeth, Macbeth, Macbeth," it piped. "Be bloody, bold and resolute . . . for none of woman born shall harm Macbeth!"

He would have asked more, but this second apparition had already vanished, and its place was taken by a third. Another child. But now it was a child wearing a crown and holding out the branch of a tree.

"Macbeth shall never vanquished be," this apparition told him, "until great Birnam Wood to high Dunsinane hill shall come against him."

"That will never be!" cried Macbeth, as the third apparition sank into smoky nothingness. What he had been told lifted up his heart and bewitched his spirits as if with wine! No man born of woman could ever harm him; and he would never fall till Birnam Wood came to Dunsinane. Such things could never happen, so he would never fall!

Yet there was still one thing he wanted to know. "Shall Banquo's issue ever reign in this kingdom?" he asked. "Seek to know no more," he was told. But he insisted, and, at length, he had his answer. Before his peering eyes the cauldron sank away and out of the thick air, silent and gleaming, there stalked a procession of kings. One by one they passed him by, each with a stare and each with a nod: five; six; seven; eight in all. And then came Banquo! Banquo, thick and clotted with blood. He pointed to the last of the kings who held up a glass; and in the glass were kings and more kings, stretching out into future time. Banquo smiled. Those kings to come were his!

Suddenly Macbeth was alone. Banquo, the kings and the weird sisters had vanished.

"Where are they?" he cried wildly. "Gone! Let this pernicious hour stand aye accursed in the calendar!"

Banquo's children would be kings. Macbeth would be barren. He himself was the beginning and the end of his line. But that was in the future. Present matters needed present action. That very day he sent men to murder Macduff.

But Macduff had forestalled him. He had fled to England and joined Malcolm, dead King Duncan's son. But he had left his wife and children behind.

"Where is your husband?" demanded Macbeth's murderers as they burst into her home.

She would not tell them; so they killed her, and all her children, and every living soul in the house.

In England, in peaceful, sunlit England, Malcolm and Macduff talked together of the sad plight of their own land that lay under the shadow of the tyrant King. Presently a messenger approached, a nobleman from Scotland. His looks were strange, his speech, halting.

"How does my wife?" asked Macduff.

"Why, well."

"And all my children?"

"Well too."

"The tyrant has not battered at their peace?"

"No. They were well at peace when I did leave 'em."

Then the messenger could keep back his terrible news no longer.

"Your castle is surprised, your wife and babes savagely slaughtered."

The great blow fell. Grief turned Macduff to stone. The world was empty for him now. Nothing remained but revenge.

Macbeth had gone to Dunsinane, and with him, like a painted shadow, went his Queen. Malcolm and Macduff were marching against him and he must needs prepare for war. He had no fear. No man born of woman could ever harm him, and he would not be vanquished till Birnam Wood should move and come to Dunsinane. Those were the promises of Fate. Yet he must be ready because Fate, he knew of old, needed a helping hand.

It was night in the castle of Dunsinane, and two figures stood close together in the dark hall. One was a doctor, the other a waiting-woman of the Queen.

"When was it she last walked?" asked the doctor, quietly.

"Since His Majesty went into the field."

"Besides her walking, and other actual performances, what, at any time, have you heard her say?"

"That, sir, which I will not report after her."

"You may, to me . . ."

"Neither to you nor anyone," said the waiting-woman. "Lo you! Here she comes."

It was the Queen. She carried a taper and was in her night attire. Her eyes were open; but she was asleep.

"What is it she does now?" whispered the doctor. "Look how she rubs her hands."

"It is an accustomed action with her," murmured the woman, "to seem thus washing her hands. I have known her continue in this a quarter of an hour."

"Hark! She speaks," said the doctor eagerly; and he and the waiting-woman listened intently to the strange mutterings of the Queen.

"Out, damned spot! Out, I say!" Her hands seemed to gnaw at each other like feverish mice, and the taper tipped and tilted, making wild shadows behind her. Then she cried out, in a voice that filled the listeners with horror: "Who would have thought the old man to have had so much blood in him?"

"She has spoke what she should not," whispered the waiting-woman. "I am sure of that."

Then her mistress, the Queen, still rubbing at her hands, complained that the smell of blood would not go; and she who had once told her husband that a little water cleared them of the deed, now cried out in anguish:

"All the perfumes of Arabia will not sweeten this little hand!" Then she drifted away. "To bed, to bed," she sighed. "What's done cannot be undone. To bed, to bed, to bed."

Malcolm and his army drew near. Already Birnam Wood was before them. It was thick and leafy.

"Let every soldier hew him down a bough," commanded Malcolm, "and bear it before him . . ."

Quickly it was done, and presently it seemed that Birnam Wood itself was moving towards Dunsinane.

Macbeth, secure in his prophecies, awaited the oncoming army. Suddenly he heard a cry, a desolate cry of women. Once, such a sound would have alarmed him; but now he was past all feeling, past all fear. Wearily he asked the reason for the cry.

"The Queen, my Lord, is dead," he was told.

He shrugged his shoulders. "She should have died hereafter," he sighed. "There would have been a time for such a word. Tomorrow, and tomorrow, and tomorrow, creeps in this petty pace from day to day to the last syllable of recorded time . . ."

A messenger broke in upon his life-weariness, a messenger amazed and scarcely able to speak. He had been watching from a hill, and, as he watched, it had seemed to him that Birnam Wood was moving, moving towards Dunsinane.

"Liar and slave!" shouted Macbeth, rousing himself. Rage filled him, not against Malcolm, nor even against Macduff, but against the weird sisters, the Fates! They had deceived and entrapped him into destroying the great man that once he had been.

"They have tied me to a stake," he cried, "I cannot fly, but bear-like I must fight the course. What's he that was not born of woman? Such a one am I to fear, or none."

This last promise sustained him as he rushed from the castle to face his enemies. He fought like a giant, for who could harm him? His life, though he valued it at nothing, was charmed. Then, in the smoke of battle, he came face to face with Macduff.

"Of all men else I have avoided thee," he cried. "But get thee back; my soul is too much charged with blood of thine already."

"I have no words; my voice is in my sword!" shouted Macduff, and rushed upon him.

"I bear a charmed life," warned Macbeth, parrying his enemy's blows, "which must not yield to one of woman born!"

"Despair thy charm!" panted Macduff, his murdered wife and children ever in his thoughts. "Macduff was from his mother's womb untimely ripped!"

The last promise had been broken, and the last prophecy fulfilled. The end had come. Nothing now remained for him but to perish bravely, like the soldier that he had been.

"Lay on, Macduff!" he cried, his sword and shield grasped firmly. "And damned be him that first cries, 'Hold, enough!'"

They fought, and Macduff killed Macbeth. Then he cut off his head and carried it, dripping, to Malcolm, the new King. He held it up on high, and its sightless glare bore witness to the double truth of Fate.